Shadows
from the Past

Shadows from the Past

*Edited, compiled and
with an introduction by*

VENETIA MURRAY

BISHOPSGATE PRESS LTD
37 UNION STREET
LONDON SE1 1SE

Shadows from the Past.
1. Wessex. Social life, ca 1900-1930.
Biographies. Collections
I. Murray, Venetia
942.3′082′0922

ISBN 1-85219-060-4

All enquiries and requests relevant
to this title should be sent to the
publisher, Bishopsgate Press Ltd.,
37 Union Street, London SE1 1SE

Printed by Whitstable Litho Printers Ltd
Millstrood Road, Whitstable, Kent

CONTENTS

INTRODUCTION

by Venetia Murray

In 1984 Lord Weymouth first conceived the idea of collecting autobiographies written by Senior Citizens who had spent much of their lives in Wessex. The sole proviso was that they should be original, unpublished manuscripts, written by 'ordinary' men and women, not professional authors. There would be a small cash payment for those accepted and a guaranteed place in the Longleat Library. The collection of Wessex manuscripts would be Lord Weymouth's personal contribution to the family tradition of adding to the Archives already housed in Longleat.

The response to his appeal has been amazing; and continues. Such was the quality of some of the material submitted that we decided it deserved a wider audience. The first anthology, composed of extracts from some of the early manuscripts sent in — "Where Have All the Cowslips Gone?" — has already been published, in an illustrated hardback edition, and in paperback. "Shadows of the Past" is the second.

Lord Weymouth's idea has caught the imagination of literally hundreds of people who might otherwise never have thought of writing their life stories, let alone considered that anyone would be interested in reading them. A number of journalists and writers have already gone round England with a tape recorder, soliciting interviews about life at the beginning of this century from those who can still remember it. But there are certain inherent qualifications to such methods of collecting information. An interview implies direct questioning, and although the subject may talk easily, he has neither the time, nor in many cases, the ability to self-edit. The interviewer is forced to prompt, and, moreover, often imposes his own style and opinions on the end product.

"Shadows of the Past", (and 'Where have all the Cowslips Gone?' before it), is based on a different approach to social history. In an autobiography it is implicit that the writer has already decided for himself exactly what he wishes to record and what he wishes to leave to the reader's imagination. He will also have decided, in advance, what, if any, social or political point he wishes to make.

Autobiography is a relatively painless form of self-expression; and although memory is, of course, a selective editor, old age is the time of life when the mind reverts increasingly to the past. As one writer says:- "One realises that the memory plays tricks . . . and it is possible to forget, or be unable to remember, something that happened a few hours earlier, while incidents of years and years before come flooding back with startling clarity." It is this kind of instinctive recall which makes these stories ring so true.

Old age is also the time of life when detachment has set in. Events which seemed overwhelmingly traumatic when they happened can be dismissed as an inevitable hiccup fifty years later. It is noticeable that, despite the truly appalling conditions and hardships which some of these contributors had to endure at the beginning of their lives there is no flicker of self-pity in any of them. The fact that they bothered to write their autobiographies at all, at such advanced ages, shows the stamina with which they have tackled life.

In the course of seventy years or more it is not only the mechanics of daily life that have changed, it is the world's concept of society. These people grew up in a candle-lit world, a world where 'the rich man in his castle, the poor man at his gate' were the accepted inevitable structure. They were brought up to believe in the infallibility of our Empire and to use the word 'Great' in conjuction with 'Britian'. Jingoism and Colonel Blimp had yet become thought of as dangerous anachronisms; nor had Edward VIII's Abdication shaken the Monarchy.

Corporal punishment was the natural consequence of wrong-doing; and the law enforced by parental authority. The cult of the teenager had yet to be invented; nor had the phrase "I'm entitled". The words 'charity' and 'means test' conotated an attitude light years away from the modern Welfare State. Modern fury with hospital waiting lists would have been considered upside-down thinking before the First World War — hospitals, amongst the working classes, were regarded as only one step short of the cemetary; places to be avoided if humanly possible. The tally-man, who did not hesitate to take the furniture away from those who got behind with their H.P. has little in common with this world of easy credit. Food today, in England at least, is no longer the imperative priority in most household budgets. And as for education, and the role of women in society, one contributor, Mrs. Roberts, sums it up thus — "My Dad's brother begged him to let me sit for the Grammar School scholarship, Dad was adamant. No. Service for girls — yes, he was one of those. They did exist."

When I was researching this book I asked one man whether he was content with the way life had turned out for him in his old age. He looked at me as though I must be joking and replied "Listen. When I was a boy I looked at my grandparents and I took it for granted that my life would end up the same way as theirs had. Four of my grandfather's sisters actually died of malnutrition. Others finished up in the workhouse — forcibly separated from their wives. They were admitted failures after a lifetime on and off the dole, or working thankfully twelve hours a day for a pittance."

Nevertheless, the attitude of the writers in this book is ambivalant; there is a certain nostalgia, understanding; much that was good about the past has been lost — the neighbourliness, the comfort and safety of living in a small community above all; a kind of innocence, gaiety and freedom which has been swamped by ambition today. There even seems to be a certain excitement about the struggle to survive. Speaking about a bad period of unemployment one writer starts by saying "I didn't need Norman Tebbit to tell me what to do. Every Monday morning I would get on my bicycle and do the rounds.... Anyway, looking back, those first two years of unemployment were in fact wonderful days. I was free — free as the birds that I hunted — no worries, no cares, no money. I could do as I liked." He bought a second-hand gun, shot rabbits and starlings "one more for the pot....", collected limpets, crabs and peewits' eggs; caught goldfinches to sell — "the top birds fetched 2/- or more, the not so good 6d or 1/-; yes, when he is hard pushed, man will find a way to make a shilling."

The working conditions some of these reminiscences evoke seem quite unbelievable today. One of the most harrowing comes from a Bristol-born miner, describing his first job, at the age of fourteen, as an underground 'Door Boy' — "it was a lonely job as there was no-one to talk to. The hardest bit was to keep awake — there was complete silence apart from the occasional cracking or fragments of rock falling from the roof. I had to stay there eight hours with only the light of the safety lamp. If I had the misfortune to upset the lamp and extinguish it, I had to stay in the dark until the end of the shift. . . . The real danger was that if I fell asleep the trucks would smash into the unopened door, burying me alive. . . ." And yet, accepting all that, he adds "I managed to pass the time by reading some books. And sometimes I had the company of small mice who came round to collect the crumbs which I scattered, and they became very tame. . . ."

In all there are nineteen contributors to this anthology; their backgrounds range from a stately home through the back streets of Bristol and Portsmouth to an isolated farm on Exmoor. The remininscences include those of a stone mason, a bargee, a doctor, a gardener, two farmers, one comparitively richer than the other, and one of the first mechanics employed by the Automobile Association.

The book begins with an aristocratic childhood described with dry humour by Lord Weymouth. He, of course is not a Senior Citizen, but writes as the originator of the scheme. Later, we find "A Worm's Eye View", part of an autobiography by Mr. Doel, who started his career in the same household — Longleat. But as the "Hall Boy", which is the "lowest position possible in the line of male staff." He explains the hierarchy:- ". . . .two slightly older lads were my Seniors — the Steward's Room Boy and the Pantry Boy. These gentlemen in turn ranked below the second Footman. Finally, Top of the tree? — there was the Butler."

Some of the writers excel at description. Mrs. Lilian Bentley, a game-keeper's daughter, sees her country childhood as a time of magic, she writes of a sheltered garden — ". . . .Here were sky-blue larkspurs and Madonna lilies as tall as myself, borders of pinks, many coloured poppies and love-in-the-mist, crown imperials with five crystal drops in each flaming bell, roses everywhere. . . . it represented Paradise in my imagination, and I walked in it, smelling the roses, thinking pleasant secret thoughts that I would share with no-one, a different child altogether to the one who climbed trees and quarrelled with my sisters. . . ." And, later, she remembers running up Cley Hill, an 800 feet high Iron Age hill-fort in Wiltshire:- ". . . on an autumn day when a big wind was let loose in the world we became, more than at any time a part of the wilderness and freedom, as much in the power of the wind as the hurrying leaves, as the thistle-down sailing shoulder high, or the torn clouds.... Even wet days had a charm of their own — to watch the chalk track change to a milk-white river, or a rainbow give sudden birth in a frowning sky."

One woman laments — "O happy, happy days, never to return" in the context of her past; another states tersely that the games they invented for themselves were "better than television". Even, she adds, "reading tealeaves was a serious pastime." Of course childhood usually seems golden in retrospect, whatever it was like at the time. Old age forgets the agonising of youth. But, even allowing for a certain amount of fantasising, many cheap and easy pleasures are mentioned in these stories which have no modern counterpart. What child today would race grasshoppers? Or make its own bow and arrow, or kite? What happened to dressing-up chests and pressed flowers? And who, today, knows about shadowplay and pictures in the fire?

The empty streets were once the children's playground by right. And the streets used to ring with the cries of hawkers — the rag-and-bone man with his ballons and goldfish to barter for anything from an empty tin to a bundle of old newspaper; the fly-paper man; the knife-grinder and the cockle-woman; the barrel-organ man with his inevitable scarlet-jacketed monkey; the 'knocker-up', who, for a modest fee, tapped on your window with a paddle pole before five in the morning — possibly a more gentle start to the day than Radio One on the digital alarm.

In editing this book I have interfered with the writer's original copy only when it was absolutely necessary to make some points clear. It is probably just because these extracts were *not* written by professionals that their style is so spontaneous and evocative. There is nothing self-conscious or rehearsed in the way they express themselves. The stories are a mixture of anecdote and fact, spiced with much humour and self-mockery. The modern, young reader may well be astonished that this kind of world existed within living memory — but what a fascinating world it is to read about. There reminiscences are being as useful to the serious social historian as being riveting to the general public.

Venetia Murray, September 1988.

Lord Weymouth (centre) with his sister Caroline (left) now the Duchess of Beaufort, and his brother Lord Christopher.

"...an aristocratic elitism"

Alexander Thynn, (the Viscount Weymouth)*

Longleat House, Wiltshire

These are fragments from the childhood chapter of an autobiography, which I am in the process of writing, but which I shall not be publishing for many years to come. I offer them to this anthology of Wessex memories, (even if I did occasionally stray across the borders into London), by way of an introduction to the Wessex theme.

My childhood was predominantly at a Georgian manor house called Sturford Mead, which was set in a beautiful garden and situated about three miles from Longleat, the stately home belonging to our family, where my grandfather still held sway. It was at Sturford that I was brought up, and steeped in the prejudices of our clan. Some of these snobbishnesses, in retrospect, may now give rise to a smile. Perhaps we should glimpse them from the very outset of my existence.

My parents were on holiday in Venice at the time when I was probably conceived. They were the quest of Laura Corrigan, the American hostess who, despite her suspect origins (of being a sometime waitress, managing to marry an elderly millionaire who promptly expired from a heart attack) and despite the fact that New York society had turned their backs on her, was currently making quite some splash upon the European social scene. My father and mother were amongst those of la jeunesse dorée, who had been enticed to her parties with extravagant gifts of jewellery concealed within the napkins of each table setting. In fact they were particular favourites of hers and, for the summer of 1931, they had been invited to stay with her at the Palazzo Mocenigo in Venice, where Byron had formerly lived for a short while. So I have often wondered if it was in Byron's bed that I was actually conceived. Apparently I was a nuisance during the final month of pregnancy in that I did not readily submit to birth. I was late.

Yet finally, at about 19.00 hours on May 6th 1932, in 95 Seymour Place,

1

London W1, assisted by a midwife known universally as Nanny B, my mother finally gave me birth — to the great rejoicing of the Thynne family, (apart from the distant Thynne cousins, I daresay, who were thus removed yet one step further from the line of succession to Longleat). To Henry, my father, and to Thomas, my grandfather, and to all the kith and kin of my father's three sisters, it was indeed splendid news that there was finally a direct heir within the main branch of the family.

So the feeling of being much wanted, in the sense that I was in some way the fulfilment of a parental ambition, was fed to me within my mother's milk. It gave me an idea of self-importance, and in those days it produced a direct bonding between my mother and myself. It was a warmth of special regard that seemed to emanate from her.

One of my very earliest memories can be dated precisely to my third birthday. I was standing up in the back of an open car, waving a small Union Jack in acknowledgement to the joyous acclamation of a London crowd. My father was telling me that they were gathered there because it was my special day to celebrate. Only later was it admitted that there had been additional cause for the crowd's festivity in that May 6th 1935 happened to be the date of King George V's Silver Jubilee. Even then I regarded it as evidence that there must be a special relationship between the two of us. I had my picture of him hanging up in the nursery, and taking my cue from the national anthem, I referred to him always as "My Gracious King".

My parents had always been steeped in an aristocratic elitism, such as my mother's friend Nancy Mitford was to portray more openly in literary form. There were upper class ways of both doing, or saying, whatever needed to be done or said; and conversely, there were non-U ways for people to brand themselves in such judgement as coming from an inferior sort of background. In Nancy's books there is a salutary undercurrent of mirth beneath the whole snobbish business. But we children had to learn such pitfalls in either behaviour, or language, in much the same way as in Divinity Class at school we had to learn the Ten Commandments.

To mention some trivial examples, it was a sin to refer to the drawing-room by any other name — such as lounge, or parlour. We never went to the toilet — it was the lavatory, or loo. Our eating utensils must be held in the correct manner, with their handles in the centre of the palm, and with our index fingers extended down the spine of each instrument. It was inadmissible to put fish knives on the dining-table, to carry a comb, or to pronounce the letter L in the word 'golf'. Joining in a chorus of 'Cheers' — when toasting — was to stick in my throat for many years to

2

come. Instead of that, we had to say "Your good health!". We never failed to notice and to comment upon it later, if people who had come to tea, poured their milk in first, and then the tea. This branded them as 'MIF', in abbreviation of the phrase. And the ultimate shibboleth was in the use of the word 'Pardon?', which had to be avoided at all costs, unless it were integrated within some longer phrase — like "I beg your pardon." "What?" or "Sorry?" were the more acceptable upper class equivalents.

Avoidance of their gentle ridicule was the most usual incentive for learning, but my father also indulged in the tactics of the short sharp shock. The proclaimed faults in my table manners were rapidly eliminated after I had experienced one of his lightening raps from the bowl of a desert spoon upon my funny-bone, to deter me from ever again placing my elbows on the table.

We were brought up to regard ourselves as superior sort of people, without it ever getting spelt out, precisely, what that superiority entailed. There was some vague idea about us all having class, as if it must be something perceptible, like the colour of our blood literally being blue. But we were made aware how this was a delicate subject that we couldn't discuss with others, (nor even with Nanny, for example) because they didn't have class, so they wouldn't understand what we were talking about, and might even be offended if they tried. There was also an awareness that we might be accused of snobbishness, if some of the things said in private between ourselves were to be overheard by others.

The importance of who I was, and of what I was going to become, was never too far from my mind. When I was seven, a couple of our footmen put that very question to me; perhaps for the reason that they knew damn well I wasn't going to reply that I wanted to be an engine-driver, a soldier, or even a prime minister. I informed them, as indeed I had been told, that I was going to be the Marquess of Bath.

Caroline* was there from the start. She was my constant companion in those early days. Older than myself by three and three-quarter years, she knew the ropes and was protective to my interests with regard to life outside the walls of our nursery sanctuary. She knew (and probably deemed it unfair) that I was something unique within the family: the treasured heir. But she accepted her guardianship role with a possessiveness that was quite fierce. Others might display a rather special concern about my welfare, but there was never any challenge from me, to her personal dominance. I belonged to her, and could be

---

*Now the Duchess of Beaufort.

3

trained to suit her ways.

Caroline's particular method of controlling me was by sensory deprivation, by which I mean that she would suddenly refuse to communicate with me until I had bent my will to hers. I invariably felt miserable while this mode of persuasion was being applied, and my one concern was to reopen the full bonding of her grace and favour. A sense of pride in my own human rights was quite evidently lacking.

I loved Caroline, and whatever she told me I believed. Mummy and Nanny would read us fairy stories, and Caroline confided to me that she herself was a fairy. If I had been so bold as to disobey her, which I seldom did, she would have turned me into a toad. But in my obedience to her, I was rewarded with many a special treat. I sinned once, however. This was at a party in London, when I informed another boy who was neglecting to show my sister the reverence she deserved, that she was a fairy, so he'd better watch out. His ribald laughter took me by surprise and offended me, and I noted how Caroline looked put out. What disappointed me was that she refrained from turning him into a toad. She was at pains to impress on me, later, that this being-a-fairy business was secret between ourselves. I must not divulge it to others. But I heard rather less about her magic powers after that.

If Caroline told me to run errands, I would run them. I was hers to command, and pleased that this should be so. The birth of a younger brother did nothing to alter any of that. I have no distinct memory of Christopher arriving upon the scene, almost two years later than myself. Nobody (apart from Nanny) treated him as a significant addition to the family, and he was generally left behind in her care, when Caroline and myself accompanied our parents to whatever might be going on.

Christopher's initial statement of indentity was as the naughty one within the family. And it was always by naughtiness that he best gained the family attention. He was only three when father took us all to the Norfolk Broads, for a holiday on board a boat called "The Wherry". Christopher continually managed to escape from the cabin where he had been confined as a punishment, by climbing out of a port-hole. Henry tried to break this habit by beating him (lightly enough I daresay) with the top section of a fishing rod. Later, I was to hear my father say that he had been greatly impressed by the little boy's cheerfulness under such treatment; the one responding to the other perhaps, in what was the initiation of a special relationship. The exact working of this was something that I never did comprehend.

Christopher was unable to pronouce his own name, which came out sounding something like "Pip....Pip....". Hence it was Pip-Pip that we called him; or soon afterwards, just Pip. Caroline's name became abbreviated to Cal, incidentally, and my own to Al — until the time we went to school that is to say. My own viewpoint upon Pip was that he was a nuisance.

My father had rules about not leaving our toys downstairs in the drawing-room, if we did so, they would be confiscated and given away to the local orphanage. And once rules had been made they had to be strictly applied — in the interest of discipline and the development of obedience.

It is probable that I possessed many more toys than Christopher, but I seldom took this into account when he left *my* toys down in the drawing-room, with the result that they were confiscated. It was no good hoping that my father might bend the rules under such circumstances. Rules were rules, and they had to be applied.

I had a new game called Helter-Skelter, involving marbles rolled down a spiral chute, to score points in accordance with the hole they entered upon the final slope. I'd only just been given it, so I was particulary upset when Pip left *this* downstairs. The rule couldn't be broken, but I obtained Henry's permission to exchange the item that was to be confiscated for something else, of lesser personal value.

I had a large menagerie of cuddly toy animals, each with a distinct personality of its own, and I concluded that one of these must be sacrificed. Two of them were pigs, so perhaps one might be regarded as superfluous. Tommy Pig had been with me for a long time, and it was because he had lost most of his stuffing that I had recently been presented by my parents with Percy Pig, who was far classier and probably came from Harrods. But I hadn't yet developed a feeling of relationship with him, so it had to be he: a decision which nonetheless cost me many tears.

The expression on my mother's face was even more woebegone than my own, when I went to make the exchange. They had chosen Percy Pig for me with some care, and at no little expense — to wean me of my adoration of Tommy Pig. And here I was trading him in for a rubbishy game of marbles, which had cost a few shillings at the most. Rules were rules however, and they had to be strictly applied. So it was goodbye to Percy.

When I did play with Pip, it was not exactly as equals. I got into trouble on one occasion because a gardener at Sturford Mead reported to Nanny that I was dragging the poor little mite around the garden, with a rope around his neck. He made it sound as if I'd been intending to string him up, and that his life had only been saved by intervention in the nick of time. But it was simple case of grown-ups getting things

5

wrong. We'd been playing at cowboys — and Pip was my steer.

There was another occasion when we were playing robbers, and we had sticks as swords. It was old Mrs. Garrett's misfortune to come walking down the lane from Corsley at this juncture. We jumped her from the bushes and threatened to cut off her head with our swords. Nanny got to hear of this, and we were sent down to apologise to Mrs. Garrett for our assault. I always assumed that it had been the old lady herself who must have lodged a complaint. But I was to learn many years later from Nanny that it was Cal who had spotted what we were up to, and reported us. I believe that Caroline played this sort of role more often than we suspected at this time. She liked to be in control of events, and this robbers game wasn't of her own making.

I was five and a half when my youngest brother, Valentine, was born. I remember his arrival, and we all got excited about it at the time. But it wasn't as if Cal and I were going to permit him to play a significant part in our lives. He was Nanny's favourite, of course. She always treasured the youngest addition to the family, extending to him the special cloak of her protection: spoiling him, as we saw it.

There is one shameful story which had best be recounted. Valentine (or Baba, as he came to be known until his schooldays) was such an inanimate creature, and it was almost in a spirit of scientific curiosity that Pip and I put nettles at the foot of his pram — just to see if his feet were truly sensitive. They were of course, and he started howling with pain, without displaying an awareness of who might be inflicting it upon him. At this moment Nanny fortuitously arrived upon the scene, kicking up one hell of a fuss. I was the culprit of course. Pip had only been watching what I did. And Nanny flounced off declaring that she was going to tell Mummy about what I'd been up to.

I followed her at a distance, and when I looked in at the drawing-room window, I espied that she was deep in a serious conversation with my mother. Entering by the bay window, I said "I'm sorry, Mummy, I'm sorry". It then became apparent that Nanny had in fact refrained from betraying me, so that I was now obliged to come out with my own confession: which may have been the circumstance which saved me from the punishment I merited.

The distinction between Caroline's and my own attitude in general came vividly to the forefront of attention when the French cook in our house had a live cockerel to slaughter for our lunch. She imagined that this would be a spectacle that would both interest and educate us, so she brought out the bird into the garden where we were playing, and stuck a carving knife down its throat so that an artery was severed, and blood began to flow. I regret to say that my own interest was aroused. But Cal was of gentler spirit, displaying her disgust in no uncertain fashion, and when it came to her refusal to partake of flesh from the cockerel we had seen slaughtered she had me wrong-footed, torn between the demands of my hunger and my fraternal desire to display ideological solidarity. Greed won the day, and I ate my share of the bird — while Cal missed out on lunch altogether.

Cal was in fact beginning to distance herself from me over the latter part of this period. The age gap of nearly four years was in fact quite a hurdle to surmount. So long as I was prepared to be her personal servant, all had been well. Nor do I feel that she had greatly abused her status over me. It was from the fact that she never really did make too heavy demands, relying more on the nuance of the elder sister relationship to get what she wanted from me which made my affection for her so durable. But I was beginning to find that there was more I could do with Pip, than with her; and I never managed to feel comfortable when she was in the presence of her particular local girl-friend, who was Diana Phipps from Chalcot House. It was girl's talk the whole time between the two of them, even in my presence; and my efforts to participate in such conversation merely led to some snide suggestions from Diana that I was probably a girlish sort of boy. In some ways my identity felt more secure when in the company of my brothers.

I can also remember that, while I was seven years old, Cal informed me (what she had no doubt been hearing from others) that I was "passing through an awkward age". I found this to be a description which, once applied, was never to be retracted. By now however, I find that I can live with it.

During those years of early childhood, before the war, our status as members of the family was held clearly in focus by all of our domestic staff. We were addressed as Master Alexander, or Miss Caroline: never by the first name on its own. Nanny alone was permitted such intimate address, and she inferred from this that she stood somewhere in status between the family and the domestic staff: a point which she never allowed those under her to forget.

That relations between Nanny and the domestic staff could be frictional is perhaps best illustrated by the anecdote, frequently related to us over subsequent years, how a particular cook, who didn't remain with us for very long, objected to the criticisms that were relayed down to the kitchen by the footman who came to collect the dirty dishes, that the meat course on the nursery menu had been over-cooked. Next day, when the cover was removed from the plate, the sight of a raw skinned rabbit greeted our eyes. Anyway that was the fashion in which Nanny described it. And by her account, after the scene which followed, attendants from the nearest lunatic asylum were called to cart off this cook to where she belonged.

But there were clear limits to Nanny's authority, as it rapidly became evident to me that all true authority stemmed from my father. People jumped to obey what he dictated, and I knew that my mother wouldn't actually contradict what he decreed. Nanny herself didn't carry any manner of equivalent weight.

This was proven to me at an early age, when I was complaining to her about having to go downstairs for Sunday lunch, which had recently been established as a regular event, but which I was anxious to avoid because luncheons downstairs were far more disciplined than our meals upstairs in the nursery. So I was seated there at the top on the front stairs, snivelling my resentment in the hopes that Nanny would take me back under her protective wing.

She was preening herself no doubt, in such evident display of my preference for her company, and she was murmuring words of consolation in my ear about soon having her back again — or whatever. Then came Henry's trumpeting below from his study downstairs, ordering Nanny's retreat to the nursery, which was promptly obeyed. My whining also ceased instantly at his command, and I was never heard to make a fuss about going downstairs to lunch after that. We all understood that my father's authority was paramount within the household.

When it came to the subject of our grandparents, whether at Longleat or at Glynn where Grandpa Vivian (George, Lord Vivian) dwelt, we understood that their authority was then to be accepted as supreme. Each of them was quite evidently to be regarded as a considerable personality in his own right: Thomas, the 5th Marquess of Bath, in his reverenced dignity and lofty reserve, and George in his peppery individualism and coercive bombast. I was aware how each was to be respected and I revered them — without managing to feel that I ever made any special impression upon their affections.

The battle for status came to a head at gatherings of the Thynne clan, at Longleat over Christmas. Grandpa Bath allotted each family its own special nursery, with Henry (his son and heir) having what was traditionally the nursery, on the second floor of the north wing of the house. Kathleen and Mary, both of them elder sisters with families of their own, had to make do with spare nurseries up on the top floor.

Kathleen had married Oliver Stanley, heir presumptive of Lord Stanley of Alderley, and her brood consisted of four sons, all of them older than myself. Nanny Harrod was in charge of them, and was senior in age and experience to Nanny Marks. Moreover she had the support of Nanny Bolton, who looked after Mary's two boys and a girl: Mary had married John Lord Numburnholm, and her Wilson children were of approximately the same age as Henry's own. But Nanny Harrod put forward the case that nurseries should have been allotted in accordance with the order in which Lord Bath's children had been born, which would have dropped our brood to the bottom of the list: something that would have put Nanny Marks firmly in her place, as her two rivals would have liked to think. But she certainly wasn't going to stand for that, and the case was taken to my grandfather, who was content to abide by tradition and his former judgement, insisting that the allotted nurseries remain as he had ordained.

The snobbery of the upbringing was rammed home to us, not only in the acquired values of Nanny Marks, but also by Miss Vigers who became our governess. Each of them was 'sine nobilitas' of course, but they had the opportunity, often enough, to listen in on the way our parents talked about life in the company of their own family, and Miss Vigers in any case had known previous such experience in that, amongst others, she had taught George and Gerald Lascelles, the children of the Princess Royal. Many years later, when comparing family memories about Miss Vigers with the former Countess of Harwood, who had been married to George, I learnt how the Lascelles boys had observed that she would bob up and down in curtsies, whenever she had the Princess Royal speaking to her on the phone —without apparently being aware of what she was doing. But in any case, she regarded herself as a real specialist in aristocratic ways. Not that Nanny Marks was ever going to let it be said that she knew less on the subject than Miss Vigers, for the two spinsters (the former middle-aged and the latter elderly) detested each other to the core.

There had been a power struggle when Miss Vigers had first arrived, which was in 1938. She wasn't our first governess, but she was the only one to take up the thorny question of whether governess or nanny had precedence within the family hierarchy. Her subtle scheme was to persuade my mother that she could save herself a lot of bother by entrusting the house accountancy to herself: which just incidentally included the task of paying the servants. My mother unwisely agreed to the suggestion. But when Nanny learnt that she was now expected to queue up with the servants every Saturday, to receive her wages from the hand of Miss Vigers, she went on strike. She reminded everyone that she was employed by Lady Weymouth, and not by Miss Vigers. So Daphne felt obliged to acknowledge that Nanny was not to be treated as one of the servants, and hence forward was paid separately: much to the governess' chagrin.

The power struggle thereafter was more a question of who had the right to exercise influence over us children. Caroline and myself had separate bedrooms downstairs, adjacent to that of Miss Vigers, whilst Christopher and Valentine remained upstairs in the nursery, still under the care and protection of Nanny. It was only during the holidays that all four children were recombined, and even this led to problems on occasions.

For example, there was the day when Miss Vigers returned from her holiday to find that one pair of Caroline's pink knickers could not be accounted for. She made a special point of keeping lists of everything so she took the appropriate list up to the nursery, demanding an explanation. But Nanny was in no mood to be cross-examined on the subject, so held the door firmly closed in her face: something which the governess found most offensive.

There was a farcical scene with them shouting at one another through the closed door: Miss Vigers demanding instant admission, while Nanny confined herself to disclaiming any knowledge of the missing pair of pink knickers. After persistent accusation however, she changed her story, and declared that she had eaten them: not that this did anything to soften Miss Vigers' insistence that the door be opened so that she could explore the nursery wardrobe for herself. And she was now pushing vigorously against the door, in the knowledge that her superior weight must surely win the day against her far lighter opponent.

At this juncture however, Nanny chose to step aside while pulling the door open, saying: "Then come in, Miss Vigers!" — which she did of course, falling flat on her face. This story was related to us subsequently, on numerous occasions, by the triumphant nurse.

The idea of there being a cultural divide between schoolroom and nursery was promoted by Miss Vigers, rather than by Nanny. In the eyes of the governess, time was on her side. Children went through a natural progression in their process of education, and there was a point when nurses became expendible. If she were to bide her time, she anticipated that Nanny would be soon retired. But she wasn't content to bide her time. She wanted Nanny to *know* that she was on the slippery slope to enforced retirement. I can remember one fierce exchange between the two of them, when meeting on the stairs, with Nanny clutching Baba to her breast, as if the devil incarnate intended to snatch him away from her. And Miss Vigers was saying sarcastically: "Yes Nanny, I'll have that one too. He'll grow up in due course, and then he'll be mine!".

We didn't really like Miss Vigers. It was Cal who initiated our Secret Club, whose only real purpose was as a forum where our identity (uncontrolled by Miss Vigers) could be effectively discussed. Our meetings were held within the sheltering seclusion of a yew tree, down in the garden near the garage. We had recently been given a typewriter by Mrs. Corrigan, and Cal put it to instant use in drawing up the list of rules of conduct and admissability, ending up with the minutes of our first meeting. She left these on a table however, where they came to Miss Vigers' attention. We regarded it as typical of this authoritarian old cow that she should promptly read them — despite the word *'Secret'* being written in capital letters, and underlined. And the penalty she imposed upon Cal for initiating such a spirit of revolt was to make her sit down and copy it all out again, with all of her numerous spelling mistakes corrected.

We disliked Miss Vigers because she was old, ugly and fierce. Nanny might cluck like a hen, but she was kindly and one hundred per cent loyal to the entire family. We made jokes about the way the two of them were perpetually trying to run the other down but we never hoped that Miss Vigers would achieve ultimate victory. At this stage however, it rather looked as if she might.

I was still only four when Miss Russell was appointed to be Caroline's governess — several years prior to the advent of Miss Vigers. In sharp contrast to the latter, the former was a youngish, good-looking lady. She may have been even more beautiful than that, for I do seem to remember her as such. I wasn't actually taking lessons from her, but I sometimes sat in with Cal, receiving instruction in drawing and the like. I can remember Miss Russell praising my picture of a blinded Sampson pulling down the pillars of the temple, so perhaps she was reading me stories from the Bible as well.

I adored Miss Russell, and she was good with Nanny besides, I can remember us all playing together in the garden at Sturford, during the summer of the Abdication crisis, the game being for the Mr. Baldwin's team to keep King Edward and Mrs. Simpson apart. Miss Russell had a good way of combining games with tuition in current affairs. She stimulated me intellectually, quite apart from furnishing me with a visual image for a romantic prototype which was perhaps to recur with some frequence in my life. She had shoulder-length, blondish hair, and an overt friendliness; or was it just that she had a good way with children? But the relationship was entirely asexual: much as that might be cause for personal regret.

She was only with us for a year. There came a day during the following Christmas visit to Longleat, when Nanny informed me sadly that Miss

11

Russell would not be playing with us any more. She had departed without so much as a hug, or a word of adieu. I just rolled on the floor, screaming my head off.

No one explained the situation to me any deeper than that, and it was only years later when I was told, by Aunt Kathleen, how Aunt Emma had reported to my father seeing the governess accompaying Thomas, my grandfather on his constitutional walk in the Pleasure Grounds at Longleat: Thomas being a seventy-five year old widower at the time. The idea of Miss Russell being a suitable governess for us children was no longer a matter to be taken into account: nor even the idea that the revered head of the family might be entitled to a small romance in the Indian summer of his life. There were now other considerations which the clan must have found disturbing — like the prospect of an additional brood of male-line Thynnes, emerging to grasp some portion of the inheritance from under our very noses.

No, I quite understand: the nubile Miss Russell had to go. I also understand why, in selecting Miss Vigers as her replacement, due notice was doubtless taken of the fact that she was both old, and ugly.

I suppose I was the favourite of both governesses. The fact of me being the future Marquess was sufficient to ensure that status, as far as Miss Vigers was concerned, no matter what kind of personality I might display. But she bestowed upon Caroline and myself a feeling that we were the intelligensia of the family, far superior in quality to either Pip or Baba.

It was Miss Vigers who spelt out to us the snobbery that was implicit within our parent's attitudes. I learnt how the local dialect, as spoken by Tom Renyard, the gamekeeper my father had appointed to instruct me in rabbiting and shooting, was indicative of low breeding, and therefore a subject for private jokes. While friendly with his nephew, I was encouraged to preserve my distance from him. Much was made of the fact that he would not be going to the same kind of school as myself. As with members of the domestic staff, I *knew* that I should not confide my inner thoughts to him.

What I had in fact been initiated into was a system of hierarchy. The Royal Family was at the top, but my father wasn't all that far below. Where the Prime Minister might find his allotted place would depend more upon his breeding, than upon his political eminence; and neither Mr. Ramsey Macdonald, nor Mr. Stanley Baldwin were at all well bred. My father was most certainly to be regarded as supreme within the family environment, and my mother (now that she had entered the Thynne fold) would not have seen fit to dispute that she only came second. Henry had by now, in some way, replaced George Lord Vivian

12

as the necessary dominate male within Daphne's life. And below her came her children, in the order of their birth.

During this my childhood, I was brought up to defer to the wishes of Caroline. One deferred to her for two reasons, in that she was older and she was female. All females were ushered through doors before myself, and they served themselves first at table. But it went deeper than this, in that Cal's preferences on any subject were demanded before my own. And I accepted all this without demur, because my own preferences had priority over those of Christopher or Valentine. Poor little Baba, if the truth be told, was supposed to defer to everybody and would have had a wretched time if his interest hadn't been so stalwartly protected by Nanny.

We didn't see very much of our parents within a normal day's schedule. We'd go up to Daphne's bedroom to kiss her good morning, and perhaps stay with her while she finished her breakfast in bed, and took her morning bath. Henry was more usually up and away by that time, preferring to eat in the dining-room. And that might well be the last we saw of either of them until we were washed and brushed up, ready for the brief evening session downstairs in the drawing-room. The rest of the day was spent either in the garden, or in the nursery downstairs. We saw a great deal more of Nanny than we did of either of my parents.

The Christmas season always sticks in my mind as being something very different, partly because we all moved into Longleat, and partly because there were so many other children (in the form of cousins) with whom to mingle. It was a fortifying experience to learn that we were all part of an integrated clan, concerned about each other's welfare. And there were ritual games of an evening, first and foremost amongst which for anyone still youthful enough to caper and cavort, was Cocky-Olly, or Kick the Pot Out — as it was sometimes called elsewhere.

This was a matter of Cocky-Olly making sorties from a base territory, invariably sited half way up the front stairs. By pronouncing the name of any individual, on sighting, they were captured, and upon the touch of anyone who remained uncaptured — so long as the touch was delivered within the home base — they were instantly released. And Henry was the adult by far the most preferred, who ever volunteered to fulfill that role. This was because he knew how to combine the right degree of growling fierceness in pursuing us fleeing children, with the lenience of permitting us to get rescued once we had been garnered in his home den. His popularity as an uncle made me feel really proud of him actually being my father.

The excitement in the game also involved that question of hiding

13

ourselves in dark corners and cachettes within Longleat's multiple galleries and corridors. The very idea of straying too far from the touch of our human kind evoked a sense of unease, or even terror, that we might encounter one of the ghosts whom we knew with conviction to populate this building. There were all those tales of the Grey Lady searching for her lost lover; or of the footman who died when falling down the spiral staircase. And there were other fancies too, of a gory nature, relating to the monks from the original Longlete Priory. Even some inanimate objects like the two ebony statues of Negro figures (to support flower arrangements) struck fear into our hearts whenever it was necessary to pass them, unaccompanied, on our way upstairs to our respective nurseries.

Some of the fun and games engendered seasonally at Longleat were for the wider audience of those who worked upon our estate. It consisted of amateur theatricals, performed by the assembled clan in the village hall at Horningsham. On my first such appearance, at two and a half, I can remember being dressed up in a clownish attire, and required to follow my elder cousins Richard Stanley, to simulate performing animals and come down a slide at a crack of the ringmaster's (Henry's) whip. A year later I even had a speaking part. I was dressed in my pink pig-patterned pyjamas, with a top hat and soot on my face. I rushed out on stage, waving a small handbrush, exclaiming "I'm getting on like a house on fire!" There was much applause which I was given to understand that I had merited.

There were activities of a sort more typical within our social strand, to which I was introduced at the age of seven. When Henry had been a boy, and prior to being recognised as the heir to Longleat, he'd been impassioned by the outdoor life to which he was introduced by Dick Futcher, the gamekeeper to whose care and tutlage he had been entrusted by Thomas.

My father was to tell me later that he always felt more at home with the Futchers' simple life than he did under the strict formality of the Longleat household. He regarded himself as a country boy at heart, which he held in sharp contrast to Daphne's social inclinations, and general town culture. By introducing me to Tom Renyard, he imagined that he was pointing my footsteps in the same direction as his own — even if it wasn't to work out like that.

I had a liking and respect for Tom. He was uneducated, but greatly concerned about education: even a poor man's philosopher, in a small way. He was often encouraging me to compete with him in spelling bees and the like. But my spelling was atrocious at that age, and I think somewhere the idea was understood that it would be inappropriate for me to compete, and get defeated by Tom. So we never really got together on an intellectual plane. And I think there were occasions when he was offended by reports from Mrs. Sims, in the kitchen, how we all made jokes about his Wessex accent. But Mrs. Sims always was a troublemaker. During these years before I was packed off to boarding-school however, most of my activities involved Tom's participation — whether in rabbiting, ratting, beating for the shooting parties, fishing, bicycling or merely in catching butterflies. The last sport was something that I introduced him to, rather than the other way around. I had been handed down the essentials for butterfly collecting by my cousin Tom Stanley, who was Caroline's contemporary. It surprised many that Tom Renyard took to the sport with such enthusiasm. But he may have had the feeling that I wasn't really catching on to the blood-lust sports, to which it had been intended that I should be introduced, so he moved a little in my direction by way of compensation. I have visions of him with cloth cap and haversack, bounding over clumps of bracken in pursuit of fritillaries, butterfly net held aloft, and with the cyanide bottle extended in the other hand: similar to the sight of a dog bounding to retain vision of a rabbit in corn stubble.

I developed an interest, although not a passion, for natural history and animal life as a result of my days in the woods with Tom. I learnt something about birds, and the appeal of young nestlings, waiting open-beaked for the anticipated gift of worms. After seeing my first grass-snake, I spent hours in that vicinity, making noises on a toy piano-accordian which I had been given, supposing that this music would charm the reptile a second time from its lair.

I was only just beginning to participate within the activities of the local hunts (which consisted of the Wylye Valley, and the South and West Wilts) before the outbreak of war disrupted such activities. Cal was thus a far more experienced rider than I ever had the chance to be, but we were both instructed in this art by Charlie Barnes, the head groom at Longleat. I was even blooded at the hunt by John Morrison, who was later to be created Lord Margedale, and his jovial instructions that the blood be left unwashed from my cheeks, no matter how strongly Nanny might protest were solemnly fulfilled. There are some who wonder if there are still any traces of it there today, since Nanny Marks was always getting accused by my father of under-implementing his instruction that we should all be kept immaculately clean.

I was not particularly sportive in those years: not encouraged to play ball games, or even to feel competitive when running. I suffered from an unnatural fear of heights, when out in the woods with Tom Renyard, and I could never climb up to the branches he suggested to examine a jackdaw's nest — or whatever. My biggest achievement over these early years was just in learning how to swim, in the municipal pool at Bath, which I attended quite regularly with Cal.

My first ever sense of sportive achievement did come relatively early however — when I succeeded in climbing out of my pram, to join Nanny where she was sitting on the lawn. The look of surprise on her face was a delight to behold, so it's a pity that this did not inspire me towards the attainment of more accomplished endeavours. But the truth of the matter is that I was quite a shy and timid child, and quite definitely highly strung. Not that this featured within my father's own image of what I ought to be, and he did encourage me towards more boyish concerns.

I was only three when Henry decreed that I should be taught how to box: curious perhaps in that he had never himself indulged in that sport. I was accompanied by Nanny to Macpherson's gym in London, and an instructor showed me how to stand and hold my fists, before advancing step by step towards an opponent, to deliver "one to the point, and one to the mark". Having absorbed my lesson, I was matched against another toddler and told to demonstrate what I had learnt. I attempted to do just this. What they had neglected to tell me was that my opponent had been given similar instructions, so that when I moved in close enough to deliver my two punches, I was preempted by the receipt of "one to the point, and one to the mark" — ending up much embarrassed on the floor. And my instructor hastily threw in the towel on my behalf, so as to avoid the additional embarrassment of me bursting into tears.

I was in fact a cry-baby. I can remember howling with rage when Nanny refused to give me the toy panda I so desperately desired, or from pain when I fell from a table and bit my tongue. But I certainly wasn't frightened by this boxing defeat, and I remember distinctly that I didn't cry: a fact concerning which the instructor praised me at the time.

There was another aspect to these visits to Macpherson's gym which did trouble me, however. The older boys were always participating in a session of gymnastics when we arrived, right at the end of which came a joy-ride on a merry-go-round — with everyone clinging to rope ladders which revolved. To encourage me in the desire for additional participation, I daresay, the instructor would beckon me down from my seat beside Nanny in the public gallery, so that I could join in the fun with them. But I always found that long walk down the aisle from where I'd been enjoying my anonymity to be the cause for excruciating self-consciousness.

16

I felt myself an intruder into the games of the bigger boys, and that they resented my addition to their throng. But it seemed all too difficult to decline such participation, with Nanny pushing me forward and away from her, urging me not to be shy. All eyes were on me, but I had to start walking. And I developed a dread, in anticipation of that cheery call from the instructor to come down and join them, even though it was impossible to communicate this dread to others.

What I did finally was to summon up my courage, when Henry was driving us all somewhere in his car, to ask if I need go to Macpherson's gym. I am still aware of the deathly silence which greeted this request. Then Nanny hastened to what she imagined was my assistance, by trying to explain to my father how the boys were sometimes a bit rough with me in the boxing. She'd got it all wrong, but I couldn't see how to communicate my true motivations behind the request. I was conscious how there was severe disapproval, and disappointment, in their reaction. But the request was granted, and that put an end to my boxing training — for the time being in any case.

Sometimes there was a male comeraderie between my father and myself. I was three when he gave me my first sips of port to drink, and my liking for this was to remain with me. It took me long to discern anything wholesome in wine however, which lacked the former's rich sweetness, and as for beer, I found it insipid and bitter. But I acquired an instant liking for cider, when it was first given me by Tom Renyard, and there was a particular occasion not long after that, when I returned home from a night's outing to catch moths by putting treacle on the bark of trees, to receive a severe scolding from Nanny. It couldn't be decided whether I had drunk too much, or was suffering from a severe touch of flu.

Returning to the activities which were actually directed by my father, I was just three when I accompanied him to his annual Royal Wiltshire Yeomanry Camp. The colonel had taken his young son to the camp the previous summer, and my father (although only a captain in those days) was damned if he shouldn't follow suit: proud as he was of having a son and heir. I sat beside him in the mess, and was taught by his fellow officers how to swill my mouth out after a meal: a habit which Henry found hard to break once we were back in female society.

What he hadn't bargained on however, was my delight in sitting on a spectator's chair while the Royal Wiltshire Yeomanry band was rehearsing and accompanying their music with my own shrill tin whistle. They gave me sixpences to go and buy myself ice creams. But after eating them, I would return to resume my accompaniment, to demonstrate yet once again my appreciation of their band. Daphne was

17

promptly summoned from Sturford Mead to repatriate me within the family fold.

Although I was encouraged by Miss Vigers to read such books as the novels of G.A. Henty, I never engrossed myself in such activity. I had been still very young when I appreciated that I ought not to reply "The Marquess of Bath", in answer to the question of what I intended to become in life. Thenceforward I told people that I would become a writer who illustrated his own books. My talent in drawing had received some praise from Miss Russell, a previous governess: and Daphne maintained some romantic notions about me emerging as a poet, in the vein of Shelley or Byron perhaps. So the idea of becoming more or less what I am today was never really that far from my mind.

The first verses that I ever wrote (at the age of seven) were for Daphne, and in the initial two lines of the first one I stated:-

Oh the little foal has play
while his mother works all day...

If we accept that I was in some way endeavouring to describe the nature of our own relationship, it stands as admirable evidence for filial devotion perhaps, but it strikes me today there may have been a touch of irrealism about my understanding of her activities in life.

Children's parties were very much a part of our lives when we were on the London scene: sometimes at no lesser place than Buckingham Palace. I was instructed by my cousin, Ben Wilson, on how to bow to royalty, and did so with exaggerated grace, (not with the head only, as I later learnt to be the more aristocratic way of doing such things). But it was Queen Mary herself who took me by the hand and assisted me to choose my present from the pile of gifts beneath the tree. I regarded her as a dear and dignified old lady.

I was a special favourite too, of Laura Corrigan, who had been made my godmother. The huge parties she threw were sometimes in my honour, and she was apt to fix the competitions (like the one to see whose gas-filled balloon travelled the furthest) so that I finally heard that I'd won the prize. I remember one little boy complaining that it was unfair in that my card was attached to a bunch of four such balloons, whereas his card had merely three. Mrs. Corrigan's explanation about me being her godson was ill-received.

I had a special fascination for the conjurors at parties such as these. And my sister (who was a fairy of course) was on more than one occasion singled out to receive the tame rabbit that got pulled out of a top hat. The day I witnessed a repetition of this trick, but with only a toy

18

rabbit being shaken as it emerged in the conjuror's hand rank as the point when I was struck by the idea that the quality of life might be deteriorating.

To examine the beginnings to my life within a more general context, I had indeed been born with a great deal of good fortune heaped there upon my plate — or with the proverbial silver spoon protruding from my mouth. But within the first few weeks of my life, I was given some foretaste of things yet to come when some careless visitor managed to drop me on my head. I was taken to hospital for X-ray examination by one Dr. H. Graham Hodgson and his letter, dated August 29th 1932, is still on the family files stating that there was no photographic evidence of fracture or any other injury in the bones of the skull. His certificate makes no mention of the state of the material below the bones of the skull, and there have been some who have wondered about this ever since.

* Eldest son and heir of Frederick Henry Thynne, who was then the 10th Viscount Weymouth, and who later became the 6th Marquess of Bath; During the period of which the author is writing he was still known as Alexander Thynne; he dropped the final 'e' in the family name by deed poll in 1976. Ed.

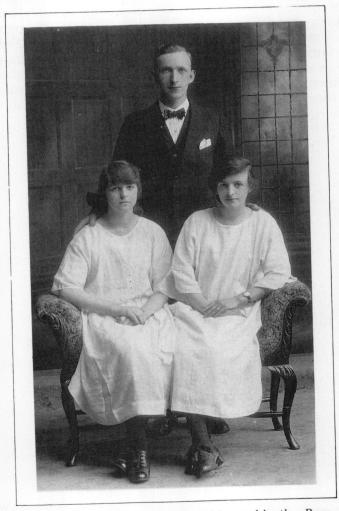

a) Mrs. Clark (left) with her sister May and brother Percy. They are both wearing their conformation dresses in 1923.

"the Post Office soon became the focal point
for all to pour out their troubles. . . ."

Mrs. E.M. Clark
Woolaston, Glos.

Those of us who were born early in this century have been privileged
to live through many changes. Perhaps they have not all been good and
some may even terrify us, if we dwell too much on what might happen,
but most of them have been little short of miracles. The many dreaded
diseases like T.B. and diphtheria have been eradicated, and, but a few
years ago, no-one would have imagined that hearts and kidneys could
be transplanted. When Bleriot flew the Channel just after I was born, the
village folk said, "Tant natural". When years later we twiddled that cat's
whisker on to a bit of crystal they said "Whatever be things coming to?"
What would the old folk have thought to see members of European
governments sitting around a table instead of fighting each other?
Probably they would have said "Well we've sin it all mate". Perhaps the
most disappointing bit of progress is the loss of our romantic notions
about the moon, for we no longer see "the man in the moon" since we
have seen the men on the moon.

The rich man in his castle,
The poor man in his gate,
God made them high or lowly
And ordered their estate.

We have come a very long way since those words were written and
accepted.

We sang that verse with same gusto that we sang the others. It is true
that we just sang words never thinking what they meant, but had we
thought about them in the early part of the century we should not have

criticized them. The days had not yet come when people thought of class distinction and when education made them think about such things as "upstairs and downstairs", or high or lowly estates.

To have questioned those things seventy years ago would have left men without work, and without work the tied cottage would no longer be available to any man not satisfied with his lot.

Working from daylight till dark meant early to bed and early to rise, and little time for thinking. On the whole, the village labourer was content to have a roof over his head, his bread and cheese and his cider, supplemented with garden produce.

Most boys could tickle a trout, poach a rabbit or a pheasant, and men went out after dark with their ferrets and nets when the moon came up. Unpolluted streams grew plenty of watercress, and mushrooms and blackberries grew in abundance.

Neighbours knew everyone's business and they saw that each other did not want.

Local fairs, dancing bears, hurdy-gurdy men, the local pubs, and a good sing song gave enough entertainment and few wanted more.

It was a long walk to seek other enjoyments if one had no donkey cart or a horse, or the money to go by train.

I was born in 1905, in the Gloucestershire village of Woolaston. At that time Lord of the Manor was still much in evidence in some places, but not in Woolaston. At the turn of the century most of the property belonged to the Duke of Beaufort and a few others, but, after 1908, they sold to the tenants and other local people. By the time I was old enough to take an interest, many people owned their own cottages and smallholdings.

How things have changed. The owners of the mansions and palaces around the country need the folk who once were of the lowly estate to finance the up-keep of their homes, the grounds of which have been considered almost holy in the past.

Woolaston, being close to a main road, was in touch with the outside world, every man was employed, and so the inhabitants were very independent, obsequious to no-one.

Good manners were the order of the day and men and boys touched their caps, especially to women. At school we learned to stand at the side of the road and to bow our heads if we should meet a funeral and we were told never to pass an older person who was carrying a basket without asking if we could help.

The dog and cat no longer wanted were shot, and the pig which died mysteriously was buried by the owner in the garden by the light of the hurricane lantern. I held the lantern on a few occasions for my father to bury pigs and I was forbidden to speak a word about it. One lesson we learned was how to keep things to ourselves, knowing full well that the leather belt was the alternative.

At the turn of the century most village dwellers did not know and did not want to know what went on outside their small world. People in adjoining villages were like foreigners and they were usually referred to in disparaging terms. Village youth spoiling for a fight went to the borders of their territory and were like terriers with their hackles up.

Men walked their animals to Chepstow market six miles away, the pigs having a rope tied to a back leg. The men spent much of their time, and the money received, in the village inns on their return. A few women took produce from house to house and others took it to the markets in Lydney or to Chepstow. My mother told me about the women who could carry baskets on their heads as well as having one on each arm but I do not remember seeing them.

Most villagers were self supporting, having a pig or two, a few hens and ducks or geese, a small orchard and a large garden.

Taps at the roadside or wells or water-spouts supplied water to most households. The buckets were fastened on to chains hanging from a strong wooden structure worn on the shoulders called a yoke. This was a splendid way to carry, and I sometimes feel that it could still be put to good use when doing outside work, fetching and carrying.

When I was four years old my mother had a telephone installed. There were very few telephones, the police station at Lydney had one but not the village police stations. The doctors had them at Chepstow and Lydney.

Before we had one, men took it in turns to walk, or go on horse-back or with a horse and cart to fetch the doctor. My father did more than his share, walking when it was his turn. We were lucky to be left in peace for more than a few weeks at a time as people seemed to be able to cope by day but at night panic would cause them to want the doctor! So to hear someone calling us up was a common occurance. Babies seem to have the habit of arriving in batches (our doctor swore by the moon phases) and I remember one week in particular when we were called up every night for a week.

The postal authorities wanted mother to have a post office so our sitting room became a busy place. The telephone was boxed in and the few people who were brave enough to use it thought that, as they could not be seen, they could not be heard. At first, of course, apart from emergencies, there were few calls for or from the locals.

With the installation of the post office came troubles. Until then we had little contact with people, except for those who came for eggs,

23

vegetables, pig-meat, walnuts and fruit, which my mother sold. But now, people came for mother to write letters for them and when her hands began to itch she was very ashamed to say that she had caught the 'dirty' infection, the itch from, the doctor said, handling coins and other people's materials. That started the rule of Jeyes' fluid as a cure-all for everything. We put a few spots in our washing water for hands and faces, in the bath and on cuts.

Then came illness. My sister aged seven, a most beautiful child with large blue eyes and blonde curls developed diptheria, an all too common infection at that time. I was four years old but those last days of her life are still as fresh in my mind as they were then. Until the day before she died it seemed that it was just a throat infection. I remember our doctor sitting on the edge of the table telling my mother there was nothing anyone could do. My mother was bowed with grief and my father was speaking angrily but all to no avail. That night I slept downstairs and the next day Gladys died.

In every village, before the district nurses came into being, one or two women could be relied upon to do what they could and to lay out the dead. At our end of the village was a Mrs. Harris, the wife of a fisherman, and the mother of a large family. She was what was then known as a "comfortable body", not very tall and with a reasonable figure.

The order of the day for ordinary wear was the black apron, which was changed to the white one for the sick room. I can see her standing midway down the stairs just after Gladys had died. She was waiting for a vest to put on her, and when she called downstairs to ask Mother if she had it ready, I can see Mother holding the vest in front of the fire and saying "I'm just making sure it is aired". As I have grown older and I think of those words, I feel choked. How deeply one can be touched by a simple statement made at such a time.

On the day of the funeral I was taken to a neighbour at the Tan House on the corner but the lady there wanted to see the funeral pass so she raised the blind a little and I also watched the procession. Of course, all coffins were carried to the church and every house on the route drew the blinds as a mark of respect, and everyone in the village able to follow the coffin did so. Immediately a death occurred, whether it be in that house, or if it were a relative living hundreds of miles away the blinds would be drawn and voices lowered. Black or dark clothes or black arm bands were worn, for some time.

The mourners attended the evening service on the following Sunday at the church where the burial took place and they all walked to the grave afterwards. From the time my sister died my mother was afraid that I would get diphtheria and I was watched over and, as folk said, the wind was hardly allowed to blow on me.

Having the post office, the telephone, a large orchard, lots of pigs and poultry, and three gardens there was far too much to do to sit down under the weight of grief.

The telephone was installed in 1913. And what fun we had with it in the early days. People came to look at it and they were afraid of it. "This new contraption" they called it. One man asked "How can ee yer anything on wires?", "I can't make that out" said another, "it don't seem right do it?". Old and young put their ears to the telephone poles to listen. We had lots of laughs.

Of course it was not used much for some time because only the banks and doctors had them and the Lydney and Chepstow police station, and perhaps a few business people. The main use was to call the doctor, or to take messages for the police. Most people only asked for doctors when babies were due, so consequently we had spells of night calls. Invariably men rushed off without bringing any money and Mother waited long spells for her money and often had to pay it herself.

A Welsh woman often came to ring her sister in Neath. If you cannot speak a language and you listen to the voice of an unseen person having a one-sided conversation, it is exceedingly funny. We dared not make a noise or we would have been sent outside, so with our handkerchiefs stuffed in our mouths we nearly died laughing, aching all over from being so doubled up.

There were few free moments and people on their way to the station, the inn or the shop found excuses to call at the post office, many because they hoped to pick up some scrap of information. They had a lot to learn because mother never divulged any business and we were told never to tell anything which we heard over the telephone or what was talked of in the post office or the house. A few women tried to ask me questions but I always had the same answer, "I don't know. You must ask Mother". I was referred to as the little girl who didn't know. Funnily enough I never had the urge to tell. Friends were not encouraged indoors in the daytime in case they gossiped outside.

We knew everyone's business, bad as well as good. The village police station had no telephone so we took all their phone calls. The station was at the top of the hill and many times I ran up with messages, written down by Mother but I knew what they were. Usually the policeman came down to telephone back again, but he always put Mother in the picture as to what was going on if she did not know the full facts.

There were very few forms to fill in but there was the occasional letter to be written for the few with relatives living some distance away. Sometimes there were long ways to walk with the telephone messages

25

but if they were not urgent the postman, who called twice a day on deliveries, took them in the morning.

What a different relationship there was between the Head Postmaster and the Sub Postmaster then and now. The Head and his wife often came to tea and we knew the clerks by name and had many friendly conversations with them.

It is easy to see that the post office soon became the focal point for all who wanted to pour out their troubles, or for those who hoped to learn something of interest, so we knew almost everything that went on in the village.

We heard of the family quarrels and skeletons in the cupboards. We knew before anyone else when women said they were "that way again", and the joy if a miscarriage helped them back to happiness again. Old women were experts at "reading the signs" and all the denials would not convince them when told that they were wrong.

In one or two cases children left home when they could no longer tolerate the strict discipline of the home. In two cases when this happened, we knew that on certain nights of the week the kitchen window would be unlatched so that the prodigal could come for food in the night. Mothers were usually last to bed and first to rise and a tramp could be blamed for a break-in. Being on the main road tramps were always passing but it was food they needed and they were seldom turned away. On two occasions tramps appeared to be the cause of the break-in. In the one instance terrifying the blind woman who heard them, and in the other the cupboard (there were no fridges) was raided and when the owner came down in the morning it was to find the kitchen table littered with the empty pie dish, in which had been the apple pie made for the next day, and a few crumbs were all that remained of the loaf of bread.

We were told exactly how much money people had, if they were lucky enough to have anything after the beginning of the week. One woman had a bank account and at times she would come to ring the bank about her pass book, very few knew what that was, and she would ask my mother or sister to write down items, so we knew what she had and what she spent.

Few people would have trusted a bank if they had money to spare. The teapot on the mantelpiece, a cup on the top shelf of the dresser, a drawer or a corner of the cupboard were the hiding places, if that is what they could be called. When the landlord came for the rent or the insurance man for his few pence, they openly lifted down the vessel containing the money to pay. Doors were seldom locked, even at night, but the small amounts were not worth stealing in any case. The favourite place, of course, was under the mattress and through all my childhood I slept on Mother's money. All beds were iron ones with laths on which were straw mattresses and then a feather bed.

Mother had her salary as post-mistress, rents from her three cottages and her three fields, money from the eggs and poultry, money from her two railway lodgers, from fruit, vegetables and joints of pig-meat and bacon when we killed our pigs, home-cured lard and perhaps home preserves, much of which she gave away. This was not all profit by any means for the pigs had to be bought and fed, so did the poultry, and gardens must be well stocked to produce abundance. Father, being a ganger on the Great Western Railway, had a better wage than most. With a large orchard we were self-supporting and we made several hogsheads of cider which were stored in the cellar.

If Father had charge of the money it would not have been so well looked after, especially on Christmas Eve when he and his friends spent the night in playing half-penny nap, and the inn was only next door.

Each week Mother sent her order to the head post office at Lydney with an account of what business had been transacted and the new supplies came in large brown registered envelopes. Several of these envelopes were used to hold the various monies, each duly labelled and put under my mattress beneath my feather bed. Also placed there was her own money, household money, the rents, money for the rates and so on. Only my mother, my sister and myself knew it was there.

In my bedroom was a chest of drawers with two smaller drawers side by side at the top. Every night the post office money, the stamps, postal orders and other post office stock was put in the drawers. Why this was not all kept in Mother's room I do not know. One Christmas Eve I remember Father came back from his annual card party having lost all his money and wanting more to go back and try again, so perhaps it was to keep temptation out of his way that my mother did this.

Money was not of first importance though. Enough to eat and drink, a fire and a bed, and a job was all most village people hoped for. The modern good neighbour schemes will find that they have nothing to add to the good neighbourliness of the past. "Draw thee cha-er up and 'ave a tater", "cum an' 'ave a bite, thee da looked starved", "sit thee down a bit, have a drop of cider", was the welcome at almost every door. No rush, no hurry, nowhere to go, life plodded on.

The funniest person who came to use the telephone was old Mr. Hall who decided he would start a fish round in the village. He was not too wholesome Mother said, but few knew the word hygiene in those days and there were too many germs around so a few more was no "great shakes" someone said.

27

No-one had to have permits so all he needed was his old horse and cart. He came to ask Mother if she would make out his order for him, add up the amount and telephone his order to Newport market twice a week. The market was twenty-three miles away but all trains stopped at Woolaston station so the next morning his order would be at the station ready for him to pick up. Folk who could not do sums on paper were sharp enough with the money in their hands. So Mother sorted out the order and the money side for him but he was terrified of the telephone, and would not try to use it, but he stood by while the order was given. He often had a boil or a carbuncle on his neck, so I christened him Buncle.

It was only in school holidays that I was able to listen to and enjoy the pantomime of the telephoning of the order. It went something like this:-

The old man, chewing his quid of twist tobaco, looking none too clean, his clothes, mole-skin trousers, an old jacket and a cap, stood by the counter.

"Mornin' Ma'am, here I be agen to worry ya." Mother would give him a cheery "Good Morning" and ask after his health.

"I got another of they carbuncles Ma'am and it da 'urt somethin' cruel" was often the reply.

After a word of sympathy, Mother would ask if he knew what he wanted to order and she would then attend to it. When he was satisfied that everything was on order Mother would say "you must learn to talk to Mr. Flack you know. It is quite easy — like talking to anyone else."

"Oh no" he would say, "I can't abide they things. They da frighten I. They da make me all of a tremble. But I should like to let 'em know as I ent very well and I got this yer carbuncle."

"Very well" said Mother, "when I have given him your order you can tell him yourself." "Don't give I that thing, just 'old it by me and I'll shout and tell um" was the reply.

When the order had been given Mother would say "Mr. Flack, Mr. Hall wants a word with you" and she would hold the receiver near to the old man, who would shout loud enough to be heard outside.

"How be Sir. I bent very well. I want ya to know."

Mr. Flack must have asked what was the matter. "I got a carbuncle on me neck. A gert big un. Ah, as big as a honion. Ah, a honion I said."

His repetition of the word onion must have made his hearer think that he was ordering onions for he shouted "No, no, I don't want honions, I be talking about me neck. This yer carbuncle as big as a gert big turnup an' it da 'urt sumut cruel." Mother would be there of course and say, "let me tell him" and he would say "Aye Mam you teln, I can't make un unnerstan." Mother would bring the conversation to an end by

28

repeating what the old man wanted Mr. Flack to know after which she would offer the poor fellow words of sympathy purporting to have come from Mr. Flack who had said something very different. But old Mr. Hall went away very pleased.

At one of the big houses in the district a family arrived with much style. Everyone gave them credit and looked up to them as being of the "upper class". The sister of the wife came to stay and she often came to use our telephone to ring a gentleman (married) at the local town. The conversation were about dogs and it was usually found necessary for them to meet it seemed, always to do with the dogs of course. Another little secret we had to keep. A year or so later the family quietly left, and people local and from the towns came to the post office to know if Mother knew where they had gone. Of course they had taken good care not to leave any address, and we often wondered if any had traced them.

If we had repeated half that we heard on the telephone we should have upset many people. It was the thing to run to us to ring the doctor for the least thing. The doctors soon got wise to this and to us they made some disparaging remarks which we could not pass on. They knew, as we did, that within a short time after any visit or prescription, the person would soon be out again possibly enjoying a pint in the local.

One of the Lydney doctors, fed up with one man's constant moanings, gave him sixpence and told him to get a couple of pints of cider which would do him more good than doctor's medicine.

Then there were the calls to the firm in Gloucester who collected dead horses and cows and the farmer whose animal had died in the field or stable was too upset to use the telephone himself.

People rang us and expected us to get relations a long way off to come to the telephone, or to deliver messages at some outlandish place, but we soon put a stop to that and told them to write. Often the postman would pass the messages on, verbally, if necessary, because few people *could* write letters before the First World War.

Mother was asked to help people write letters. I remember sniggering at a love letter written by a young soldier, not at the wording so much as at the spelling, but then I was too young to realize that to a mother, a wife or a girl friend, these letters were as precious as gold regardless of errors. But I did not learn that lesson until the Second World War.

The inn next door was often first stop for men who drew their war pensions or the "Lord George" as they called the old age pension. Wives often came with them or in their place and then went off to the shop. It was easy to sign a name or put a cross or write a good imitation of the man's signature and this often caused trouble. One couple, in particular, had many rows over this. Mother knew that if the man collected the

29

pension not a penny would find its way home to the large family, so often Mother put up with abuse when she let the woman draw the money.

Some old age pensioners were not well enough to come to the post office and a few of them were blind. Many of these lived in remote cottages across fields. Mother and Father often walked many miles at weekends to take the ten shillings to these folk and often added a bit of bacon, a few eggs, a bit of home cured lard or something from the garden. Sometimes I went with them.

The blind were so grateful and so gentle and one old man used to ask me to sit near him. He would put his hand on my head and say "such lovely soft curls and the parting is dead over your left eye. I've got no hair and no eyes but I thank God every day for the kind friends that help me."

What a different world it was then. Oil lamps and candles, stone floors, dirty great fire places and often a newspaper on the table to do duty as a tablecloth.

The house in which I was born stood on the side of the main road, between two hills, with an inn next door, and a brook with a deep trough, across the road. The roadside by the brook was of some importance as it was a stopping place for so many travellers, and upon it pigs were killed and the cider mill came to make our cider.

The motor car was a curiosity, and the splendid traction engines pulled along side to rake out the ashes and build up their fires and the steam rollers used it for a parking space. Piles of stone were also deposited for the old stone breaker to break up into smaller sizes for mending the roads.

The first of the charabancs parked there and riders stopped for their horses to drink. And, during the First World War, convoys of soldiers, with horse drawn wagons, guns, loads of hay and foot soldiers often halted beside the stream. On many occasions my mother woke me to see them outside the house.

Greater excitement for me was when the circus animals walked by or when the traction egines, pulling the fair, stopped to see to their engines and to take up water. It was a grand place to live, so full of excitement and I did not need to get out of bed to see all these things and the early morning travellers.

Needless to say, the brook was a favourite play place and I had more than one lot of punishment for falling in. What was the punishment? The usual one for that age, being sent to bed and then Father came up with the strap. Boys often had the buckle end of the strap but if anyone accidently caught a cut from the buckle it was considered just punishment. Luckily, I didn't.

That same brook flowed through fields where we picked mushrooms, watercress, orchids and cowslips, where we ate Sour Sally and spent many an hour making daisy chains.

We roamed those same fields to try to find the nests of the many plovers or lapwings, listening to their constant call of "peewit". Their eggs were a delicacy and we had them for breakfast. What endless joy we found in the fields and the brooks. We picked lots of cowslips and washed them, then we poured hot water over them and how we enjoyed our cowslip wine; it was wine indeed to us.

We also picked a variety of flowers which we pressed between two pieces of glass and asked all we saw to give a pin to see a poppy show. What simple pleasures were ours.

In our favourite fields there were ponds green and slimy, but the haunts of so many interesting creatures. We took home tadpoles and put them in old boilers and when they became baby frogs we went to the Severn to pick up pieces of cork on which the tiny frogs sat until the sad day when they jumped out to leave us.

Newts fascinated us for a while and we kept those in water, taking them out to watch their movements. But to see the lovely dragon flies and watch other tiny creatures in the ponds took up much of our time, rather to the annoyance of our parents when we returned looking like urchins.

The old cottages were built of stone and even on the hottest day one felt cold when first going inside. Our fireplace had a big open chimney and one could look up and see the sky. Soot was the everpresent menace and often it fell just as a lid was lifted to check on the contents of the saucepan. One day there was a large saucepan of blackcurrant jam ready to pot when down came the soot. As a skin had formed on the top of the jam, with a lot of care and a lot of blowing the jam was reclaimed, more or less edible.

Getting the fire going in the morning to boil the kettle and to fry the bacon was a miserable business. But it got done. I can see the Sunday morning breakfast pan with bacon and kidneys sizzling away. On Saturday mornings the emery board came out and knives had to be cleaned. One day I discovered that steel knives cleaned very well in the soil so I stuck them in and went to play in the road. Not for long. I soon got hauled back to do the job properly. Another task was hammering bits of china until they were as fine as dust to help the hens lay eggs with stronger shells.

Most houses had floors of large flag stones, which sweated in damp or sultry weather. Between the stones the filling looked more like dirt than

31

cement and the constant damp from scrubbing often made gaps through which mice appeared. I often made a lasso with cotton and lay in wait when mice were active but only once had a success.

Linoleum soon rotted on stone floors so most people made rug mats for warmth and comfort. Most winter evenings some time was spent making these mats and every possible bit of material was kept to be cut into strips.

Our house was one of the first to have a water tap indoors. There was a tap outside but when Mother decided to have water laid on to our house and also to her three cottages, there was no shortage of volunteers to dig the trenches for the pipes. There was no thought of hot water, of course; that had to be obtained by lighting a fire under the large copper or boiler.

The candle which lighted us to bed was taken away and we lay in utter darkness and in fear. I used to hold my own hand to fool myself that I was not alone. Then I would start calling for my sister to come to bed and she would give me a thumping when she was sent up before she wanted to come. Gladys had died in that bedroom and I could not forget it.

In Mother's bedroom was a large chest and what child could resist a peep inside such a treasure trove? I spent many happy hours delving in that chest. I loved to dress up as most girls do, and the high necked gowns with their boned laced collars were a great attraction. The velvet neck bands, the gold guard watches, the feather boa, and the fur stole, the ponyskin coat and trinkets which were going out of fashion, were all stored away.

I could be happy for hours draping myself, but something else was a greater attraction for at the very bottom of the chest there were two books which held my attention. One must have been a medical book for I stared at the skeletons drawn there and thought they were strange and weird; they fascinated me. As I looked at them I felt that I was being very wicked but I did not know why and the need to put them out of sight was ever present if I should hear the slightest sound.

The other book was even more of an attraction. How I wish that I had it now. It was either the Bible or only the Old Testament, but it was a huge book with the most gorgeous pictures in colour and each picture had a sheet of tissue paper over it. Decorated capital letters started each page and two pictures I still see clearly.

One was of Sampson with his hands in the lion's mouth, the other was of Solomon's judgement. Sampson was depicted as a strong boy with thick legs. He wore a short loose robe tied with a cord.

When I first saw the picture of Solomon, I was horrified for he was holding a baby by the foot and the child's head hung down. In his other hand Solomon held the sword to cut the child in half to settle the dispute between the two women, knowing that the real mother would be the first to react to the gesture. On the face of the one woman was the look of horror while the face of the other showed little emotion. At the first sight of the picture I took it to Mother to ask about it so that later I could look at it without fear, knowing that the child had come to no harm.

Our house was an 18th Century one and Mother's bedroom originally had three windows but one had been filled in and the window sill made a splendid shelf and standing in the middle was a bust of Julius Caesar. Where it had come from I do not know and somehow it scared me and I was afraid to touch it. It was white but of what it was made I do not remember, but to a small child it was a weird object. Sometimes, as I looked at the books from the chest, I imagined that it looked at me and that one day it would come to life and speak.

All the pictures of outside scenes in the big book had the same types of clouds. These clouds were fat and billowy with silver linings but peeping out around lots of clouds were fat little faces of cherubs and pretty angels. I stared at the real clouds in the hope that one day a cherub or an angel would appear but they never did. Over sixty years later, cloud formations still fascinate me, especially the billowy ones and I am still fanciful enough to look for shapes.

We also spent evenings looking at pictures in the fire; how real they were. We roasted chestnuts in the fire, toasted cheese on the trivet hooked on the bars, and the oven was always hot to roast an apple, an onion or a potato. What a joy an always-hot oven was, and the kettle was always singing on the hob.

But my greatest pleasure was to climb trees in our orchard on a windy day and to sing as loudly as I could as I swayed and imagined myself on a ship. I made up my songs about anything I saw around me: the hens, the pigs, the fruit on the trees — just anything.

There were times when I loved the orchard and could climb the trees, when I could talk to the pigs and the hens; when I could pick the apples of my choice. But there were times when I hated it. These were when apples had to be picked and put in sacks for cider making, when the trees were shaken and the walnuts had to be picked up and set aside for selling at Christmas. It was my job then to count and bag the walnuts which were sold by the hundred. One hundred and nine was the number for each bag, somewhat like thirteen being the baker's dozen.

On cold, frosty mornings, gloves would not keep out the cold when we picked up the apples which had to be collected before the animals

33

and the hens ate them. In one of our gardens, which we called The Patch, was an apple tree which was called the Batheer. How I wished that lightening would strike it, for it was huge and cropped heavily every year. I sometimes got my friends to help but they soon tired.

Living on the main road we had many callers; some welcome and some not so welcome; some caused no trouble and some who hung around and had to be watched. But all in all the doubtful ones were few and far between.

The tramps, we called milestone inspectors, were numerous. Almost every day at least one called. Some we remembered from previous calls. We were happy about these, knowing that they wanted only food or a hot drink. Most of them looked reasonably well, their flesh more or less clean and they did quite well for clothes. Mother kept all cast-offs in the cupboard under the stairs right by the front door so that they were get-at-able when any tramp called. How grateful they were.

They were never refused tea and food. Sometimes they had some tea in the bottom of their billy cans, and occasionally some sugar. We never touched their cans; we let them hold them while we poured in the boiling water and the milk or whatever was needed. Many cooked dinners were eaten on our back wall and many hundreds of chunks of bread and cheese were carried away. We thought that our place was marked but whatever signs were used, we never knew, but often searched for marks outside.

We preferred the tramps to the gypsies who also were regular callers. The gypsies were most persistent and were foot-in-the-door types and expert wheedlers. Most people were afraid of them and there were stories of spells and so on; people were very superstitious about so many things. Gypsies had learned their psychology in the School of Life. They needed no books. Gypsies knew the right approach, they knew how to flatter, how to break down any resistance, and how to make a person believe that they really had the powers of telling the future.

"You have a lucky face my dear" melted my heart. "I can see great happiness coming your way. Just cross my palm with silver and I will tell you your fortune." Who could resist it? Certainly not the young folk.

The long black plaits wound around the gypsies 'heads, their swarthy complexions, their black shawls, their long dresses and enormous baskets made them easily distinguishable. Children would often hide or turn back rather than run the risk of the gypsies casting a spell over them. Of course the gypsies were expert poachers and no doubt some of them helped themselves to fruit or vegetables at times, but I cannot remember hearing of them doing anything to earn the discredit which was always associated with their tribes.

Mother was very fond of Aunty Mary Anne, and they had so much to talk about. I can recall some of the family troubles she talked of. Those things would be commonplace today. She was a beautiful woman and I loved to sit and look at her.

Mother had a friend at Lydney. Her husband was an engine driver on the Great Western Railway. On Thursdays, when the post office closed for the half day, Mother went to tea with her on occasions. We went by train, and the house was close to the station. Mother took a starched pinafore for me to wear at the tea table, over my velvet dress.

In our house, and most others, in those days the mantel shelves were draped with 'pelmets' made of heavy material like mohair or a serge material trimmed with heavy bobbles. They must have been a great fire risk as well as a harbour for soot and dirt. Chairs were draped with antimacassars and shawls were very much needed in the cold draughty places. All beds had valances as much to hide what was underneath as for the appearance.

Equally, windows needed blinds as much to be drawn at the time of a death or when a funeral passed by as for the real purpose. Horse hair sofas were a misery to sit on, they were stuffed too hard and it felt as if you were sitting on a pack of needles or thistles. The old harmonium with its carpet-clad pedals found a place in many homes.

A lot of the light from the small windows was blotted out by pots, most beautiful ones, in which were Christmas cactus and maindenhair ferns of great size, while the aspidistra stood to gather dust in corners or on side tables. Eight-day clocks competed with the groaning old grandfathers to boom out the hour and its quarters. My Uncle's clock terrified me when it let out such a groan between each stroke, midnight being the most dreaded hour.

We must not forget the what-nots, which stood in the corners of the parlours, and were well stocked with ornaments and other bric-a-brac treasured by the owners. In the early nineteen hundreds the fourth commandment was kept quite rigidly. After six days of dawn to dark toil it was good to rest. Our church was out of the way and many villagers went to the chapels nearer to them. Sunday school was held in the church on Sunday afternoons. Several children walked together and we were eager to get there early to "play" the organ but few wanted to go into the little cubby hole to blow the bellows by pressing the long wooden shaft up and down. Someone was left to keep watch for the teachers and the rector so that we could rush to our seats and look as innocent as angels. We rang the church bell, swinging the rope in turns,

35

never thinking we were in any danger. We chose our hymns, enjoyed our lessons but most of all on summer days we loved to be taken around the rectory garden when we were told to choose a rose which would be cut for us.

Confirmation day was a great day in our lives. We were the V.I.P's of course, and we had new white dresses and we wore confirmation veils in which we felt like the Virgin Mary.

Funerals, whenever possible, were held on Saturdays, so that as many men as possible could attend. There were no hearses; the coffin being carried shoulder high to the church, often-times a matter of two or three miles. Most villagers attended. It was somewhere to go, something to talk about. At the height of the flu epidemic in 1919 many young people were brought home for burial. One I remember in particular was when the sister of the young woman being buried screamed as the coffin was lowered, "Don't put her down there. Bring her back". Many children died. I can still picture a child dying of tuberculosis, as thin as a skeleton, sitting in the front desk, not long before her death. No-one realised the gravity of the infection. In one week I attended three child funerals, T.B. and meningitis being the cause of the deaths.

At home, Sundays were what I call the No-days. Everything could wait until Monday, no matter how urgent.

No singing of songs, no knitting, no mending, no gardening, no sewing, no whistling, no reading of anything except from the Bible or some religious book, no wearing of weekday clothes, no going out to play in the road. It was for me, church at 8am if there was a communion service, church at 11am, Sunday school at 3pm and church again at 6.30pm when often Father and Mother came too. After church some members of the choir came to our home and we sang around the piano while Father played the hymn tunes on his flute. We each chose a hymn. Whenever I was asked to choose one it was always "Fair waved the golden corn" but I have no idea why.

The first car owners were mine owners from Wales. The first ones were not very reliable and those who drove them had very little or no idea what to do when they broke down which was often. Our house lay in the dip between two hills. Many came to grief through going too fast or too slow or mostly braking too harshly. Some turned over so we were quite a clearing station for those in trouble.

Often, on a Sunday morning, I would see every chair in our living room occupied by a stranger who had broken down and who had been taken pity on by my parents.

The first open tourers had the running boards on the sides, and the ladies wore big hats with veils tied over the hats and under the chin. The pace was slow and the motorists often stopped to talk to passers by. I remember going home after a carnival all in yellow, when a large car stopped and the driver and his lady told me how nice I looked and each gave me a sixpence.

Village people resented the coming of the car and many old folk refused to walk on the side of the road when one came along.

One evening I was a passenger in a large open tourer on the outskirts of the village when we came upon an old man who was walking home to his cottage, which was luckily not far away. A blast on the big bulbous horn was ignored a couple of times and the car had to be stopped. Turning round the angry man shouted "Stop blowing that bloody horn. I bin on this yer road a seventy years or more and I bent a-going to move for thee nor that bloody new gadget. Thee cast stay behind and wait till I da to my gate and then thee cast have all the road to theeself and I hope thee dost end up in the ditch." So there was nothing for it but to wait and as he leaned over his gate he shook his fist and shouted "Bloody things."

I am sure that the winters of the early 1900's were colder than they are now.

I had to collect the milk from the farm, and the number of times I fell on the ice I couldn't count. It was good that we collected the milk in cans with tight fitting lids or I should have had many more double journeys. All children and most grown-ups had terrible chilblains on hands and feet and on backs of their legs. The usual way of trying to bring relief was by rubbing raw onion on them.

More than one winter farm ponds froze solid and horse drawn wagons were driven over them by the farmers to cut hedges and load up the debris.

Village folk took lanterns to place around the edges of the ponds so we could see to skate or slide. Horses fell often too and the first cars overturned at the foot of the hill outside our house. The animals had to have hot food; the hens sliding on the frozen orchard had to have Indian corn made into a kind of gruel by pouring boiling water over it and their water thawed, while the hungry rats and foxes paid many more visits, and the egg production fell off badly. They were hard times for the keeper of a small-holding if he was dependent on his stock for his sustenance. I can still see myself as I ran home from school crying with the cold. But then came the spring and all the lovely produce from the garden. Spring cabbage and gooseberries arrived in time for Whitsun, kidney beans in July and plenty of peas in June when the Severn salmon were at their best and not too big.

A salmon weighing six to eight pounds was bought from the local

37

fishermen who sent most of their catch to Long's at Gloucester by train. Duck, salmon, chicken, picnic ham or a goose we did not consider luxuries. Country people reared their own pigs and poultry.

Almost all Palm Sundays I remember as being wet and windy. On the flowering day folk came from far and near and Mother enjoyed talking to folk about days gone by. One of the women had been Mother's bridesmaid so they had plenty to talk about.

On the verge beside the brook an old one-legged stone breaker sat. How he managed to sit on those sharp stones all day and hammer them was a mystery to the children. We tried to use his hammer on our own to no avail. Mother often gave him hot drinks and food on cold days as he sat there with the sack around his shoulders to keep out the weather.

Although my mother was born at a small country inn she had an aversion to drink and we saw the results of so much of it when we lived next door to the Woolaston Inn.

In my earliest recollections I hear singing in her lovely centralto voice in the early morning when I woke. As she worked the treadle sewing machine she sang the Sanky and Moody hymns which she had sung so often when she was a member of the Methodist church. As she made Father's shirts, and all the garments we wore the air was filled with sounds of "The Old Rugged Cross", "We Will Gather at the River" and "Yes, Jesus Loves Me".

What a wonderful sound to awake to each day. She made beautiful velvet dresses for herself and for my sister and I, in blue, in brown or in crush-strawberry, a pink shade. She sent to Manchester to J.D. Williams for the material and how excited we were when the parcel arrived. She was always smart with her velvet and lace, stiff boned collars, long full sleeves, and sometimes a band of black velvet around her throat with a jewel inset in it. I liked to dress in these things. Her feather boa, or her fur stole set off her dresses. Her hair was combed straight back from her face which needed no artificial aids.

Her blue eyes shone when she was happy but they had not always shone that way. She had wanted to marry her cousin, a smart dapper man, but her father would not allow it. The belief was that if cousins married the children would be of low mentality or even "daft" which was a word in common use.

Living near her home was my Father who was a handsome man, and an old man often said to me, "You know, your Father and Mother were the most handsome couple who ever walked out." Whether on the rebound or not I do not know but they were married in a Gloucester church.

We kept several pigs, for breeding, for pork and for selling live. When the colder weather came they were fattened on the boiled mangolds and lots of meal. Dates were marked when killing should commence and everything was ready so that pig-meat could be ready for Christmas.

My bedroom window looked out on the road and the brook and how I hated the mornings when the killing took place. It was so awful to think that the pigs which had been treated almost like humans should, on a cold dark winter morning, be rudely taken to the brookside to become meat.

Straw was placed in readiness, and the pig bench put beside it with buckets and cloths, pumice stone and that awful butcher's knife. The poor creature would be manhandled on to the bench, its screams cutting through the air; how I dreaded it. I pulled the clothes over my head to try to deaden the sound.

The pigs were not stunned. The poor creatures were held fast while their throats were cut. I still shudder when I think of it. When all was quiet I would peep out, but often at the wrong moment, in time to see one of the men gleefully catching the blood in a bucket. This was later used in the making of black puddings.

Then the flames would leap up by my window as the pig was laid on the burning straw to burn off the hairs. If it was a porker, boiling water was used for scrubbing it. When the pig was returned to the bench it was cleaned and the clean-flowing water of the brook was put to good use.

The pig was then carried around to our back kitchen where it was hung from a big beam, head downwards. It was then cut open and all the organs were removed and examined by my father. Bowls, buckets and baths were everywhere, for the liver and the intestines. When all was removed the inside was washed and the carcase left to cool and "set". A piece of hazel branch about a foot long was inserted to keep the body well open.

A day or two later the butcher came in the evening to cut out the joints and several people came to order or to take away such things as griskins, spare-ribs, sweetbread, lard, chitterlings and bacon. All these had to be noted while boys came to ask for the bladder which, when blown up, made a good foootball.

The washing of the chitterlings was a horrible job. Gallons of water washed through the intestines and they had to be turned inside-out with a stick. We had cold water laid on but people who did not have this luxury took the things either to the tap at the roadside or to the nearest brook.

While the pig hung in the back kitchen I was terrified. I could not sleep at night in case it moved, it really haunted me. I would not go near it and made detours around the house not to see it.

The sides of the pigs were laid on a bench to be salted, another horrible job. One of us would have the salt, the saltpetre or the dredger of plain flour ready. For, I think, about three weeks this went on and then the sides were ready to hang on the kitchen wall.

After some weeks the bacon was fit to cut. It had to be tasted and tested first so I kept out of sight because to see my father cut off and eat a small piece raw made me thoroughly sick.

The smell of the bacon first thing in the morning always made me feel ill and it is small wonder that I did not taste bacon until I was fifteen years old and even now the sight of pig's liver in the butcher's shop almost turns my stomach.

Nothing was wasted. The lard was melted and eaten on bread. The old adage went:

> On Monday we had bread and dripping,
> On Tuesday we had dripping and bread,
> On Wednesday and Thursday we had
> dripping on toast,
> But that's only dripping and bread.

Our lard was kept mostly for winter coughs and it was a proven remedy. 'It will grease the inner pipes', the old ones explained. It was warmed and put on top of jam and it set and made an airtight seal.

The pig's head, of course, was made into brawn, and the feet and trotters were boiled and thoroughly enjoyed by the men of the household as were the faggots.

When pigs were not well or when their tails hung straight the remedy was coal. A shovel of small coal was put into the trough and it acted as a medicine.

An old sailor told me that sailors also ate small coal when they were off colour.

When there are animals there will be rats so that it was not unusual to look into the pig troughs and see rats or to open the bins in which food was kept and find them. This meant, of course, that ratting became quite a sport.

Guns, ferrets, sticks, stones, gin traps and rat cages were used. The gin traps, now illegal, were in common use and cats were often the victims. It was usual to see cats with deformed or with part of a leg missing but these crippled animals were usually shot. My own cats were often victims and some of those had to be disposed of and many times I cried when cats with legs hanging by a thread had dragged themselves home after being released from a trap. I released cats on two occasions from these cruel traps being badly bitten in the process.

Most merciful were the rat cages in which some bait was put and once the rats were in they could not get out. Mothers and their families crowded in and it was quite a ceremony when Father took the cages to the brook and all the children and some adults came to see the drowning in the trough. Guns were brought by neighbours and a watch was kept for the rats coming to feed at the trough when the pigs moved away. Loaded guns were often stacked against the wall in readiness and children were warned to keep away, and luckily they did. Rats also ate the hen eggs, and the baby chicks and ducks and it was not safe to put the hand into a nest without looking first.

I was four years old when my seven year old sister died of diphtheria so that when I started school shortly afterwards, the headmistress, who taught the reception class, was very kind to me.

When I moved into the first class I must have been able to read fairly well because I remember staying in from drill as we called our physical training then, to teach a boy to read. We sat on the end of the desk near the old tortoise stove which suited me well in the winter as I hated the cold.

The new school master who came just before I moved up to the big school was tall, thin and very severe. When he came he had a poor opinion of the village in general and the school in particular. His first words were a promise to lick us into shape and to put the fear of God into us, which was no idle threat.

In those days, no allowance was made for those who lagged behind. The misbegotten idea that all children could learn and failing other methods, the method of hitting it into them was tried out, not only in Charles Dicken's day.

Let me go through a typical day. When the last bell rang or the whistle was blown, we all rushed to our lines in a set order. There we were inspected. Clean necks, clean nails, tidy hair, no loose buttons or safety pins, no dirty shoes. Those who fell short were told to improve on the morrow.

Then into the classrooms in dead silence. We remained standing until told we could sit, upright, and with our hands behind our backs. The register was called and we went to assembly. After prayers and Bible reading we returned to our classes for scripture and to memorise the commandments and certain Bible passages.

Then came arithmetic and the chanting of tables, and some easy rhymes to help us to remember these rules. At seven we were expected

41

to read well and know all our tables and to be able to apply the four rules with number capacity, length, time and weight. I was always good with figures so I was happy but many had no play and were kept in after school to correct their work.

There were rules for everything. Geography was learned like tables going all around the British Isles chanting Newcastle-on-the-Tyne, Stockton-on-the-Tees, Hull-on-the-Humber etc., and the names of the rivers in their order. There was some way to remember lots of other places like "Long-legged Italy kicked poor Sicily into the Mediterranean Sea."

Smoke blown by the wind and the look of the river Severn provided our weather forecasts.

History was learned like tables. Dates were most important. Our "Bible of History" was Arnold Foster's book and how we revelled in our victories, the British were always right; I wish we had known a little of the other side, but we were great patriots and were proud of the pink patches on the map of the world. We learned the kings and queens of England like a poem:

> First William the Norman
> Then William his son
> Henry, Stephen and Henry
> Then Richard and John (and so on, to end)
> Came good Queen Victoria and
> And seventh Edward her son.

Then the dates to go with these were learned: 1066-1087, 1087-1100, 1100-1135.

I still use this and find it very easy to sort out periods in history through it.

Reading was all important and there were no abridged editions for us. Sir Walter Scott was hard going, as to get the gist of the story, we had to read so many descriptive passages. The Headmaster guided us through many of these passages and pointed out the beauty of them but for ten year olds to be enthusiastic about Scott was asking quite a lot.

Scott, Thackeray, Shakespeare, Longfellow, Dickens, Matthew Arnold, Mrs. Harriett Beacher Stowe and Rudyard Kipling were but a few authors we had at our fingertips.

How he made the people live again for us. We wept for Topsy and Little Eva, for Oliver Twist and David Copperfield, for Sohrab and Rustum, for Coriolanus, Uncle Tom and for Dora.

We learned passages of Hiawatha, and of Morte d'Arthur, the whole of such patriotic poems as 'The Revenge', 'If' and 'The Thousandth Man' and many more. Mrs. Beesley's History of Rome was a great favourite and so were Aesop's Fables.

Thinking back, I am amazed at the amount of English literature we absorbed in those few years and I pay tribute to the man who made all this possible. I would also add to that, he never ceased to teach the lesson that he knew and to quote from Morte d'Arthur: "It is better for a man to leave behind a good portrait of his character than a finely painted portrait of his face."

Our biggest worry was handwriting, especially when we were in the lower classes. We copied beautiful copperplate writing with loops just right, thin upstrokes and thicker downstrokes; every letter so perfect. The Head would come to the classroom door and say "Pens down". That was enough to scare us but when he brought the cane, how we trembled.

We were used to being called fools, blockheads and idiots, and sarcasm was cruel. We hated being asked questions in case we gave the wrong or silly answer to be greeted with, "Oh wise young man how I do honour thee" or "The genius hath spoken". Then would come the usual pause and we knew what was coming. "Did I say geni-US? I made a mistake. I should have said geni-ASS." He often informed us that it was easier to get blood out of a stone than to get any sense out of us.

Picture study lessons were always interesting and we could at least look and say what we saw and what we thought, but the expressions we learned and were taught to apply were used too often. Everyone's nose was 'roman' or 'aquiline', horses of the Stuarts were always 'richly caparisoned', all hands were 'expressive', smiles were 'enigmatic' or 'sad' and I remember them all so well as I see in galleries, on the television, or in the cities, the paintings of the great artists.

Today the teachers have no jurisdiction outside school, but the village schoolmaster went for a walk after school each day with an ever watchful eye for wrongdoers. Children watched him too and they breathed a sigh of relief when they saw him on his homeward journey. Who was that in a certain orchard last evening? Who did not raise his hat to Mrs. James? Who was playing outside when he was too ill to come to school yesterday? And so on. It was difficult to try to get out of it as he had a way of knowing or of getting someone to tell tales. So assembly time was not only the time to praise God, it was also the time for the wrath of God through his exponent. We were pleased when the session was over.

I well remember one family who lived quite three miles from school. They were poor and often they had no boots to wear across the sodden

43

fields but young though we were we saw the injustice of the punishment they had for being late.

Dirty heads were very common. It was a constant worry to keep them clean. I wonder how many notes stated "please move Mary away from Jane because she has come home with nits in her hair"? At home we had only to put a hand to our scalps when we were told to get the small-toothed comb and lean over the sheet of white paper spread over the table while the hair was raked through and the paper minutely examined. Fleas were common, especially in public places. Luckily there were not public cinemas or halls to go to.

Silence in schools was a must unless the lesson called for reading aloud, chanting verse or tables, or answering questions. A teacher would often drop a pin and we were expected to hear it having been warned previously that we were to listen. In sewing, the teacher used to insist that we were not sewing correctly if she could not hear the click of thimbles.

My sister, after her marriage, went to live in a Cotswold village which was still under the dominance of the Lord and Lady of the manor. Most of the people in the village lived in houses belonging to the estate and some of the older residents were out of touch with the goings on beyond a small radius. In the 'twenties, I went to visit my sister. I liked to keep abreast with the fashion which then was the very short, sleeveless dress which was considered by the young as being "it" and by the elderly as being shameful.

During the afternoon a man came to the door and when he was asked inside he took one look at me and in great confusion said, "I be so sorry miss, I'll come back when you be dressed." He hastily made for the door and when I told him that I was dressed and this was the latest fashion he said "Well all I can say miss is I hope you don't catch yer death of cold. You da make me feel cold to look at ya". Needless to say the poor man was too embarrassed to stay long.

When later I had some Hebden cord riding breeches made to wear for touring round the country on the back of a motor cycle I was told that I should be ashamed and asked "Whatever is the world coming to?" In that outfit I caused quite a commotion in St Ives when a child drew attention to me by saying "Oh do look Mummy, there is a woman in trousers."

What fun we had from small things. At the Tan House around the corner lived a lady who wore beautiful bonnets with plumes and ribbons. We were allowed to play in the road in the evenings as long as

b) Mrs. Clark wearing a dress about 1929. The one when a country man who called was so embarrassed he said 'I'll come back when you be dressed'.

we did not go out of sight of our house. One night, while the lady was there, we saw her shadows on the blind and we watched as the feathers danced as she talked to Mother. It then became a regular thing for me to invite her round and to tell the children around to come and watch and we had as much enjoyment from looking at the blind as children today would have from a spectacular film.

We spent a lot of time by the river Severn. Everyone loved to go to the Severn and it was the worry of every parent. Many children were drowned, and even fishermen lost their lives but the river was like a magnet. The fields around grew mushrooms, plovers nested in the grass, curlews, wild duck and partridge were there for the man with the gun, wood for fires was in abundance on the shore, it was an ideal place for picnic fires and the air was good to help the children sleep at night.

We swam in the dirty water and we waded to rock pools which were clean. Several went together to pull each other out of the deep mud. They were wonderful times and we did not see the danger.

I have a Parish Magazine for 1914 and these are a few extracts:

"We English are fond of washing. There is no need to wash every day. A capital plan is to dip a towel in a basin of water and then standing , rub yourself all over with wet towel. We should have a hot sponge down once a week.

Don't waste soap. Put scraps in a pan, pour on a little water, and leave in a warm oven until the water evaporates.

Onions are wholesome and good for the digestion. Potatoes are over-rated being 76% water and the rest starch. Never eat meat more than twice a day and never drink while eating meat."

Gambling. The Chief Constable of Manchester has said that "gambling is on the increase and runs drink close as a cause of social and moral ruin."

Enormous prizes are offered and a member of Parliament asked the Postmaster General whether there had been a marked increase in the number of sixpenny postal orders sold recently.

The Postmaster General replied that the sale was two hundred and twenty-seven thousand per week more than in the twelve months previously, and that the increase was due to certain newspaper competitions.

A lengthy explanation of what a competition was followed, and a Mr. John Hobson summed it up "Gambling is the determination of the ownership of property by appeal to chance."

Not too clear a definition to the folk in 1914 I imagine.

The advertisements are many and varied, with great claims

made in cures. "A completely paralized man cured by Dr. Cassells tablets in six weeks." Domestic servants were needed in New Zealand. "By any steamer, £2.16.0d. If girls pay their own fares they will not be refunded. If they borrow their fares the amount will be taken from their wages." Members of the Church Traveller's Club could holiday in Switzerland for £7.19.6d and by the Italian Lakes for £8.12.6d.

Home entertainment was simple, telling stories, gossip, singing, playing cards, whist or draughts, which we played for hours.

The gramophone was considered a poor substitute of which most older folk did not approve. A young man living close by had an 'His Master's Voice' with a big horn. Children sat on the bank outside his cottage to listen to the records. I was quite obsessed by it and one day in the school holidays he told me that I could borrow it. It took me some time to collect the gramophone, the horn and the records but at last I had it all set up.

Mother warned me how angry Father would be if I did not get it all back before he came home. As he enjoyed music and he played the flute, and in his younger days had been a splendid dancer "running" dances and dancing classes at the Town Hall in Lydney, I was sure that he would like the gramophone.

I sat spell-bound at the old songs, "Harvest Moon", "Poor Old Joe", and the twanging banjo was wonderful filling the air when Father walked in. Before he shut the door he said "Shut that thing off! I will not have that canned rubbish in here! Get that thing out of here. You can sing and play better than that twanging rubbish." So there was nothing for it but to trudge back with all the records and the big horn and the gramophone. I did not think that they were heavy to bring home but they were terribly heavy to carry back.

When the radio came the older folk said "Taint natural" and they hated that too for a while. The first folk to have one would have not only a room full to listen but more listened outside as well. Music on the radio was described as caterwauling and one man said he would far rather listen to his old tom cat on the roof than that horrible row. Like all new things, there was suspicion that it would bring harm.

The vicar was persuaded to have a generator and lights put in the church. The idea was not a good one. The lovely lamps were taken down but the lights broke down so often that eventually the lamps came into their own again. How we loved it and how we laughed when during the service the electric light failed. It was great fun.

Even when electricity came to the village, lots of people had no faith in it and they always kept lamps trimmed and took their candles to bed.

It was not until the 'thirties that a district nurse came to the village. Until that time any woman who was capable and willing to attend the sick was allowed to do so. They officiated at births and deaths and they gave a lot of their time to their duties.

One cannot picture how difficult it was for these woman who had no transport and very few materials to use when they got to the house of the sick. Called out at night they trudged through fields and lanes often carrying sheets and something to put on the new baby. They took home with them clothes and bed linen to wash and occasionally a child who could not be looked after at his own home. Morning and evening they attended the sick, often taking food to the very poor, and some of their own children's cast off clothing. Gratitude was all many had to offer for the services. A lift on a farm cart or later on the pillion of a motor cycle was help indeed.

Such a woman was Mrs. Kingston who devoted many years to such work and received no pay in return. She sat all night with the dying, made and administered remedies like elderflower tea, for influenza and for pneumonia, and in her quiet and efficient way she did much to comfort and to reassure her patients. She laid out the dead and was called upon to help clear up after suicides, and some of those tasks were horrible. She needed the constitution of a horse to do some of the things she carried out.

Everywhere superstitions were rife. It was a wonder anyone surived the bad luck which was always threatened.

If two met on a stair, one must go back. It was very unlucky to pass. It was also unlucky to turn on the stairs, one should go to the top or bottom before retracing the steps.

One must not view a new moon through glass, and it was not safe to sleep in a moonlit room, the moon did strange things to the brain.

Knives crossed meant a quarrel, and if knives were given as gifts a coin must be tendered or the friendship would be cut.

Pearls meant tears and they also broke friendships.

To meet a funeral, a load of hay or a cross-eyed woman on a journey meant trouble.

If a bee, a bird, a frog or a toad came indoors that was a sure sign of a death in the family, as was a crowing hen which was immediately killed. To cut one's nails on a Friday or on a Sunday was to encourage the devil.

To see one crow meant sorrow, and to wear a green outfit was asking for bad luck. I wore a green hat to the hospital the day before my father died and I was told that I should not have done so.

Never move house on a Friday, you will be out again before the year has gone.

Some things brought good luck. Seeing a black cat cross your path, putting a garment on inside out, meeting a chimney sweep, picking up a pin, or a dark haired man bringing a piece of coal to the house at the New Year, were among the best known.

Reading tea leaves was a serious pastime.

When my parents moved into the house where I was born, an old Irish woman named Mother Liza Delaney laid Bibles and prayer books on the floor in the doorway and insisted that the family walked on them to keep the devil from entering.

She was a strange woman who people said had strange powers. They were afraid to meet her in case they upset her as one man named John O'Hare had done. When the woman got angry with him she cast a spell on him with the words "May your hair fall out in patches."

Whether she had detected some scalp trouble or whether she really had powers no-one would say but my parents said the poor man in a very short time had lost most of his hair, so that when the woman died there was a great sense of relief.

When the first cars came, Mother Shipton's predictions about the horseless carriages were told and retold, and her prediction that ships would go without sails and men would be seen in the air.

Three aeroplanes came down in the village fields and we all ran to look at them. Two of them had to be dismantled to be taken away by train, much to the amusement of the local people who had not yet accepted these things. One managed to get airborn and crowds ran to the fields to see it take off.

If one had to pin-point the time when the villagers came out of their small corner it would no doubt have been during the First World War. It became necessary for women to take the place of men in many jobs, some of them having to dress like men and a whole new way of life opened up for many.

Some of our local girls drove tram cars and ambulances and we were all excited when they told us about their work. After the war, these girls and women were no longer content to stay at home and there was a drift away. Several young men went to Australia but most of them returned after a few years. A few men and women went to Canada and most of those stayed.

I do not remember much about the War but some things stand out clearly. The troops who marched by in the early mornings; the horse drawn loads of hay; the horses stopping to drink at the brook; and the rationing of food. We were lucky as most of our food we produced but some things were certainly in short supply.

The coming of television and radio has, of course, penetrated all the small corners, and with the various forms of travel and the equality of the sexes, the breaking down of the idea of the rich man in his castle and the poor man at his gate, we moved along into the future, and who knows what that will bring?

Astonishing "things" have happened during my life-time. We dare not think what the next decade will produce.

"Water Under The Bridge"

John Smith

I was born on 21st October 1902 son of Josiah and Rosina Smith, and my early life was spent in poor circumstances. My father was serving a sentence of imprisonment for desertion from the army. He had joined the regular army, then one night he had been involved in a fight in the barrack room. He was placed in the guardhouse under arrest. In the morning he escaped in a baker's cart that was leaving the barracks.

He subsequently joined five other regiments during the next twelve months. He deserted from each and burned the army uniforms in an effort to cover his tracks. He succeeded, and went to work in the South Wales coal mines but eventually returned to Bristol to seek a job nearer the family. He was looking at the job advertisements in the local paper when the police came in from Bedminster Police Station next door and arrested him as an army deserter. He was sentenced to a term of imprisonment.

My mother had a hard struggle to keep herself and me. She managed to do so by working hard at home, doing tailoring work for several clothing factories. Todd's Factory, in Chatterton Square, near Temple Meads Station, was one. She worked at home from 5am until often after midnight to provide food and clothing for us, and first of all, when my father was in Horfield Prison, to take him something as prison fare was very meagre.

My father was released from prison, then worked in several Bristol coal mines, but latterly in the South Liberty coal mine, near Ashton Vale. There was a long strike of coal miners before the 1914 war; it lasted thirteen weeks, I believe. Things became very hard and we used to get free meals at the Bedminster Salvation Army Hall, Dean Lane. We were given mugs of cocoa and large slices of bread and margarine.

a) John Henry Smith aged 16 in 1918.

I had to take my two sisters to the Temperance Hall, Bedmister Parade for a free dinner, walking from West Street as we had no money for the tram fares. We were given boiled fish and potatoes with a heavy layer of sauce, and thick slices of bread and a mug of tea. At weekends I walked to an old coffee shop on Radcliffe Hill. It was a shop with a bay window, and inside one could see the array of steaming hot faggots, peas and potatoes. What a glorious smell that was, on a cold winter's day! I had a free ticket for a jug of soup only. I carried it along the pavements for some two miles — in both hands, chest high, to prevent slopping it over. The shop is no longer there but it will always remain in my memory.

I went to work as a baker's boy. Starting at 6 o'clock in the morning, I helped to bake the bread in a coal-fired oven until school began at 9am. Then at dinner time I delivered bread in the Ashton and Bedminster district until afternoon school started; then again after school until dark, or even later. My wage was one shilling and sixpence, plus a loaf of bread on Saturday, for a sixty or seventy hour week. One Friday the baker, who was a very religious man, told me the world was going to end the next day — Saturday at 12 noon. I asked him if he would pay me my one shilling and sixpence and give the loaf of bread to me on Friday instead of Saturday evening as the world was going to end. He gave me the sack for asking.

At 5 o'clock each morning the cotton factory hooter sounded, and farm carts began climbing Fire Engines Hill with their hurricane lamps alight, and the driver fast asleep as his horse plodded on its way. The carts contained vegetables for the Bristol Market, brought in each morning from Cheddar and Axbridge.

Each morning the knocker-up, for modest fee, would tap on your bedroom window with his padded pole to wake you for work. Night and morning the miner's wooden clogs clattered along the pavement, as they went to and from the mines, carrying their four pint tin of water and food tin, wearing corduroy or moleskin trousers. A pair of yorks, or straps, were tied just beneath the knees to help take the weight of their heavy trousers. These yorks, or straps, were also worn by labourers or navvies. The navvy usually had a 'little man' tucked inside one of these knee straps. This 'little man' was a piece of wood, cut like a spade, to scrape his shovel when it got clogged with thick mud.

Shops were open from early morning, 5am or so, until late at night. Often their wares were displayed on the pavement, and tradesmen stood outside touting for customers. On Saturday nights mother visited the fish or meat market. In those days there was little refrigeration, and perishable food had to be disposed of if unsold on Saturday night late, so poorer people did their shopping then, as it was sold off cheaply.

Pawn shops were numerous and well patronised. We children used to earn a penny on Saturday for going to the pawn shop to get a neighbour's Sunday suit out of pawn. All sorts of things were pawned — suits, watches, clocks and blankets. The favourite tale was that people had even pawned a sheep's head wrapped up, as the pawnbroker did not always open the parcel! The usual thing was to put the parcel on the counter and say "Mum says the same as last week." There was a comic card of a beery-nosed woman carrying a grandfather clock into the pawn shop; the captain said "Grandmother puts the clock back."

With the penny earned we would go to the latest film at the cinema.

Pearl White in 'The Perils of Pauline'; 'The Black Box'; Charlie Chaplin; Cowboys and Indians; 'Lieutenant Pimple'; 'The Keystone Cops', or Fatty Arbuckle. What thrills one could have for a penny! A bar of chocolate or a comic paper thrown in — smoking a Woodbine and being sick!

What were our chief fears in those days? There was the School Board man, terror of all truants, and the police constable with his steady gait. He wore a cape which he threw at your legs when you were running away from him. This brought you flat on your face. There was the fear of getting the 'birch' if found guilty of breaking the law; and there was always the chance of the bailiffs taking away your furniture for debts unpaid. Another unwelcome caller was 'The Duffer' who called weekly to collect credit money for clothes obtained. Every so often it was necessary to do a 'moonlight flit' — when you disappeared with your furniture and all to dodge your debts. My father came home one night from work and found an empty house. Mother had moved all the furniture with a hand cart whilst he was at work, and he had to enquire from neighbours where she had gone.

Towards dusk the lamplighter went his rounds, with a pole and a ladder to light the street lamps. Electric carbon lamps sizzling away lit the main roads, but oil and gas lamps were still used in the side streets. The town streets were alive at night as shops kept open until late. From the club rooms of the pubs could be heard the singing of the 'Buffalos' or 'Druids'. There was the hot chestnut cart and the hot potato man, and struggling drunks taken to the police station on a four-wheeled stretcher.

At last came the weekend. On Saturday and Sunday the youth of Bedminster paraded the local parks or Bedminster Parade. Lads sported a buttonhole flower in their coats. Oxford bags and blazers were the order of the day. Bowler hats were still in fashion, and it was quite the thing to carry a swagger cane under your arm. Brass bands were playing in the parks — each had a bandstand and a dancing area around it where the lads did a turn with the lasses.

At weekends the pigeon fanciers organised races. Once there was a gas explosion in the street where we lived. The recently laid gas main leaked. One chap was in bed and he ran into the street in his shirt and no trousers shouting "Save my pigeons" — Andy Capp style! In summer, we Scouts pulled a trek cart out to Hancocks Woods and camped by the stream — cocoa like mud and scorched toast!

It was a favourite trip on Saturday or Sunday evening to take the penny steamer from the Nova Scotia public house wharf at the Cumberland Basin, to the steps opposite the Bristol Hippodrome. You passed the Mardyke Ferry and the training ship for boys — into the heart of the old docks — in those days crowded with steam and sailing ships. Sailing ships berthed beside the quays right up to the City centre; cargoes of hides, hogsheads of tobacco, locust beans, monkey nuts, and a smell of tar and rope. What dreams of far-off lands they conjured up in our boyish minds.

What a sight for us younger ones to see the fire engines come charging out of Bedminster Fire Station! The engine was drawn by horses. The harness hung over the central draught pole and could be lowered quickly on to the horses' backs when they were placed underneath. The glass sliding doors enable a quick take-off, and away they went — galloping hooves, clanging bells, smoke from the water-pumps and the tenders with water and ladders. Horses and carts pulled in to the side of the road. Tram cars halted, children ran after the engine, and then came the clang of the bell of the horse-drawn ambulance.

Beside the Fire Station was the Police Station, with the Black Maria in the yard. This was a closed, horse-drawn van for the transportation of prisoners and police. The scaffold for the public execution of persons convicted on a capital charge was erected over this gate. I believe the last person executed in this way was a servant girl who killed her mistress in a fit of anger.

A walk through Bedminster before 1914 presented many sights which have long since disappeared. Horse-drawn bakery drays and railway carts, teams of Shire horses returning to their stables, the horse-drawn hearse proceeding to a funeral with bearers walking in front, wearing top hats and frock-tailed coats. Barrel organs playing merry tunes in the streets, with the operator collecting pennies in a tin. Shops with sawdust on the floor. Drinking water troughs for horses and dogs at strategic spots, especially near hills. Tram cars trolley poles, sparking overhead. The horse-drawn ice cream cart with a fellow we called 'Johnny Ice Cream', who played a concertina as he toured the streets. The old knife-grinder with his pedal-driven grindstone. The rag and bone man with his balloons and goldfish in exchange for rags, bones or bottles. The fly-paper man with his sticky fly-papers, and his song:

"Oh, those tormenting flies; catch 'em alive"

There were street traders with horses and carts, costermongers two-wheeled barrows. Women in Welsh shawls balancing wooden tubs of Welsh cockles on their heads crying "Cockles a dweli". Boys selling hot cross buns at Easter time, carrying a basket and handbell and shouting 'One a penny, two a penny, hot cross buns". The baker's shop where, before we had a gas stove, we took our cakes or roast and paid a penny to have it baked or roasted for Sunday dinner or tea. Polly Reynolds, who kept a second-hand clothes shop — she was a Salvation Army woman and had an open Bible in the window. She turned over a page every day and gave you a tract every time you made a purchase. And Cloggy Davies, who made and sold the wooden clogs worn by labourers and miners. All this, and so much else, is now "water under the bridge".

There was also the trolley made with four pram wheels and a plank, with rope reins for steering, on which we made trips into the countryside. We also ran behind the four-horse brakes loaded with people taking a day trip to Weston-Super-Mare or Clevedon — the people would throw pennies to us.

Trips to Leigh Woods and many a slide on what we called 'The Donkey Slide' — that huge slab of rock just underneath the Suspension Bridge — highly polished by the seats of many trousers and pants — many of us returning home with seats of our trousers worn through. Today the same rock slab is covered with slogans and grafitti. In those far off days they would soon have been erased by the friction of many pants.

There were so many thrills for us children. The Coliseum in Park Row where they had a 'Menagerie of Wild, Untamed Beasts'. Once Professor Stevens, the Demon Barber, shaved a man in the lion's cage in the Coliseum menagerie. There were peep shows in Castle Street — the tattooed lady, the strongest man on earth, the bearded lady, the fat boy, the human beast from the jungle. All sights for a penny. A childrens' roundabout on a horse-drawn trolley toured the streets, a penny a ride. In winter there was ice skating in the flooded fields at St. John's Lane, Bedminster, and South Liberty Lane. One could earn sixpence by leaning a chair for the skaters to sit on and screw on their scates. Paraffin flares lit the scene.

On 5th November there were fireworks and a fire baloon in J. Cooper's Yard, West Street. One half-penny entrance fee to see the greatest fire-work display in Bedminster. There were fair grounds in town, and Charlie Heal's Roundabout — or a visit to Woolworth's where nothing cost over 6d.

I saw my first film at the Victoria Rooms, Clifton. We were taken by the teachers from South Street School to see 'Sixty Years a Queen' — the life of Queen Victoria; 'Birth of a Nation' and 'Quo Vardis'. On Empire Day the school children formed the Union flag on the Bristol City Football Ground, Ashton Gate, dressed in the national colours they moved and gave the effect of the flag waving. On May Day the young ladies used to have a coming-out day. They dressed in white, hired taxis to the Drill Hall, Old Market Street, and there danced around the maypole. There were summer carnivals at the Bristol Zoo, with fair and fire-works until after dark, and boat rides on the Zoo lake, and donkey rides on the Downs.

Never to be forgotten were the trips to the 'Old Gaff' as the Theatre Royal in King Street was called. We sat in the front of the gallery and used to drop orange peel, apple cores and sundry other things on the heads of the elite who sat in the stalls below. We made up our own street games — played hop-scotch on the flagstones, 'weak horses', tally-ho, knock-up ginger, five stones, shoot for goal, which way to London —

b) John Smith, as a child, with his mother & father. About 1906.

and we bowled our iron hoops. The girls played skipping games, one called 'higher and higher', and we all took part in 'dare' games. We gathered on the railway bridge in Bartletts Terrace in the evening to sing old-time songs, or we went swimming in the Malago — a place for catching tiddlers and bathing.

The coming of amateur photography provided new pastimes for us. We used an old cupboard as a dark room, where we developed our plates, and we printed the photos by the sunlight. Later we used gaslight and electricity to print.

At school 'do's' a man used to show magic lantern slides with various devices to animate them, and organised shadowgraph shows. He stood before a white sheet and threw shadows with a lamp or candle, representing cartoon animals with his hands. Sometimes they played us a phonograph, forerunner of the gramophone, with it's cylindrical records and ruby pick-up, huge trumpet and pedestal stand.

We took long walks over the fields in the Malago district. Then there were fields towards Dundry and Headley of wheat and corn, with poppies growing in the midst. We could watch the horses crossing and re-crossing the fields on the Dundry slopes as they ploughed or reaped.

The days that followed the outbreak of the 1914-18 war brought adult responsibility to many of us younger children. Fathers and elder brothers went away on military service, leaving the women and youths to carry the responsibilities of home and civil life. We grew up quickly in those days of shortages, queues, blackouts and black markets. At first it meant long queues for essential foods. Starting sometimes at 6 o'clock in the morning we queued outside the Maypole Shop, East Street, the queue stretching back a long way down Warden Road, keeping a place in the queue until mother came to relieve us in time for morning school. Often after waiting hours we got to the shop door and found the supply of margarine had run out and we went away empty-handed. There was a shortage of sugar and sweets, and we often had lard on our sandwiches.

There were horse-drawn gun carriages in the streets and Scottish regiments, like the Black Watch or the Argyll and Sutherland Highlanders, thrilled us boys as we marched along with them to the sound of the bagpipes playing 'Roamin' in the Gloaming' etc. We saw the wounded transferred to ambulances at Temple Meads Station for transport to hospital, and the German prisoners of war escorted to farms to work.

I had left school at the age of twelve and six months, having been in the top class for two years. I obtained employment with the British American Tobacco Company at Raleigh Road, Ashton, at a wage of four shillings a week, with one shilling War Bonus. I was engaged in soldering the tin linings of cases containing cigarettes and tobacco for the troops of the expeditionary force in France, the Navy and soldiers in many places overseas.

After the war I went to work in the South Liberty Lane Colliery, as a door-boy in the mine, on the night shift. I well remember my first night in the mine. I got my safety lamp from the lamp room at the pit-head at 10pm, and I was shown how to test it for safety by blowing around the joints between the glass and safety gauze of the lamp for air leaks. With eleven others I then entered the cage or lift that was to take us down the shaft. The gates were shut, a bell was rung, the cage rose slightly to release the safety catches, and then it dropped away at breathtaking speed — you just dropped away into space. The cage swerved from side to side as it rattled in the guides, then came the sensation of rising back up the shaft as it slowed up midway in it's descent to pass the ascending cage. The two cages passed each other and we dropped away again into space. Then came the same jerking, ascending sensation as we slowed to a stop at the bottom of the shaft.

Here a few electric lights lit the scene. Below the cage was a large sump containing water that constantly dripped from the shaft walls. Pumps were continually pumping the water to the surface to prevent the flooding of the mine. At the bottom of the shaft were the stables for the pit ponies. They were kept here, but were taken after a time for a spell in the fields on the surface. Here an overseer or fireman searched us for matches or cigarettes, and again tested our lamps.

Narrow roads led away in various directions — they were about six feet high and six feet wide. A single narrow track of rail lines ran along the road centre, and the walls and roof were supported with pit props, some being bent and broken under the stress of the weight above. We walked in single file along the passage-way between the rail lines, ducking our heads when the roof timbers were low. We placed a piece of tin or cardboard at the back of the safety lamp to prevent the person behind having the light shining in his eyes. We walked on, descending to a lower level for a couple of miles. The air was becoming stagnant and there was an odour of coal dust and damp, decaying timber.

We carried a gallon tin of cold drinking water and a tin of sandwiches. There were no canteens underground, and the coal dust made one continually thirsty. We also carried a small block of wood on our belts which was called a 'donkey'. We had walked a distance of two or three miles when we came to a place where there was a fork in the road. Here we stopped for a brief rest and took off some of our clothes, each man choosing a place behind one of the timbers to place them, until he retrieved them at the end of the shift. The miners sat in what was called a 'miner's squat', with their lamp between their knees at the roadside. There was talk of race horses, pigeons, whippets and pubs. Then the men split into two parties; our party took the road to the left which descended a steep gradient.

Now the purpose of the 'donkey' becomes clear. This block of wood was a length of log about a foot long and split in two. A groove had been cut in the concave side and a length of spring steel was attached to the forward end of the groove. The 'donkey' was placed on the tram line on the left, then one balanced oneself on it and placed the right clog on the other tram rail. Holding the safety lamp as steady as possible, you then slid away on the wet rails to the bottom of the incline. It was a rough ride and full of painful spills until some proficiency was gained — still it was much better than the hazardous descent on foot.

The younger chaps often let the older men have a start of a few seconds, as the older men travelled at a slower pace. Then we would slide down after them, shouting and laughing. Often this would end in a glorious tumble of men and boys, with some lamps being extinguished. This was very awkward as it meant a walk back to the bottom of the pit shaft to get the lamp re-lit, there being no way of re-lighting them in a working area owing to the danger of an explosion. At the bottom of this incline we came to another, steeper slope. We descended this until we came to a wooden door — it was here that I was to do my job.

The air system of the mine was operated by drawing the foul, gas-laden air up one shaft, while the fresh air descended the other shaft. This was done by the operation of a huge fan. There was a danger that with the many passages in the mine, the air would take short cuts back to the surface fan and so deprive the further workings of air, and create an accumulation of gas. To prevent this, doors and sometimes canvas sheets were placed across some roads to regulate the supply of air. The door I was to operate was one such. The coal trucks were hauled up the incline by a wire rope attached to the winding drum of an electric engine. The door had to be opened at intervals to allow the passage of the trucks. This was done by pulling on a chain passing over a pulley, which enabled me to open or shut the door at about half-hourly intervals. The door had to be kept closed as long as possible to ensure the greatest supply of air to the workings.

It was a lonely job, as there was no one to talk to. The hardest job was to keep awake — there was complete silence apart from the occasional cracking, and a dribble of dust or fragments of rock falling from the roof. I had to stay there eight hours with only the light of the safety lamp. I managed to pass the time, however, by reading some books.

Sometimes I had the company of small mice who came around to collect crumbs which I scattered, and they became very tame. The time passed slowly and I think they were some of the longest nights I have ever experienced. The danger was that, if I fell asleep, the trucks would smash into the unopened door and bring down the roof, burying me underneath. A young boy who relieved me at the end of my shift thought he had an answer to this. He attached a cord to his leg and tied the other end to the wire rope that pulled the trucks. The idea was that when the rope started to pull the trucks it would awaken him. Unfortunately the truck wire moved so suddenly that he did not have time to release himself, and he was badly injured before the cord broke. If I had the misfortune to upset my lamp and extinguish it, I had to stay in the dark until the end of the shift.

After two years of this, I started work at the coal face. I worked alongside two miners, filling the trucks with the coal they cut. It was a hard job; the roof of the coal face was only three feet high and the coal seams sloped at an acute angle. I had to kneel on the rocky surface and toss the coal by the shovelful over my shoulder for a distance of several yards from heap to heap until it was close enough to load it into the trams. I then had to push the laden tram along the low passages, keeping my head and hands well below the level of the top of the truck, as this only just cleared the roof. I carried my lamp by the hook with my teeth, leaving my hands free to push the truck.

Sometimes the truck became de-railed, and I had to exert all my strength to replace it on the rails. It weighed seven hundredweight, and it was only by bracing myself at one end that it was possible to lift the truck back onto the rails. When I reached the spot where there was a double set of tram rails, a pony would take over as there was more height. I would then return to the coal face with another empty truck.

This was heavy work and the coal dust filled the air. It collected in a thick paste inside my mouth. Ones back and head collected many cuts and scratches through contact with the rocky roof or sides of the passage. The miners were a jolly lot, some of the best I ever worked with; they laughed, joked and often sang at their work.

At times some of the rocky roof or floor bottom had to be blasted away to make enough height for the trucks. Holes were drilled into the rock manually by sledge-hammer and drill, and an explosive charge was inserted in the holes. We would then have to retire along the passage to a safe distance. The charges were detonated by an electric current from a small battery. After the explosion the workings would be full of acrid fumes and we would have to wave our shirts around to clear the air.

The pit ponies were very interesting, and soon learned some cunning habits. When you brought in the empty trucks you unshackled the pony from the couplings; you than had to make sure you coupled the shackles quickly on to a full truck or the pony, feeling itself free, would immediately bolt away into the darkness and back to the stables at the pit shaft bottom, a distance often of some four miles. There were three horses working in turn. They did two runs with the trucks, and then rested for one run. Sometimes only two horses or ponies were available, because of sickness or injuries, which meant that they had to work hard continuously. They would do the two runs, but would jib violently on being asked to do a third. It was unwise to get into a position where you had to get past the pony and the side of the passage, it would lean over with all its weight and stop you getting by, sometimes gnashing its teeth and rearing up at you.

Occasionally we had to get out quickly from the workings owing to the accumulation of poisonous gas, or because of roof falls. At times, accidents to the winding gear caused a delay of several hours in getting up the shaft. There is nothing like the experience one got on a fine summer morning after a night shift, to come from the darkness of the mine into the clear morning sunshine and to walk past the green fields towards home and a bath, and to hear the lark singing overhead.

The spinning wheels above us spin
The cage swaying from side to side
As we speedily rise from darkness.
The retaining gates swing open wide
Releasing us into the sunshine.

It was the end of the night shift.
From out of the darkness into light
From out of dusty depths
Into the clear air of a summers' morn.
It was like being reborn
The spinning wheels above us spin
The cage swaying from side to side
As we speedily rise from darkness.
The retaining gates swing open wide
Releasing us into the sunshine.

It was the end of the night shift.
From out of the darkness into light
From out of dusty depths
Into the clear air of a summer's morn.

It was like being reborn
To see again the bright blue sky
To feel the crunch of the frosty grass
To hear the birds singing on high.

To fill one's lungs with sweet air
Laden with the dampness of glist'ning dew.
To hear the lowing of the cattle there
In the misty dale beside the stream.

Day after day I relived that miracle
When the night shift ended
And once again I was free
To walk again on the surface
Of God's good earth.

Among the many interesting characters I met in the years following the First World War was an old chap called Dick. Dick was an itinerant — some called him a tramp; he called himself a 'Knight of the Road'.

The usual picture of a tramp was a fellow in tattered clothes, unshaven and unbathed, sleeping rough under haystacks or hedges. Dick was not like that. He was clean and tidily dressed. He travelled the country in the summer months working on railways, building sites, tunnels, the underground railways, and any public works. He was the fore-runner of the modern hitch-hiker or hippie. There was no social security in those times, and Dick stayed just long enough to earn money to take him on his travels. After doing one day's work he would ask for a sub or advance of wages equal to the day's pay he had earned. This gave him enough money for the night's lodgings.

He had a big silver pocket watch, which he would take to the local pawn shop and pawn it for fifty shillings on a Monday. When he obtained his wages at the weekend he would re-possess his watch for fifty shillings, then he would pawn it again for forty-five shillings to be retrieved the following pay day for forty-five shillings; to be pawned again for forty shillings. This went on until it required only ten shillings to retrieve his watch, then Dick would proudly boast 'The watch is mine again'. The advantage of this system was that Dick always had a watch at weekends. In fact, he called it his 'weekend watch' and was proud to be the inventor of his system of diminishing returns (to the pawn shop!).

He usually stayed in one place during the winter months, but when spring came along, Dick would get restless. He would gaze at the sky and say 'Just hear those birds'. The green buds would show on the trees,

63

the sun rise earlier each day, and the days would grow warmer. Then the call of the road would become too much for Dick, or as I nicknamed him 'Ding-dong'.

He would then collect his pay, pay his debts, and would again become a 'Knight of the Road'. He would walk the country road again, going from workhouse to workhouse, tramping the roads by day and sleeping as an inmate of the workhouse at night.

In the cell of the workhouse where he spent the night was placed a huge slab of rock. This he would have to break into small pieces with a sledge-hammer, small enough to be passed out through a small grill of iron in the cell wall, before they gave him a mug of cocoa and some bread and released him to go on his way. This stone was used in the making of roads, and was in payment for his night's lodging and food.

Dick knew how to brew a drink from herbs, and nettles, or berries; what nature could provide by the wayside in the way of food; how to bake a hedgehog in a pat of mud, and so be able to peel off it's quills; how to set a snare for a rabbit; how to fashion all sorts of useful things for his everyday use from wood, with his big pocket knife. He could remain motionless like a cat stalking it's prey when required to do so in the process of survival. He knew all the weather signs, and the bird and animal signals. He was an expert in the art of survival.

"Rainbows in a frowning sky"

Lillian Bentley

Corsley, Wilts

Our nearest neighbours lived in a small cottage in the lane adjacent to our house. At the back lay a sheltered garden where ozmunda ferns and yellow flags grew and where, to my eyes at least, all the flowers of the world seemed gathered.

Here were sky-blue larkspurs and Madonna lilies as tall as myself, borders of pinks, many coloured poppies and love-in-the-mist, crown imperials with five crystal drops in each flaming bell, roses everywhere, and dozens of other beautiful plants. In springtime carpets of crocus, daffodils, snowdrops and violets breathtakingly beautiful.

Whether it was the heavenly blue of the larkspurs or the saintliness of the lilies, or the sweet drowsy warmth that seemed to be imprisoned in the garden, I do not know, but it represented Paradise in my imagination, and I walked in it, smelling the roses, thinking pleasant secret thoughts that I would share with no-one, a different child altogether from the one who climbed trees and quarrelled with my sister.

At the bottom of our garden near the stream stood a beautiful weeping willow tree. A swing hung from an upper bough. Standing on it and working your legs with all your might you could attain the giddiest heights, and yet always there was the possibility of going still higher. Short of turning a complete somersault it seemed as though that glorious rush through the air grew swifter and more glorious every time you flew into the green heart of the tree. Always you thought, "Now I can go no higher", and yet the next day you went higher still. To push a small brother or sister who wanted their turn on the swing when you longed to be soaring aloft yourself — how tedious it was. Nothing but the thought that the next day one could have it for one's own private delight made this last labour endurable.

With the exception of a few particular friends, flowers and birds were more real to us than human beings, and we greeted each new-comer with shouts of joy. The first thrushes nest, the first snowdrop on a cold January day and the first catkins, these were the things that made our hearts leap, I can remember, in Clear Wood one March evening finding the first primrose and the sight of it when gazed upon filled me with all beauty and fragrance of the world gathered in that soft pale face. My Father had the same love for this flower and he always wished to die when the primroses were in bloom. God granted his wish, several baskets of them scattered on him as he was lowered into the ground.

On Good Friday afternoon we would, whatever the weather, hasten forth armed with baskets in search of flowers to decorate the church for Easter, and every year we went the same way, for to deviate would have been in defiance of all Good Friday traditions. We would search the gulleys, hedgerows and woods rather soberly, hugging to ourselves the thought that after all this expedition was not just for our own satisfaction but that Christ would be pleased with us for wanting to make the church look beautiful.

Death — our own, anyone's, became unbelievable to us as we raced along up and down banks, over fields where we turned somersaults, disturbing the peewits as they ran through the grass with lifted crests. This was the real world where larks sprang heaven-wards on all sides from the turf under our feet.

Soon flowers began to appear, dog-violets, celendines, starry anaemonies, and the earliest cowslips. Filling our hands as we went we entered the copse which was the paradise of primroses. Nowhere else did they grow so large, so moist, so fragrant and with such wealth of enveloping leaves. I can still smell the intoxicating scent of the pollen and hear the hum of innumerable bees among them. At last, when baskets were full and our fingers ached with picking, our thoughts would turn to tea. On Good Friday there was a ritual about tea as with everything else that day — hot cross buns heavy with butter and cakes covered with pink sugar icing.

We lived in a thatched cottage surrounded by fields, woods and streams on the outskirts of the village of Corsley in the county of Wiltshire.

My father was the local Gamekeeper in the employment of the Marquess of Bath. I was born in July 1919 obviously the result of a happy husband returning home after the armistice.

Where we lived one could walk for hours and never see another human being, but I feel sure that did not upset my father who was happy to potter about amongst his rabbits, pheasants and other wild

a) Lillian Bentley's father (top back row, right) in a group of Longleat staff, 1919.

creatures. One of my early memories is going through the woods with the game-bag to feed the pheasants. Of course it was essential to learn the correct whistle in order to call the pheasants and this took me a long time to accomplish much to my Father's dismay; and only to be used when he was indisposed.

Our cottage was separated by a field from Trusenhayes Wood with a smaller Ladies Copse three fields away. Behind the cottage, about one mile away, was Clear Wood which seemed large and frightening to me until I found my way through the many rides and thickets.

The Marquess of Bath's estate was a very large one 50 years ago taking in Horningham, Maiden Bradley, Temple Crockerton, Corsley, in fact reaching almost to Warminster on one side and Frome on the other.

The seat of the Marquess was and still is "Longleat House" a magnificent stately home built on the site of a priory and completed in 1579.

There were nine under-keepers and one head-keeper. In the days of which I am relating the estate was teaming with game, pheasant, partridge, mallard, snipe and woodcock. There were also thousands of rabbits. Each under-keeper was expected to rear 1000 pheasants a season and was allowed casual help from one youth who was called a "bird boy", between 1st April and 31st October. We children loved this exciting time. Firstly the collecting of the broody fowls from farmers and cottagers and placing them in the hatchery or nest boxes. Then the enormous task of collecting sufficient pheasants eggs and keeping them at the correct temperature before placing them under the broody foster hens. Many is the time I have seen my father with a shirt full of eggs supported by his large leather belt which held up his trousers. I used to say "Give me a big hug Dad", hoping he would so that I could laugh at the awful mess which would have resulted.

As soon as the chicks hatched they were transferred to a field where the required row upon row of coops had been placed along with the drinking vessels. Each coop contained one hen and her brood of about 14 pheasant chicks. This of course meant constant vigilance on behalf of the bird boy or the keeper in order to ward off any marauders such as foxes, stoats, weasels, magpies or any other predators. The galvanized hut in which the sacks of rice and dozens of poultry eggs were kept was a special place for us children. On the way home from school, or if we were in the vicinity playing, we were always sure of a feast of boiled rice and hard boiled egg which did not please our mother who would have prepared a meal for her hungry children only to find that they had already feasted on a meal much more exciting than perhaps boiled rabbit, boiled potato with onions and swede followed by a suet pudding.

The pheasant chicks also enjoyed their food but alas their lives were short-lived for when they were about three weeks old they were transferred to the woods and fattened up for the kill.

Good drives were enjoyed by the Marquess and his quests. They were spectacular shooting times with bags of 500-1000 pheasants a day. Arrangements were made to serve lunches to guns, loaders and keepers. The beaters were given half a loaf of bread with half a pound of cheese and two pints of draught beer. I can remember our cottage being used for such an occasion. The polishing of brass and beating of carpets, not forgetting the sorting out of best linen and china for use in the best room for the Marquess and his guests caused my Mother to be in a tizzy for days. We children had strict instructions to keep out of the way or "Woe betide us". Forty men were employed as beaters, plus a dozen boys, who took up positions as blocks (stops). At the end of the day all the keepers and loaders would be in the Gun Room cleaning their masters' guns and talking about the events of the day. Not only were the gun barrels oiled but the men also were "oiled" with the gin which they drank while discussing the next shoot.

The keeper's life was a varied and busy one. He needed to know much about woods, animals, birds, guns, traps, poaching, weather and the law.

My Father obtained an intimate acquaintance with every field and tree in his area, and no little knowledge of natural history. By a kind of instinct he knew where any particular bird or animal was at any particular hour. He was bitter against poachers, and would have liked to see harder measures dealt over to them. He needed his robust health and his constitution was capable of with-standing the wear and tear of a keeper's life. The Game-keeper is often about the best part of the night; he cannot stay indoors because it rains.

Proud of his vigour and strength, my Father could keep on his feet without fatigue from morning until evening, going his rounds without abating one inch of the distance.

On a tree in a field near our cottage hung rows of dead and dried vermin, furred and feathered, impaled for their misdeeds, proof of an observant and conscientious game-keeper.

Our cottage was thatched and oddly gabled with walls three feet thick which kept out the cold of winter and the heat of summer. The front and only door opened directly into a square brick floored living room from which the stairs wound with their steep wedge-shaped treads up to our parent's bedroom, through which you had to go to reach the second bedroom, used only by us children. A window faced onto the orchard and the huge elm tree in the lane.

Our parent's bedroom overlooked the front garden and woods beyond the fields. The kitchen or scullery was the room which contained just about everything from boots to butts of trees split for firewood.

The living room ceiling was low and crossed by one huge square oak beam, darkened by smoke and age. Sometimes a peculiar odour filled the low-pitched room — it was emitted by roots burning on the fire, hissing as the sap exuded and boiled in the fierce heat. From oak, ash, elm and fir the aromic odour the scent of the earth was exhaled as they burnt. Above the wide fireplace my Father's double barrelled gun rested on it's rack along with others out of the reach of inquisitive children. Every Monday morning Mother did her washing in the huge copper that was part of the scullery. All houses boasted one of these important features. The copper was set in a huge mould of cement, and it was lined with zinc. The actual fire heated the water from underneath, the fuel being kept in place by an iron lattice-type door. Like most children too young for school, I used to "help" although tensions of her labours meant that I would end up being scolded or smacked as I was persistantly attempting to put my doll's clothes in the wash-tub. In those days washing day was extremely hard going for women who could not afford to send the dirty clothes to the laundry. Swirling the clothes round in the copper, then scrubbing them on the drubbing board and putting them through the huge and cumbersome mangle must have been hard for even the toughest female. In between all this, of course, she had to continually rake out the cinders and feed the fire.

The kitchen range was the only heating, the lighting was from oil lamps and candles at bed time.

Water had to be fetched from a well sunk about 20 yards down the garden. We were forbidden to go near the well which was reputed to be sixty feet or more deep and covered by a wooden lid. There was no safety rail or wall and the windlass with it's rusty chain and iron handle was the only thing on which to cling when lowering the galvanized bucket to the water. If you were careless the weight of the bucket pulled the chain too rapidly off the roller, and the handle of the windlass would fly round at a fearsome pace and deal you a blow on the head. The excellent water came from a spring deep in the rock below and no matter how long the summer drought, the bucket always came up filled to the brim with cold sparkling water that tasted clean and fresh. During the heat of the summer the shaft of the well was used as a means of cold storage by suspending food such as meats and jellies for setting, in the well bucket.

One day the mechanism broke causing the bucket containing a ham to drop down into the water. After much swearing and struggling Father had to get help as the water would be contaminated. Looking back at this episode I am always horrified. We watched from a distance, having been banished from the scene. Bucket after bucket of thick black mud came up and as the water was drained from the mud the bleached bones of small animals could be seen buried in it. I listened in horror as the men hazarded their guesses. "That be a cat, I reckon" one said. Another picked out a printed skull. "That be a rat's head, bain't it?" As well as mud and bones the bucket brought up several old boots, a shrunken trilby hat along with big, black, slimy slugs which must have been living on the sides of the shaft near the water line. I had never seen such slugs and ever after cowered away when one crossed my path.

Eventually the well was said to be clean and a brand new bucket was attached to the chain, the cogs that controlled the handle were oiled, and the well went into use again. The water tasted the same — no better, no worse, but for a long time my Mother insisted on boiling it, although my Father said this was shutting the stable door when the horse had bolted. Eventually we forget about the episode and drank the water as

70

freely as before.

I was confronted at the age of four with my first real glimpse into the outside world when I started at the village school. Then I remember the bewilderment of being surrounded by what seemed like hundreds of other children. After the protection of my family I was terrified.

b) Mrs. Bentley's father, John Charles Hole, with her mother Elsie Jane and her sisters, 1917.

When the mixture of boys and girls of all shapes and sizes closed in on me in the playground on that first day, I felt like the rabbit in one of my Father's traps. They stared at me, pulled my hair, spun me around like a top until I was dizzy and called me names. At last I was rescued by one of my older sisters who had not been aware of my plight, having been with friends in a different playground.

71

I was marched smartly off to the cloak-room and divested of my outer garments and introduced to the Infant teacher. The classroom was a seemingly secure haven after the rodeo roar of the play-ground but not for long.

In a very short time we played, wept, broke things, quarrelled, fell asleep and on waking discovered our ability for self preservation. Or at least I thought I had until I was dragged off howling to the Big-room to face the Head-master. I had actually bitten another girl for grabbing the toy I was playing with. Even now I remember the disgrace of standing in the corner with my hands on my head in the Big-room with the eyes of children glued to my back and the anger and scorn of my two older sisters who I knew would have plenty to say about the matter on the way home. My punishment from them was that they ran from me at the first field leaving me to find my own way home. Incidentally they received a severe reprimand and were sent up to bed early whilst I got away with it, my Father as usual saying "The young 'un be only larning how to stand up for herself, bain't she?"

We learnt simple patterns of facts and letters and through the seemingly long hours of the morning and sleepy afternoons we chanted away at our tables. Possible passers-by could have heard our voices rising, "Twelve-inches-one-foot. Three-feet-make-a-yard. Fourteen-pounds-make-a-stone. Eight-stone-a-hundred-weight." We absorbed these figures as gospel truths declared by ultimate power. Unhearing, unquestioning, we rocked to our chanting. "Twice-two-are-four. One-God-is-Love. One-Lord-is-King. One-King-is-George. One-George-is-Fifth." So it was always; had been; would be for ever; we asked no questions, we didn't hear what we said; yet neither did we forget it.

One nice thing about the school and this I think was universal all over the country, was the wonderful patriotic attitude on Empire Day. We all foregathered in the play-ground and we sang "Land of Hope and Glory", "Rule Britannia", "There will always be an England" and other appropriate songs, at the top of our voices. Everyone had a Union Jack flag and it gave us a wonderful thrill, a feeling of belonging, when the Union Jack flag was hoisted on the school flag pole.

With my two older sisters in the awesome "Big-room" and my younger sister now with me in the "Infants" I too looked for promotion at the age of seven. I found that I could write my name in both large and small letters, and subtract certain numbers from each other and count up to a hundred. The "Big-room" was ready for me. I found there was a world both adult and tough, with desks and inkwells, scratching pens, strange maps, strange words and possible perfection.

Gone for ever were the infant excuses, now I was alone and

unprotected, faced by a struggle which required new techniques, where one made pacts and split them, made friends and betrayed them, and fought for ones place near the stove.

I was in Standard One. We sat two to a desk and the first week I kept shooting scared glances at the walls on which were pictures of how the world came into being covering millions of years, showing Darwin's theory of evolution. I hardly dared to look at it because I knew the world had been made in seven days — it said so in the Bible and to think anything else was blasphemy.

School taught me that everyone was not equal. I noticed that some of us were brighter, cleaner, better fed and better dressed than others. From some of the outlying places in the village came the children who wore leaky boots and shoes and ill fitting cast-offs. They suffered permanent snuffy colds and came from a very large family whose father, a farm labourer, did not earn enough to support his family. The Mother dragged down by perpetual pregnancies was too busy trying to eke out the food in an almost empty cupboard to keep her children clean and healthy. The children often had lice in their hair.

The annual family outing was a day at the seaside. This was arranged and paid for by my Grandfather and was an event we looked forward to and talked about for a long time.

The last days before the trip were almost unbearable. We were almost too excited to eat or sleep. When the day finally dawned we were up at the crack of daybreak making sure that buckets and spades, bathing suits, beach towels and sun hats were safely packed.

The open-topped char-a-banc rumbled noisily along drowning our tuneless expression of a song. We drove up hill and down dale past churches and villages, through towns and twisting lanes; behind thickets and copses and suddenly, there before us was the sea, blue as the bluebells in the woods at home. We could taste the salt on our lips and the coast shimmered in the sunshine. Nearer the sea the sand was wet and littered with shining shells. My sisters and I were soon shedding our clothes behind our towels. We wrapped our small garments and shoes in our dresses and placed them in a tidy pile beneath the deckchairs before scooting off to the water's edge.

The sea stretched before us, vast, endless. The sand was coarse and cold beneath our feet and the ripples of cool water crept over our ankles before stepping forward knee deep into the unknown. Around about other children paddled, a few venturing to lie on their backs, lashing the water with their heels. Suddenly, I felt small and scared. I ran back across the sand to the safety of my family and the comfort of food, already I was hungry.

At last the sandwiches were unpacked, gritty with sand but delicious. My arms and legs were soon burned red and I frequently rushed into the sea to cool off. The sand was scorchingly hot so that it was painful to walk on with bare feet.

I settled down to make sandcastles with the other children. We dug deeper and deeper filling the moats with water from our buckets but soon the tide was already lapping at the battered remains of our sand castle, the fortifications crumbled and the castle was doomed.

A cool breeze sprang up as the sun sank and the pier cast long dark shadows on the sand. It was time to go home.

The char-a-banc was waiting by the pier and before boarding it we slipped our remaining pennies into a machine which dispensed bars of chocolate. We were tired and quiet on the way home remembering the day. The walk back across the fields passing the sleeping cows was almost done in my sleep and I did not remember going to bed.

We did not eat a lot of sweets when I was a child, it was considered bad for our health and for another thing we could not afford them. One special treat was to have an orange with sugar lumps inserted halfway in it. You sucked the orange juice through the sugar but oranges were only obtainable at Christmas time, when they were in season, not all the year round as now.

Sometimes Mother used to wrap up a few currants in a piece of paper in lieu of sweets or give us the sugar from inside the candied peel of lemons and oranges which was delicious but now practically unheard of. Occasionally she would sprinkle sugar on a piece of bread to satisfy the "sweet tooth". Even the poorest children ate better food than they do today. It was good wholesome food, very nourishing, nothing synthetic.

People indulged themselves especially on Sundays. As a general rule we had a joint of meat once a week with rabbits and bacon to fill in the other days along with fresh vegetables from the garden. The occasional pigeon pie was a treat as was the joint of venison on the day the deer were shot and about once a year we received a brace of pheasants from the Marquess. My Father always insisted the pheasants were to be hung for a week before being plucked and cooked.

Cley Hill, 800ft high Iron Age hill-fort, situated in the parish of Corsley (now owned by the National Trust) was one of our special heights of delight. The little troubles and disappointments of childhood fell away when we climbed high on the lonely hill-top, nothing seemed impossible to us. We would shout aloud in ecstasy, roll ourselves down the slopes and make the most amazing and preposterous plans.

In this region of bygone ages we pursued each other round and round the indent of the long gone hill-fort imagining ourselves among a horde of shaggy ancestors, advancing into battle with those flint headed arrows or bronze axes in the local museum. Try as we might we could never step backwards into the past.

In all weathers, at all seasons of the year, the hill enchanted us. We loved it when it was white with snow and the shadows marked its shape a cold and lovely blue. No matter how bitter the wind, we would climb up and pass one of those days that stand out in my memory as clear and white as the hill itself.

We loved it in the spring when it grew green again, when peewits cried and tumbled and the cornfields below took on a hundred tender tints. Summer, who flung across the hill a web of many colours that blended into one perfect whole and played a tune made up of a dozen minor tunes; of the broken music of sheep bells, the swish of wind through yielding grasses, the tiny tinkle of seedpods, the hum of bees and ecstasy of larks, the distant bleating of sheep — all these and other nameless sounds combining into one perfect harmony. How good then to lie in the grass, to feel the sun on our bare legs and to turn our eyes from slowly drifting clouds to the blue valley below, that seemed scarcely less remote.

Even wet days had a charm of their own — to watch the chalk track change to a milk-white river, or a rainbow give sudden birth in the frowning sky.

On an autumn day when a big wind was let loose in the world we became, more than at any time a part of the wilderness and freedom, as much in the power of the wind as the hurrying leaves, as the thistle-down sailing shoulder high, or the torn clouds.

We moved without effort, scarcely conscious of the ground beneath our feet asking nothing better than to be swept on and on by that tremendous presence. But, panting and radiant, we asked no questions, felt no fatigue when at last the wind dropped. Like all children we pined for a wild and dangerous earth, we wanted to feel that though savage beasts and half naked men no longer wandered abroad on our hills, there were still certain things that would never be tamed and such another mighty wind might one day rush upon us.

Out of the blue one day my Father announced we were to leave our cottage to live in a brand new brick dwelling situated on the Bath Road on the edge of the Longleat Estate boundary. We were not at all happy, least of all our Mother who feared for our safety on the busy main road. I was then ten years old with three sisters and four brothers, far too large a family for a two bedroomed cottage to house any longer. There was

75

not, we were sure, a chance of our lives ever being the same again.

Eventually we began to feel a dawning curiosity as to what this other place might be like so we took ourselves off across the fields and through Clear Wood, to view this unknown place. Here we found a half finished brick house in the corner of a field on the edge of the road.

We walked slowly home under the darkening sky. The wind had grown wild and cold, the ploughed fields looked strangely desolate in the twilight. Never had the grass seemed so green as in these last days. Never had the church bells sounded so sweet or the flowers so colourful, as they did these Spring-time days. We roamed out into the fields looking back for some fresh aspect of the place, laying up one more memory, binding our hearts with one more thread.

But the final day arrived and with it the large farm wagon and horses in which we travelled to our new home and a new life.

"It is time I confessed my passion for trams."

Sir Ronald Johnson

Portsmouth, Hampshire

These notes are an attempt to write down impressions of the physical, economic and social circumstances of a boyhood in Portsmouth sixty or so years ago. Reminiscences are inevitably liable to errors and omissions, and most of my statements must be qualified by an "If I remember aright...". Most of the events to which I refer occurred in about 1919-1925.

I was the only child of Ernest Bertram Johnson and Amelia Grace, née Kneller. My father was a cook in the Royal Navy; he was born in 1889 in Model Dwellings, a tenement built by housing reformers at the Arundel Street end of Church Path. My mother was born in 1884 in Winchester. She was a bright pupil, but an illness prevented her from becoming a teacher. My mother's father, Charles Henry Kneller, was the only grandparent I knew. He was an expert shoemaker and came to Portsmouth from Winchester to be employed in a high-class business in High Street. (Lillington's). Later he kept his own shoe-repair shop in Chichester Road. As a young man he was an active cycling-club member: this would be in the cycling boom years of the '80s or '90s. At different dates I inherited two bicycles from him.

Our friends were either ship-mates of my father's, or chapel friends, or fellow-Esperantists. My father was absorbed by enthusiasm for Esperanto, though he was prevented by long absences at sea from doing as much for it as he wished. I was aware even as a small boy that our Esperantist friends included several people of unusual goodness of character. Mr. and Mrs. Gall, who kept a chemist's shop in Arundel Street, a few steps from my father's birth-place, were benefactors of the surrounding poor for many years. Mr. Gall, to a small boy, was a man of awe-inspiring appearance with a long beard; a patriarch. Mrs. Gall wore her hair tightly brushed and had high cheek-bones, rather like an American Indian. Mr. Gall was a qualified chemist (as was his son after him), in whose name the business was run; but Mrs. Gall saw countless poor women in the back shop, advising them on domestic ailments and their troubles generally and making up bottles of medicine for them. (In those days medicine was not tablets or injections but bottles, to be taken by the spoonful after thorough shaking.) On Sundays the shop was opened in the evening; and early in the morning the Galls went forth botanising with a tin for specimens. They went to places I had not then heard of — for instance by train to Warblington Halt, from where they culled the hedgerows in what were then the lanes towards Westbourne. Sometimes the Galls had a musical evening, at which we sang around the table. Mr. Gall played the flute; I disliked being next to him, because the end of the flute dribbled on me, but that is where I learned the hymn tune "Wareham", which proved more durable than anything we sang at Sunday-school. It amazed me that people who apparently did not go to church were so good.

Naturally, a substantial proportion of our acquaintances were naval ratings, dockyard men or Admiralty clerks. The most superior people we knew were teachers, and still I think with deep respect of several names as people of dedication and intellect. They were not of course graduates, but had taken a certificate at a teacher training college.

On their marriage my parents rented two rooms at 8 Garnier Street, Fratton, and that is where I was born on 3 May 1913. Before May 1918 we moved to 35 Netley Street. Here we rented the whole house except two rooms, which the owner kept for her own use. She was an old lady to my eyes, who wore a long black dress, went out in a black bonnet and had a great collection of jet beads and a crystal chandelier. One day she went out and sold the house to the local undertaker for £200; she did not realise until it was too late that my father then became the tenant and she the lodger. I think we stayed in Netley Street about three years. Other people's misfortunes then enable us to move to a more attractive district — a house in Drayton Road.

Neither house had a bathroom, and the biggest room at Drayton Road, a bigger house than Netley Street, was 14ft by 9ft. In both houses one had to go out into weather to "go to the back". But at least it was a W.C. I do not know when I first saw toilet paper. In early days we cut up newspaper into squares, and later in life an Irish lady I knew used to say of unwanted circular letters "You can stick that on the nail behind the door".

We were never short of food; indeed as a small boy I was fat. Meals were simple and no doubt as cheap as possible. I remember lentil soup and a dish of mashed potatoes with cheese beaten into them, baked in the oven, and also being late for school because it took so long to eat a herring at breakfast. (My mother believed that fish fed the brain.) Thousands of families must have had a similiar routine; many dockyardmen went home for dinner at mid-day. I once called on a school friend aged about six, who lived in a poor court off Church Path, and was shocked to find him and his mother eating nothing but potatoes for dinner; we were never reduced to that. My father took his breakfast and dinner "on board", i.e. in Royal Naval Barracks, and came home to tea with bacon. But my mother and I did not share it, though the cat did.

a) Ronald Johnson with his mother about 1924.

In both houses there was a copper, i.e. a semi-spherical vessel for boiling water, built into a corner of the kitchen. In Netley Street the copper had a fireplace under it, in Drayton Road it was heated by gas, but both coppers had to be filled and emptied by ladling. The kitchen tap was the only one in the house. We took baths in a portable zinc bath filled from the copper. The range was "blackleaded", that is to say it was kept clean, black and shiny by the application of a black liquid with a brush, followed by polishing. When convenient, kettles were boiled on the fire in the living room. This arrangement was facilitated by the trivet, a triangular bracket clipped on the bars of the grate, where the kettle could stand and keep hot when not actually "put on to boil". The house was lit by gas, and we had a gas fire in the front room at Drayton Road. The living room had a "by-pass", by which the light could be reduced to a mere spot when one went out, so that on return one did not have to fumble for matches in the dark. My father's sister in Gosport lived in a house which had no lighting upstairs, and other friends (they were Scots) said that they never had a light on in the front bedroom but relied on the gas-lit lamp post on the pavement outside.

My mother obviously had no electrical aids to housework such as a vacuum cleaner or a refrigerator. Neither did we have a wireless or gramophone. We had to amuse ourselves. My father and I sometimes played cards, especially cribbage; my mother did competitions in Answers and John Bull and very occasionally won a small prize; my father translated songs and other items into Esperanto; I had a Meccano outfit and a clockwork train, and when I was 14 my mother bought me a Little Nipper box camera (with plates) in a sale for 2s 9d. Our grocer once invited us to spend an evening listening to his crystal wireless set with headphones. We were not tempted to buy one.

Our household goods included a rosewood cabinet with a glass door which contained sets of Hamsworth's Encyclopaedia and a medical encyclopaedia and few pieces of crest china — small objects bearing the coats of arms of various holiday resorts. There were also small models, in some kind of white ceramic, of Westminster Abbey and St. Paul's Cathedral, which I greatly admired long before I saw either of those churches. Stainless steel we had none, not even in our knives, which were cleaned by the application of "knife powder" (brown and pungent), again with strong rubbing, which gradually wore the knives away.

The meal at which friends were entertained especially on Sundays, was tea. There would be bread and jam, cake and stewed (or tinned) fruit and custard. (I discovered when I went to Cambridge that tinned peaches are not universally regarded as the high-spot of a good tea.) Housewives who could afford to do so took great pride in their tea cups and plates, and frequently bought new and supposedly prettier sets even though the old were not damaged. These admired tea-cups often had irregular rims which were very awkward to drink from, at least to a big boy.

At one time we were taken up with a craze called "spiritualism", in which a tumbler was inverted on a smooth table, everyone put a finger on it, and questions were asked of the spirit supposed to be inside it. We were favoured with visits from a spirit called Obadiah Neverlive. The game of pit also hit us (fresh from Wall Street) and I have not quite recovered yet.

The pattern of Portsmouth streets as it existed in my childhood has largely been obliterated by war damage and rebuilding on more airy and more logical lines. The streets I knew curved and twisted about in intricate patterns which one would suppose greatly added to the cost of building. The lines they followed, as Dr. John Chapman has explained in The Common Lands of Portsea Island, were those of the fields and cultivation strips which existed before the island was built over. As a boy I loved exploring not only the streets, but also the alleys; and these, as Dr. Chapman explains, are often ancient rights of way which street builders could not disturb.

When we lived in Netley Street the surrounding network of streets and alleys fascinated me, and as I grew older I extended my explorations, on foot or bicycle, over the whole town, including the opposite extreme of the social spectrum, the secluded residential lanes known as the Thicket and the Retreat off Grove Road.

Perhaps I inherited my taste for back streets from my father. The Esperanto group met in the Co-operative Women's Guild room on the corner of Besant Road and Garnier Street. We used to walk there on Tuesday evenings, and my father insisted on a short cut through the back streets. My mother hated this route because it was so gloomy, with only occasional gas lamps; there was no thought that these dark streets might be dangerous. After the meeting we came home on the tram. That is where I learned what people smell like after an evening in the public house.

There were more tradesmen in the street than there are now. The milkman pushed a small truck carrying a churn, from which he ladled out milk into small oval cans with a handle, which customers hung on a hook on their doorposts — where no doubt they were safe from cats. The baker called with a van drawn by a horse. The muffin man, pushing a hand-cart and ringing a bell, was an occasional visitor. So were the cats' meat man, the scissors grinder and the rag-and-bone man. The last had a singing call "rag-o-bone" — and gave paper windmills to children in exchange for jam jars. Coal was sold from drays by the hundred-weight bag. A regular caller at the house was the man from the Refuge Insurance, with whom my mother had insured her father's life at a weekly premium of three pence a week and mine for a penny. It was long afterwards that I realised that these policies were a provision against funeral expenses. I doubt whether we were the man's favourite clients. My mother firmly resisted all blandishments to increase her weekly investment, and I once jumped up to touch his waxed and pointed moustache, to see what it was made of. Another regular caller was the grocer's boy, who took an order for items totalling a few shillings and delivered what my mother had ordered the week before. These boys had presumably attended school for nine years, but none of them could give change for a £1 note. The boy usually arrived with the correct change ready made up, but if there was a query or mistake, he was helpless.

It is time that I confessed my passion for the trams. I would go anywhere for a tram ride, and when I had a bike would often follow a favourite tram round its whole route to observe how fast it ran and what difficulties it met in keeping up to it's timetable. When I was small there were only open-topped trams, but in 1920 the Corporation bought twelve with covered tops and glass protection for the driver, and these were my pride and joy. I noted the routes on which they were employed each day and when after 1924 I had to travel to school it was bliss if I could board one of them.

The 100 open-topped cars were not of uniform design. Nos. 81-84 had smaller windows than the others and upholstered seats with a stuffy smell. I supposed that they had been converted when the horse trams were given up in 1905. They only came out on days when the system was fully stretched such as Bank Holidays, or as football specials. Nos. 85-100 differed from 1-80 in the style of their stairs, in having lights on the top deck and in other details. Nos. 101-3 were low cars carrying tanks to water the street; they were not often seen. No. 104 was the "toastrack car", with open sides and no roof, for sight-seeing in good weather. I seem to remember that it first appeared in 1919, gaily festooned with lights.

All the Portsmouth trams ran on four wheels with a short axle base and "wagged their tails" badly at speed; their bodies also creaked and visibly gave at the joints at rough places in the track, of which there were plenty. In about 1930 car No. 1 was rebuilt with an improved truck, steel-framed body and domed roof, but the experiment was not followed up.

Trams carried a conductor as well as a driver and he was equipped with a bundle of tickets, a machine for punching a hole in them and a pouch for money. Even a penny ticket — and a grown-up could ride, for instance, from North Road to Kingston Church for a penny — had the names of the fare stages printed down each side. The conductor punched your ticket to show the stage to which you were entitled to ride. Inside passengers sat facing each other — room for eleven each side — and the conductor walked along calling "Any more fares please?".

One humourist used to add: "Anyone want to pay twice?".

The nine tram routes each had it's own tickets, so my wanderings about the streets also had the motive of collecting discarded tickets on routes far from home. The shops sold "conductor's outfits" for children. But I also had a large model tram and a copy of a route and destination indicator, both made by a friend of my grandfather's. So I could play at being driver or conductor with more realism than other children.

The network of tramways was remarkably complete and elaborate, but the fact that so many of the streets were too narrow for two tracks presented severe difficulties. The service was too frequent for a single-track system with passing places to be acceptable, so the streets carried as much double track as possible, with pinches for getting past obstacles. In the days when the rails were laid down there was no thought of the trams being an obstacle to faster vehicles, but horse-drawn carts were an obstacle to them. So in the busier streets trams were always crawling behind carts and the tram-drivers were clanging their bells to urge the carters to get to the next pinch as soon as possible and let them pass. In some streets, such as New Road, the double-track tramway was close to the kerb on each side. In such a place a van conducting a house removal would block one track altogether and the tram would have to run on one track only using crossovers at each end of the road. Such an incident enlivened a boy's journey to school.

I was particularly interested in the tram pinch at the point where the line came out of Bradford Road and crossed Somers Road into Blackfriars Road, because my grandfather's house was hard by. This corner was so difficult that orginally (so my mother said) movement was controlled by a signal. But over the years the Corporation were able to edge the pavements back and relax the curves. However, trams could never pass at this point and always had to take care not to collide. There were six routes in each direction, so the screeching of driving wheels without differentials which was characteristic of trams on severe curves, was more or less continuous. A great delight to a small boy.

The green trams which ran from Cosham to Horndean (a separate company) were superior to the Corporation fleet. They were quicker and did not wag their tails at speed; the inside seats faced in the forward direction and they had brakes which pressed on the rail, which were screwed down before descending Portsdown Hill. The service was infrequent enough to allow single-track working with passing places. There was a reserved track from Cosham to the top of the hill and from Waterlooville to Horndean. In 1926 or so these trams began to run right through town to Southsea. Presumably this was intended as an answer to bus competition, but it did not avert the decline of the tram.

In 1917 the Corporation expanded their transport network by buying buses for a route from Copnor to the dockyard main gate via St. Mary's Road and Arundel Street. I was delighted when we went to live near these strange vehicles. They were narrow at the bottom, and the inside seats faced each other; wider on the open top deck, where the seats faced forwards. They looked top-heavy and they had solid tyres. But they remained in service for many years.

The bolder spirits in Drayton Road spent afternoons at the tram depot — still known as the "stables" twenty years after the last horse-tram — at the bottom of Gladys Avenue. The mischief we got up to was very mild, but the more genteel mothers did not allow their children to join in these expeditions.

When I was small the streets were still liable to the thick mud described in the Sherlock Holmes stories, which was a mixture of horse-droppings and rain trampled under foot. It was particularly pernicious to women's long skirts, and I remember the queer way in which our old lady in Netley Street held up the back of her skirt when she walked down the street. Drayton Road did not suffer from that disadvantage, but when we first knew it, it had never seen the tar boiler and in dry weather the sandy road surface was blown about very unpleasantly.

The tar boiler looked like a small version of a Locomotion or Puffing Billy and filled the street with a pungent smell; always an attraction to boys. There was much less clutter in the streets in those days than there is now. Tram stops were indicated by metal shields fixed to lamp-posts — red for "All cars stop here" and green for request stops. I first saw traffic lights at Cambridge in 1930. Pedestrian crossings were later than that, as were lines in the road, so complicated today. There were no direction signs for motorists in the town of Portsmouth and in the country sign posts were still conveniently placed for perusal from horse-back. However, all villages were identified by circular plates about two feet across with black lettering and a yellow background, put up by the A.A. Even in 1925 a motorist had to be driving slowly to read the information they offered, but it was warmly appreciated by young cyclists.

Mass production of cars was in its infancy. ("Motors" or "motor cars" they were when I was ten: "car" meant a tram.) So, though there were few cars, there was a great variety of manufacturers, and boys went round the streets with small notebooks in which they entered the names of makes of cars; it was amazing how many pages could be filled. Many makes could be identified by the shape of the bonnet or by radiator badges, others gave rise to disputes between rival spotters.

84

(Train spotting, by the way, had not yet been invented.)

I had two years in the Infants' School but soon after going up into the "big boys" we moved to Drayton Road, where we lived opposite what was regarded as one of the best elementary schools in the town. There I was lucky to sit under a Mr. Warren, who was dedicated to his best pupils though perhaps less patient with the tail of his class of sixty. What did we learn? Arithmetic; to write legibly from a copy-book (containing maxims such as "Joshua rose up early in the morning"); to read Ivanhoe; to record the weather; to admire Biblical prose; to recite the rivers of England; to believe that most of the map of the world was red.

About ten of us were taken to the Empire Exhibition at Wembley and we wrote "compositions" about it ever after. We also had an outing to Winchester and St. Cross, in the course of which we were enlightened as to the meaning of that learned word, char-a-banc. Mr. Warren's aim was to get his best pupils through the entrance competition for the secondary school, but at a late stage it was decided that I should try for a free place at the grammar school. This decision determined the whole course of my life since, but I think that in taking it my parents had their minds on the immediate advantages. The place at the grammar school, if won, was free, whereas it was not easy to be let off the modest fees at the secondary school. Moreover, I had recently been ill, and the grammar school examination, which came later, gave me more time to get better. The grammar school set not so much a formal examination as a morning of tests of general ability. For instance, we were required to draft an advertisement, and we each had to read aloud to a member of the staff, who questioned us on what we had read. I was caught out, not knowing the meaning of "terrace" (as a feature of mountain scenery) and I thought I had failed. But in fact I tasted grandeur of taking the first place in the competition.

The daily transition from a working-class home to a school for the sons of professional and business men was difficult, and it was made harder when Canon Walter J. Barton became headmaster, he set about a programme of up-grading the school from its old-fashioned role of a place where middle-class parents bought learning for their sons into a rigorous society demanding the primary allegiance of its members in the name of academic, sporting and patriotic ideals. Several of the old-style free place boys, I think, found themselves side-stepping some of the headmaster's reforms. So there were tensions. But I was happy at school so long as it was a place for acquiring knowledge.

When I was 16 my free place (much to my parents' surprise) was supplemented by a small grant and I passed into the enthusiastic hands of Frank E. Harrison, and the humane scholarship and sardonic humour of Philip Sidney Richards. These two equipped me for Cambridge; Richards was the only schoolmaster that I ever had who made friends with my father, when he found that he had had a naval service in the Greek islands.

When I was small I seemed to be surrounded by relations and friends who regarded ill-health as normal. My mother was always incapable of sustained exertion and was liable to be exhausted by warm weather or shortage of air. She had her heart sounded for the first time in her life when I was four and was told that she had valvular disease. In 1918 both she and I succumbed to the virulent influenza which was supposed to have come over from the trenches and which carried off the youngest member of the Royal Family, Prince John. It also killed the mother of five children who lived next door to us in Netley Street. Diptheria was then greatly feared, and once when I had a sore throat the doctor took a swab and had it analysed "at the Town Hall". The diagnosis was tonsillitis, which was treated by painting with a very bitter glutinous substance applied by sticking a crooked brush down my throat.

After we moved to Drayton Road my mother became a patient of D.A.V. Maybury, who practised from a fine old house a few doors up from Charles Dickens' birth-place. Dr. Maybury was in partnership with his venerable father, who was driven on his round in a pony and trap. A doctor did not in those days coarsen his hands by driving himself. The Maybury's employed a dispenser who made up their prescriptions, and their waiting room usually contained more people bringing bottles for renewal at the dispensary than there were waiting to consult the doctor. The only occasion I went to the surgery on my own account was when I was hurt in a bicycle accident; the doctor put two stitches into my chin. One would not take such a casualty to a general practitioner now-a-days. Dr. Maybury had a very grave manner and a slow, deep voice. My mother had implicit confidence in him, but he was not a man to get the wrong side of.

All this of course was long before the National Health Service. Dr. Maybury sent us bills from time to time, but our friends who were in civilian employment paid insurance contributions and were "on the panel", a list of patients treated without charge. The health insurance system was administered through friendly societies, who paid benefit to members who were off work through illness, also sent round agents to check their state of health. Woe betide the person in receipt of benefit who was found to be out after eight in the evening!

As toddlers my generation wore frocks like girls until we were "britched" at age 2 or 3. Then we were at risk of being put into velvet suits. Unlike our fathers, who as boys had covered their knees in knicker-bockers, and our grand-children, who wear trousers, boys and girls alike. We wore shorts — "boys' knickers" to the shops, "trucks" to their wearers. This was sensible. Children fall over a hundred times a day, and the human knee is more easily washed and repaired than any garment. At the age of 12 or so I had a suit for Sundays, jacket and shorts from a tailor's shop, and for school a blazer and collar and tie, the collar being washable celluloid. Boots were more usual than shoes, but I never had wellingtons. When I was about six I wanted a bright red jersey, but my mother was horrified; clothes were in dark, serviceable colours. I will not pretend that I was not susceptible to girls, but I had no idea how they dressed.

My parents were Liberal supporters who believed that the country would pull through so long as Sir Thomas Bramsdom* retained his seat, but public affairs were not much discussed at home. When the Liberal party declined they did not transfer their allegiance. It was, I think, a grief to them that Esperanto attracted people who saw in it a means of promoting international socialism. However, for a time we were friendly with some Esperantists whose children attended a socialist Sunday school in the Trades Council hall in Fratton Road. I once joined with them in a May Day procession (in 1920, I suppose) of which the worth while bit was the return after it was all over, riding on an empty dray drawn by a trotting horse.

I think it was at the 1924 General Election that Sir Bertram Falle adopted the slogan: "Vote for Falle who works for all". Some of us boys thereupon ran about the streets shouting "Vote for Falle and vote for a fool", more for the pleasure of being rude in public than from political conviction. Was I in fact surprised at the age of 11 how many houses in poor alleys displayed "true blue" posters, or was this a later reflection? This was the election which led to the first Labour Government. Two years later came the General Strike, of which all that I remember is that I wished I were old enough to offer to drive a tram. At the time of the 1929 election, which reduced the Liberal Party to fewer than 60 M.P.'s, my mother was ill, and I sat on her bed commiserating with her on the results as published in the Evening News.

My parents married (I was told) on 13 shillings a week. When I was first old enough to notice such things, my mother used to go to the post

* Sir Thomas Bramsdon, 1857-1935, solicitor, many eminent public activities, Portsmouth M.P. off and on between 1900 and 1924.

office every Thursday to collect her allotment from my father's pay — 54 shillings. A few years later a friend of my mother's once protested that you "could not do such-and-such on £3 a week", but my mother believed that her husband in fact earned more. Later than that, I heard a middle-aged lady express great sympathy with a newly married girl who would have to manage on less than £3. How did people live on such wages? Prices were low — a herring for a penny, butter went down to 9d a pound during the depression, there was a three-pound jar of marmalade for 1/3d. Life was simpler; many things which are now necessities had not been invented; people developed the habit of not even wanting what they could not afford; mending was universal; things were not bought on deferred payments, unless perhaps the piano. Moreover for about ten years prices went down, so that the struggle to live tended to grow less critical.

But with so small a margin of safety conscious of differences of income threw up barriers between friends. My mother had a friend whose husband was a Petty Officer Artificer, and she had no children. She liked to go to afternoon entertainments on Clarence Pier; my mother begrudged the money and spent her afternoons at women's meetings at the chapel and Sailors' Rest. My Copnor aunt and her husband and children went, like us, on the tram to Horndean, but since they spent a little money in the Red Lion and we ate our picnic in the woods, we never went together. And there were other differences. We might notice that some friends went "on the panel" if they were ill, but they in return might observe that my father had some meals "on board". Among Admiralty and dockyard employees "establishment" (i.e. a permanent, pensionable post) was a prize which separated the "have nots" from the "haves". Unemployment was not severe in Portsmouth, but at the same time as life became a little easier for those with an assured wage, however small, others were exposed to an increasing hazard of losing their jobs. But whereas I caught from my mother a strong consciousness that we were poor, I was only occasionally aware that others were much worse off.

him 8/- for it when I had my first chickens.

He was in great pain during his last years, and was unable to breathe easily. He used to put Potters Asthma Cure powder on a saucer, cover his head with a cloth and inhale. I think it used to give him a little relief. He died in 1936 and was sadly missed, he was always very polite and would touch his hat and say 'Sir' when meeting and talking to people who employed him, or the vicar, doctor or other gentry.

Mr. Nicholas (a farmer who was to have a tremendous influence on my later life) used to come down at about 6.30 a.m. to get his cows for milking. While he was talking to either my father, mother or the postman I would run out and round up the cows, the name of the field was Bridge-close, and the cows had to walk over the old packhorse bridge single file. I was only about 4 years old and I remember feeling very proud walking up the hill behind the cows. I was sometimes given a penny on Saturdays. As I got older I would help tie the cows up and do other little jobs which included getting 'Jolly' the horse in, he was a very big chestnut and if you weren't careful he would step on your toe.

How I started helping with the milking was like this; I was about 10 years old and whilst Mr. N. was hand milking in the stable I would go up to the house and Mrs. N. would give me a cup of tea to take down for Mr. N. After he had drunk it I would go into the skilling next door where there was a lovely quiet Guernsey cow, having washed the cup out I would squirt milk from this cow's teats into the cup and drink it, it was delicious.

One morning I was busy milking into the cup and didn't hear Mr. N. coming, I think he must have known that I was up to something, anyway he looked over the half door and caught me redhanded. He said "Ah, then you can milk then, me sonny!" I think I blushed and was frightened he would be angry. I said, "Not very well". He smiled and said, "Ah we must see what we can do about this, I can do with some help." Anyway within a couple of days I was given a 3 gallon pail and a 3 legged stool, and Mrs. N. had made me a round hat and an apron with tapes at the neck and waist, so I was a fully fledged milker. The usual size for a milk pail was 4 or 5 gallons, they were the same diameter top to bottom with a T shaped handle riveted on the top.

I started milking the Guernsey and soon found out that it was very wrist aching, then it was two cows and as I was getting more proficient, three cows. I began to enjoy milking and felt very important, I was given twopence on Saturdays which was given to my mother towards living expenses. After a couple of weeks Mr. N. said I should try my hand at milking a black and white cow named Spot. I had noticed that he was a long time milking her, and wondered why. She gave about 4 gallons a day, her teats were like thick rubber and you had to squeeze and pull very hard to get just a thin trickle of milk, it was very hard on my wrists and it seemed I would never finish her, but I stuck to her, and I can remember now what a great feeling of relief it was when she was 'dried off' to have another calf. Although I had wished all sorts of things to happen to Spot, I was very upset and cried all day when, a year or so after I started milking her again, she had, I think, meningitis and had to be slaughtered, it was heartbreaking to see her being winched up into the knackers cart.

I used to go up from Buckland school when I was ten years old to the field named Close, which is now Rogers Close council estate. I knew that the hay would be fit for turning and I would drive the horse with the hay turner round and round the field turning the swaths two at a time.

Then I would eat some bread and cheese and have a drink of lemonade, which Mr. N. had brought for me, then run back to school in time for afternoon lessons. I'm afraid my mind would wander though, to the hay field, and I'd wonder when we would be hauling it. I would have to lead the horse which pulled the sweep or collector along the swathes. After we finished in the evening we would sit under the elm trees and eat crusty bread and real Cheddar cheese and drink cider and listen to all the yarns being told by older men. Of course with the coming of the tractor and baler, the combine and other modern implements, it didn't need many workmen, so the lovely evenings, like so many other things are just things of the past.

When still at school, I used to love going along the hedgerows after milking, looking for hens nests, if I found one with several eggs, I would leave it if it was in a safe place from foxes. A hen would usually lay about thirteen eggs, then go broody, and you can be sure if you left her alone she would hatch out thirteen chicks. On the farm we had a lean-to hen house, and in the spring, I would put about ten or twelve nest boxes in it and fill them with broody hens, putting thirteen eggs for each. My job was to let the broodies out every day to feed and water, usually two at a time, then shut them in again, keeping the dates of sitting in a book. Sometimes when hatching, the hen would step on a chick and the chick would die. I brought many chicks back to life, by what I now know as resuscitation (the kiss of life). I would blow in the chick's beak very gently and revive it, it seemed the natural thing to do, and as I was paid 1d for each live chick, it meant a lot to me.

I used to put mole traps and rabbit wires down the top ground, (Lynch). One Saturday morning I took a load of manure along that field, I had to make about four heaps to one load. After I finished unloading, I

94

b) Fred Chant, far right, in 1935 with his seven brothers.

went to look at my traps and wires. I had put one wire on the bank coming down from the neighbours field, I was shocked to find that a cock pheasant had crept through the hedge and got caught in my wire, it was dead. I got my old overcoat off the cart and put the pheasant in it, and wrapped it up hoping nobody had seen me, Mr. N. was very pleased when I took it to him and he set me picking it straight away, I had dinner with them on Sunday and the pheasant was lovely.

On the Tuesday when I was milking at about 5 p.m. the game keeper from the Orchardleigh estate looked over the door, I thought, "he knows", and was very worried. He carried on a conversation with Mr. N. (they were very good friends), then he said to me "I see you've got a few wires down the field", I said "Yes" and wondered what was coming next. He said "If you come along the field later on, I will show you how to put them down properly". So after milking I went with him, I had to take up all the wires first, then he made me walk forty paces from the hedge into the field. He didn't show me how to set the wire, but said "Now I don't want to see any rabbit wires closer to the hedge than that". He didn't mention anything about the pheasant but he knew alright, afterwards he took me along to the copse and shot two rabbits, which he gave me to take home. Gamekeepers are very crafty, they are also very clever and know almost all there is to know about nature.

One Saturday morning I was sent down to Mrs. Bush's at the bottom of the hill, to drive her sow along to Elliots farm to be mated with Alfie M's boar, it was about half a mile. It was not too bad. On the following Saturday I had to drive it back, it was a very hot day, as I was passing the cottage at Poor Patch, a large dog, which was chained up just inside the gate, jumped up and started barking, I had a terrible job getting the sow past it, she went just past the lay-by and flopped down in the ditch in an awful temper. Well you've heard the saying 'you can take a horse to water, but you can't make it drink', it was something like that here, that sow just wouldn't budge, I sat on the bank crying in frustration for about two hours waiting for it to move. I thought about going home to dinner, but knew that as soon as I was gone the pig would have got up and gone back to Elliott's. Of course, I had my leg pulled again, but I tell you, it was no laughing matter.

Doctor Helps called one day to see father, my mother asked him if he would look at my sister who was poorly, she would have been about seventeen years old, he said to her "What are you sitting there for like a little Dutch doll, get up and help your mother with housework" I think it cured her. He looked at me and said "Hello, long, thin and ugly". Well, I'll admit to being long and thin, but I didn't like being called ugly! But he was a good doctor and friend to us all.

One sight I shall never forget is Taylor's steam engine. It was massive, and was used for hauling timber on big four-wheeled pole trailers. It would get to Buckland from Midsomer Norton at about 8 a.m. on a Monday morning, the two brothers in charge would put three or four bags of coal by the round house wall near where we lived, this was for the return journey next day. They would put a long pipe with a nozzle on down over the bridge into the river, and fill their tank with water, then they would continue their journey. What I thought was wonderful was that Tom Hill had a wooden leg (I expect he lost it in the war, or perhaps a tree rolled on it), anyway he could get around and climb into that engine as well as anyone with two good legs.

Next day when we got home from school the engine would be back with several massive trees on the trailer, mother would make them a cup of tea and give them some homemade cake, they would show their appreciation by giving her a few lumps of coal. Taylors also had a team of six lovely horses and a timber carriage. On hot days in the summer on the return journey with their load, the carters would unhitch the horses and let them walk a little way up the stream to cool them down, the engine would take its load up to the other end of the village and unhitch and reverse all the way to the bottom to help pull the horses' load up, it was a truly magnificent sight.

At this time, too, I would wait for hours if I knew that Barnes thresher from Southwick was coming to Murtry Hill farm. Bill Lucas and 'Titch' Freeman were in charge, it always amazed me how they got that great steam engine through some of the narrow gateways and awkward lanes. Hitched behind the engine was thresher, then their four wheeled living van, and behind that was a two wheeled machine called a tier which tied the straw, which dropped into it straight from the thresher, into bundles of about 14lbs weight for thatching ricks.

The living van would be left on a wide verge at the bottom of the lane, the two men would cook and care for themselves all week, then ride their bikes home on Saturday afternoon after pulling the canvas curtains down round the engine and covering the thresher and tier with tarpaulins. They came back on Sunday evening because they had to be up at 5 a.m. to light the fire in the engine ready for 8 a.m. start. Bill would pull a cord which blew the whistle dead on the hour, then he would push a lever forward and the pulley wheels would start turning, slowly gathering speed until there was a droning, roaring noise and 'Titch' would start feeding the sheaves of corn into the drum, which had to be done evenly.

On Christmas Eve every year, my brothers, sisters and I would walk into Frome to do our Christmas shopping, I don't suppose any of us had more than three shillings to spend but it was wonderful what presents we bought. I bought a cake stand for Mrs. N., a pipe for Mr. N. and presents for my parents. I think it was a tobacco pouch for father and a sugar dish for mother. We did most of our shopping in Dykes Bazaar in Catherine Street, soon though, along came Woolworths where everything was 3d and 6d. I'm sure we had more fun spending 3/- then than the children today with several pounds to spend. All our little presents, given or received, were appreciated.

The first time I ever heard a radio or wireless was at the Bell Inn. Sammy Hillier the landlord invited some of us village children in to 'listen in'. I remember seeing a small box with a horn sticking out, after a bit of crackling you could hear voices and music. Later I used to hear football commentaries on a crystal set that Mr. Nicholas had, you had to put headphones on, again there was a lot of whistling and crackling.

The blacksmith shop or Smithy was also a meeting place. You could often find C. Pearce, the Parish Council Clerk, and other top villagers, also Sammy Hillier of the Bell in deep discussion there. Our village blacksmith was a very hard working man named Bert Davis or 'Dinky' as he was affectionately called. He had an outsized pair of bellows to keep his fire burning red, this was operated by pulling a long piece of wood down and up. Sometimes he would let us children work it for him, but you had to be very careful as a hard pull would blow the red embers all over the place. He would shoe all the farm horses and Charltons six or seven timber pulling horses; these were all big strong horses and Dinky would sweat profusely, especially if they leaned on him whilst he had their leg between his knees.

He would put bonds on wagon wheels, I think he worked on these in conjunction with Frank Gray the carpenter who had the building almost adjoining. These bonds were put on the wooden wheels hot, there was a great round flat piece of metal outside the blacksmith's shop, it had a hole in the centre where the hub, or I think they called it 'the billy' fitted. Dinky would do little jobs for the children — mending their hoops and trolleys etc. He was a very quiet spoken, kindly man. He mended all sorts of farm tools and implements. When he put a handle in a hay or dung fork his bill would be like this: 'handle 9d, to putting 6d.' Both these men were experts. Dinky depended on his eye as a measure for most things.

Harry Beacham was our shop keeper, he also had the Post Office. Paraffin oil was kept up the garden in a large tank for all the oil lamps which people had. He was the church warden and bell ringer for many years, I think he stood in as godfather to many babies during that time. He was a jovial man and used to call all the children 'My young Victoria'. He was deaf, some children would tell him it was their birthday very often and would have some sweets given them.

Our vicar, the Rev. H.S. Pugh, had the use of about seven or eight acres of glebe land, there were some stone buildings and a yard in the corner, behind the church hall. He kept about four lovely little Jersey cows, these were milked by a girl named Dolly Haines. We children were sent to the vicarage after school with a large can with a handle for some skimmed milk. We were allowed to watch her milk as long as we were quiet, then she would carry the buckets of milk up to the kitchen to the separator. I don't know how it worked, but the cream was all taken off and we bought the skimmed milk, this was almost as good as the milk (full cream) which was delivered daily. The charge for this was between ½d and 1½d per pint according to the supply. When the vicar's cows went dry we could get skimmed milk at New Close Farm, but that was a much longer walk.

Horace Putt who used to live on the batch helped the vicar with his haymaking: and if Mr. Nicholas had some ready to haul Horace would come down and ask if he could help him as well. Mr. N. would say "I thought you were helping the Parson", Horace would answer "Ah, but you've got some good cider down here, you only get tea and lemonade up there".

George Hobbs delivered the milk round the village, he would have two five gallon cans fixed to yolks which he had across his shoulders, he had a half pint and a pint measure for dipping the milk to put in the housewives jugs. His cans and measures were always scrupulously clean. His brother who lived at Mullins farm, made some really lovely ice cream. We would go out onto their lawn after chapel on a Sunday afternoon and a whacking great halfpennyworth of ice cream. I think we had to put the other halfpenny in the collection plate. I was five years old then.

Mr. Trowbridge was our village baker. It must have been very hard work. I can remember the big wooden trough in which he mixed the dough. He would burn faggots of hazel wood in the oven, and when it was red hot, he would slide dozens of tins of dough in, also cottage loaves with tops and bottoms. I used to eat much of the crust on the way home if I had been sent to buy one, it was delicious. Mr. T. would go round Buckland and other villages delivering it, first with a horse and covered wagon, then he bought a Morris Cowley car and used this, I think he removed the back seat. He would never ask for money, but if he thought it was time someone paid, he would rattle some loose change in his pocket, then he would probably be paid 5/-, although he would be owed pounds. He was a chapel preacher also, his customers were poor mine and farm workers.

I think it was about 1930 when Sir Alan Cobham brought his Flying Circus to Gypsy Lane. A gang of us children would walk (or run) as soon as we had had tea and done our little jobs, up to this large flat field, it must have been two-and-a-half or three miles. The pilots would take a couple of bi-planes up and do stunts like loops and rolls, then a man would walk out onto a wing and back and other performances, then they would go up high and a couple of men would parachute down. We were very thrilled and excited. Flips over Frome were given for 5/- and 7/6, although this was a lot of money my father had 5/- worth, he said he could see Ted Lawrence at New Close farm cleaning up the yard. We would be in trouble when we got home for being late and had to go straight to bed.

Mrs. Bush kept dozens of hens on the green, she also had a nanny goat which was tethered under the elm trees. This goat had a kid, and I saw a once in a life time sight — it was very hot, the nanny stood quietly under the tree and the kid jumped up and balanced on it's mother's back, when it was balanced it reached up to eat the elm leaves, I shall never forget that sight.

Another thing I remember was a hen which always laid her eggs in a nest in the tallet (loft), I could never make out how she got the chicks, when they hatched, out of the loft as there was a five foot drop. Anyway I waited and watched. The hen, when she thought she was alone, got three or four chicks on her back and gently jumped down onto the ground and let them off, she repeated this about three times, when all the chicks were down she would proudly take them down into the cart shed to feed, then disappear into a large patch of stinging nettles at the bottom of the yard.

I went on working for Mr. N. until I was seventeen. I had milked his cows twice a day, and sometimes I would be sent out to help other farmers between milkings. As Mrs. N. had to go up to her mother's in the village each day, I would help Mr. N. clean the house and I had to polish the old black kitchen grate until it shone. One of the things I am grateful for is that he taught me to cook good farmhouse food (nothing fancy), and we had some lovely dinners. Mrs. N. was a vegetarian so if we cooked two pigeons we would have one each, with plenty of vegetables, he would have a lot of thick cream on his but I preferred Bisto gravy.

Mr. N. could not afford to pay me more than ten shillings a week, so at seventeen he told me I could go up to Court Farm at six in the mornings to help Mr. V. with the milking, and again at four in the afternoons, for this I would be paid one shilling a milking — fourteen shillings per week. Then I would get Mr. N's cows in on the way down and milk some of them, I would thus be milking an average of fifteen cows twice a day.

Court Farm was noted for it's good cheese, the farmer who was there before made Caerphilly but Mr. W. made Cheddar which he sold for 2/-per pound.

When I was eighteen I went to work at Dangerfield Farm, I received £1. 18s. 6d. per week, we worked six full days and milked cows and fed pigs on Sundays, so that we would be free from about eleven o'clock to 2.30 p.m. If we wanted the afternoon off from milking on Sunday we could have it as long as we got someone reliable to do our milking. My mother and a gentleman called Sid Taylor would stand in for us for which we paid them 1/6.

At that time the farmer Mr. H.C.C. was letting ICI experiment on his farm with fertilizers. We would load about one ton on a trailer and lead the horse to the field, where we would start by the hedge and let the horse walk a bit at a time through the centre of the field to the other end. Mr. C. would walk from the trailer to the hedge and I would walk the other hedge. We would fill a bucket with fertilizer and loop the rope from the bucket handle over our shoulder, next we would walk four paces from the hedge to start and make a hole with our heel, walk forward four more paces and stick a stick into the ground which had some paper of a fertilizer bag tied to the top. You would then walk back to your mark in the ground and start broadcasting, you had to have rhythm, as your left leg went forward your right arm would come round in an arc and scatter the pellets. Then you get the four steps — heel — and four steps and stick, go back to your heel mark and walk back to the other stick. I think we could sow fertilizer or seed almost as evenly as a machine, but it was very tiring work.

Mr. Emlyn Jones would come from ICI and make sure that we were putting the right amount on the fields he chose for the experiment. At that time nitro-chalk and the like was fairly new to farming and I remember some of the old farm workers and others saying "Ah! he be asking for trouble putting that muck on his land, you just wait and see." Sure enough they thought they were right when eight acres of lovely wheat was laid flat in a terrific thunderstorm. That corn looked beautiful all standing straight and level three and a half feet tall. Just one storm did the damage, maybe the straw was weak (with experiments they have produced a shorter, stiffer straw), but every bit of that field was flattened, the trouble was, as with most thunderstorms, the wind came at different angles and the straw was laid all ways. You couldn't cut it with a binder, and the mowing machine, even with the knife bar as low as it would go, wouldn't go under it, so it was left to those who could use a scythe. Those who were bundling it gathered so much, then pulled out about ten straws, twisted them round the bundle and crossed the ends and tucked them under the bond to make a sheaf. As we had our regular daily jobs — milking, feeding, scrubbing stalls, etc. — quite a lot of this cutting was done in the evenings. I think it must have taken a month or more. To make matters worse we had a lot of rain which made the wheat sprout in the ear, it was a tangled mess and a thankless job, we were all very happy to see the end of it.

We had a lovely crop of grass in Southmead where we had put on some nitro-chalk. This had to be made into silage, another new thing (silage was made sometimes, but only if the grass had been cut for hay and prolonged rain made it impossible to dry it, so it was hauled into a heap and called 'sour' silage). The grass was cut by a mower and left to wilt for a few hours. Other men meanwhile were busy building the silo, we had 16 wooden sections about 3 feet wide by six feet high, these were all bolted together to form a circle, when the bottom was full we put another sixteen sections on top, this was high enough for pitching into with picks (4 prongs), but on occasions we used an elevator and went up three high. The grass was picked up and loaded into the wagons by us using the picks, while one was unloading it, the others were loading another wagon. My job was to build the silo, spreading the grass evenly and keeping the centre high like a mound. After about every two loads a mixture of treacle (mollases) and water was pumped up by a hand pump bolted to the silo boards and spread over the grass, if the weather was wet you used more treacle in the mixture. We were building a silo on Sutton near Barrow Hill one day when Mrs. Mavis Tate our Member of Parliament, came up with Mr. H.C. She was very interested and we had to build steps with several silo boards so that she could get right into the silo. To the modern farmer or worker this method of silage making would seem very slow and laborious, but I can tell you we made some very sweet and palatable feed for the cattle. We also made hay in large stacks or ricks which were thatched with straw. When thatched properly there is no sisal, polythene or any other modern methods (except covered barns) to beat straw and spar thatching.

There was no trouble in getting help at haymaking time from the Fountain Inn, there was plenty of liquid refreshment to 'wet your whistle' with whilst working, afterwards we would go into the living room where Mrs. Dowden had loaded the large table with lovely crusty bread, ham, cheese, lettuce and different pickles, and more drinks. It was a much better spread than our present day harvest suppers. Charlie would play the piano, so everyone could enjoy a sing-song. There was no shortage of volunteers to tell a 'good tale' either. We didn't need television.

In winter, usually after dinner, it was my job to take Bob and Flower, the two horses, with the wagon to cut a load of hay and haul it back to the farm buildings. You would have a very sharp (hopefully) hay knife, get up the ladder onto the rick. After removing about a square yard of thatch, you would start cutting downwards until you had a square flap of hay, getting a few rungs down the ladder you would reach up and slide this flap out onto your head, walk backwards down the ladder and place the flap on the wagon. You continued this until you had a load. The knack was to keep the knife straight so that all the flaps were equal size. I would rope the hay on when loaded, hitch Bob the trace horse in front of Flower, who was in the shafts and pull the load across the field onto the road. You held the reins of the trace horse in your left hands, and led the shaft horse by the bridle, it was quite a performance sometimes to manoeuvre through some narrow or awkward gateways.

On paper this all sounds easy, but sometimes you might forget the whetstone and the knife had no more edge, or the hay had got a bit hot and the knife would get thick with brown dust and you had to put a lot more effort into it. Then there was the wind, although you had stuck a half spar right down through the flap, the wind would take it just as you were placing it onto the wagon and blow it all over the place; it could be very exasperating.

In the autumn when all apples had been heaped up under the trees, and the farm work was dropping off a bit, we would start cider making. The apples were shovelled into the carts, slugs, snails and all, and taken to the cider house where there was a large press (it was still there in 1985). Apples were crushed in a large machine which had to be turned by handle, it took two men sometimes to turn it if the apples were hard. Straw would be placed across the press at the bottom and apple pummy would be shovelled onto the straw. A square frame of board would then be eased upwards and the straw would be bent inwards, more straw put across and more pummy added until you had a square 'cheese' containing eight layers. A very heavy board was placed on top with more baulks of wood for weight, the 'cheese' was left for an hour or so to drain gradually, then you would use a gigantic iron bar to screw down the boards and press the cider out, which would run into a lead tray and then down into a large wooden trough. It had to be screwed down gently or the 'cheese' would loose shape. When screwed right down the boards would be taken off, the corners of the 'cheese' cut off, these corners were then placed on the 'cheese' again, board replaced and screwed down again to get every drop of cider out. I think it yielded about 120 gallons to one cheese, the cider was placed in huge barrels and left with the bung out to clear, I have heard that some cider makers put large chunks of beef and other less palatable things into the barrels to make the cider 'work' and get clear. It was very potent.

I will tell you now about two 'council' men, their names were Bill Randall, the foreman, and Bob Brown, or to give him his real name, Robert Brownjohn. They were very hard working men and kept the village streets clean. Their tools consisted of spades and grubbers, a line which was used to keep the grass verges level, a reap hook, scythe and of course a whetstone. They had about seven miles of roads to care for and it was only if there were extra jobs such as gravelling or ditch digging that they had extra help.

Some people treated Bob as if he was the village idiot. I know he said things wrong sometimes, what I mean to say is that he knew what he wanted to say but got a bit mixed up. I'd rather say he was quaint, but he was a gentleman because he never spoke ill of anyone or interfered, worked hard and always looked tidy and respectable. He was one of the last people in the village to work one of the allotments along Poor Parch, or as on the old maps, allotment fields. He loved a bit of water-cress, he used to say to me "Bring me up a few cresses Freddy, I like the dark ones." It was my pleasure to take him up some cress as there was plenty growing in the lovely spring water in Bridge Close, some cress had green leaves and some very dark, almost mauve leaves, the latter was hot to the taste. It grows there to this day and I always think of old Bob when I pick some.

I can truthfully say that those two men and their barrows, kept our village street cleaner by far than what they have been since with all the lorries, tractors and modern tools.

Every Saturday morning Bob would brush the pavements and roadsides from the Bell to the church porch, and you must remember that there were two large herds of cows over those roads twice a day. Bob would be very angry with farmers concerned if the cows fouled the pavements on Sunday mornings and would brush up the offending mess so that people could go to church with clean boots and shoes. All a labour of love.

Mr. Ted Cary who farmed at Dangerfield when I was younger was said to have powers to heal cows. I was told that Mr. Bert Helps who

c) Riverside Cottage where Fred Chant was born in 1920 after the storm which washed a small round haystack into the garden. Picture taken 1905.

farmed in Kent and had a good herd of cows came down to Buckland one Sunday and arrived as Mr. Cary was going to church. He told Mr. Cary that his cows were dying, they had red-water, this was a dreaded disease, I think it was caused by a bug but I've never seen a cow with it.

Mr. Helps told his friend his trouble and said "You are the only one I know who can help me." Mr. Cary said "I'm in a hurry to go to church, but if you will write down the names and breed of your cows I will do what I can. Now you go home and not worry." What he did I don't know, but from that day no more cows died and they all made a good recovery.

In the years before the 1939 War there was very little building done, two council houses were built near the Methodist chapel between 1920 and 1930 with another two built at the bottom of the hill in 1936. I don't believe either pair cost more than £500. A house at Sands Cross built by Farmer Gillings in about 1934 cost £360.

Wages were very low, if anyone earned more than £4 a week he was well paid. Unemployment pay was about £1.50. Many families were living in 'tied' houses with a rent of four or five shillings which was deducted from their wages. Bicycles were the main form of transport. Cost of living was very cheap. When I had my first bicycle it was second hand and cost 10/-. I bought a new Hercules bike in 1935 for £3. 19s. 9d. When I bought my first motor bike in 1938 petrol was 1/3d (7 pence) a gallon.

It would take a long time for new families moving into the village to become accepted as 'villagers', everyone was polite and passed the time of day, they would even lend a hand if asked, but friendships were made very slowly.

Buckland today is very different from what it was when I was young. Our bakery closed when Mr. Trowbridge retired. I think he must have been well past retirement age when he baked his last loaf, but he and his family still kept the Methodist Chapel going. It was only a few years ago in the late '70s when Miss Trowbridge and her sister Mrs. Wilson had to close the Sunday School on account of age and health. These two lovely sisters are loved by everyone.

Our milk is delivered in bottles by van from Frome. The Smithy closed in the '50s has been demolished now, and the carpenter's shop is a thing of the past. Our vicarage was also sold and is now a private house. The new vicarage was also sold when our village was joined with several other villages under one rector I think anyone brave enough to be a rector of so many parishes must be a superman.

During the 1930s (and before) the village had a very strong and

105

enthusiastic cricket club and tennis club, both played in Court orchard before moving to Southmead. When I was seventeen I played for the village cricket team. We had Saturday and Thursday evening teams. Geoff Hibberd was our star batsman at that time, a tremendous hitter, many times the ball was hit into the Churchyard and on one occasion it cleared the Post Office into the main street. Tea was taken on the lawn behind the grocery shop in Lower Street. It was all very enjoyable. Most villages around had a cricket team but then the war put an end to it. Later attempts to restart the club failed through lack of interest.

The motor car and television has spoiled some aspects of village life and the activities which gave so much pleasure.

Farming only needs a fraction of the workers today. Hedge cutting is done by machine. Silage making and harvesting is done under contract. One man can milk a large herd of cows. 'Tied' cottages have largely disappeared. Farmer and workers have a greater knowledge of animal health than ever before which must be good for the animals.

I suppose it is because I was born in Buckland and spent most of my days here, but when we come back from our rare holidays or even day trips I say to my wife Jean "Well, we've seen some lovely places, but there's none to beat this."

"the fireplace in the front room held a fire only twice a year..."

Mrs. Udell

I was born in Southampton on the 23rd July, 1922, in a small terraced house which was an end one of three.

My first recollection is of sitting in a pram and being handed a biscuit with hard icing on one side and of screaming with fright when I turned it over and saw a face on the reverse side. When I told my mother of this recollection, many, many years later she said it was only a clown's face but I wouldn't accept that particular kind of biscuit for a long while after. I also recall going into the lodger's room, seeing something shining on the washstand, feeling the blade of the open razor cutting into the finger of my right hand yelling with terror when the blood spurted. The long scar is still visible.

Being an only child I was spoilt and early photos reveal all too clearly my wilful nature. All that changed, however, when I was three-and-a-half and my mother found she was pregnant again. My mother, born in 1889 never really overcame her Victorian up-bringing. She considered pregnancy a "delicate condition" and was ashamed of her expanding shape, always looping a towel over her arm and holding it in front of her whenever she answered the door. She had the baby, a girl, at home and on that occasion my only remaining grandparents, my paternal grandmother, came from Norfolk to look after her. When my brother was born eighteen months later, I was the little "skivvy" fetching and carrying up and down the stairs. I clearly recall sitting down on the stairs one day, looking at the blue bottle in my hand (which contained camphorated oil) and wondering why it had the same name as the insect my father had killed the day before.

Our house consisted of two bedrooms, with a boxroom leading off one, a "front room" and a living room (called the kitchen) with a small scullery leading off. The kitchen had an oven-range and the coal was

107

kept in a cupboard in the scullery. The only water supply was a tap over a low, brown shallow sink in the scullery. The lavatory was in the yard, the door having cut-out "vees" all along the top and bottom for ventilation. Very draughty in the winter. The pan was narrow and deep and the wooden seat went from wall to wall. Toilet paper was newspaper, cut into squares and hung on string on a nail. People were often a long time in the lavatory reading interesting "little bits".

a) Mrs. Udell's maternal grandfather William Richardson Gale a railway foreman. He was a descendant of Dr. Gale of Winchester.

When we were little my parents slept in the middle bedroom with my brother in a cot and the two girls in the boxroom leading off. We shared a single white iron bedstead.

One of our visitors was my aunt (my father's sister) who lived in America. I thought she was really glamorous — although that word wasn't in use in those days. She was tall and slim with the most beautiful reddish-brown hair. She had originally gone to Canada when very young and had been a model for "Harlene" hair products — very daring for those times. I have a photo of how she appeared in one of the adverts.

Our coal was bought from a horse-drawn cart, the coalman's name being Jimmie Reid and he worked for the Co-op. The coal was paid for with a £5 Co-op check: this was paid back at five shillings per week. When times were very hard Jimmie Reid could sometimes be cajoled into changing a check for money (to buy food) but more often than not he refused. At first our house was lit by gas only, the mantles having frequently to be replaced. Candles sufficed for the bedrooms.

The front room (or "frontfroom" as my young brother always called it) was the "holy of holies" used only at Christmas or when the Vicar called. Sparsely furnished at first, it later contained a piano and a hide three-piece suite, bought by my mother from Ralph's, a second-hand shop, on the never-never, much to my father's annoyance.

The fireplace in the front room held a fire only twice a year — Christmas Day and Boxing Day — but the impressive brass fender and firedogs had to be cleaned at least once a month. The brass stair-rods had to be cleaned once a week and the brass letter-box and front doorstep almost every day. There was a step by the front gate which my mother daily whitened with wet hearthstone and a cement strip in front of the kitchen range received the same treatment. I loved the smell and taste of wet hearthstone and often pinched a little piece off a corner and ate it.

In the kitchen, which was the hub of the family, a high wire-meshed fireguard stood in front of the range and this was always festooned with washing, either drying or airing. There was also a string line under the mantlepiece valance which again held small washed or ironed articles. A door in the kitchen led into the pantry which was really the area under the stairs. There were cockroaches and silverfish therein so it really wasn't very hygienic, although my mother was very fussy about covering things. An ornate gold-coloured clock under a glass dome stood on the mantlepiece, also two tall, blue china vases decorated in gold leaf, the fronts bearing circlets of coloured flowers and cherubs. Into these two vases went everything imaginable — shoe buttons, garment buttons, buckles, puncture-mending pieces, pipe cleaners, hair-grips, screws, tacks, knitting needles, crotchet hooks, chalks, pencils, etc., etc. If you wanted anything you just up-ended the vases on a piece of newspaper placed on the chenille table cloth and searched.

My mother, short, plump and pretty, was a creature of habit, as were most women of her day. She was always neatly dressed in the mornings in a sleeveless coat-apron (6¾d in Hawkin's sale) to protect her dress, with a toning cotton "cap" on her head. The latter she made herself; there were tail-pieces which buttoned at the back. She always changed after "dinner" which we ate at 12.30 p.m. and which was the main meal of the day. This change even included her elastic-legged knickers — interlock in the mornings, Celanese in the afternoons.

Every member of the family had a bath once a week, taken in a tin bath which lived on a nail on an outside wall. Later on we went more up-market and had a "bungalow" bath. This hung on the same nail but was of better galvanised steel and different in shape, being long and narrow, wider one end than the other. Water was heated in the brick copper in the scullery (where the bath was taken) by means of a fire lit underneath. Thus one had a nice warm bath in cold weather and a real sweaty one when the weather was warm. Water was baled into the bath by the means of a smell grey enamelled bowl on a long wooden handle. The bath was emptied by the same method, the dirty water being baled out and emptied down the sink. When the bath was light enough it was tilted over the sink to get rid of the remaining water. We three children shared one lot of water, the two adults another. That dealt with our nether ends. For the rest of the week we just washed faces and hands, drying on a linen roller towel placed on the inside of the back door.

It was a close-knit community, everyone struggling to pay their way, some slightly better-off than others but not that much. As there were no freezers, the prices of fresh produce were controlled by the seasons. It seems to me now that all other prices stayed the same for years. Employees had a wage increase on their birthday if they had been punctual and hard-working during the year, or if they obtained promotion. One was given credit for merit and folk seemed happier that way.

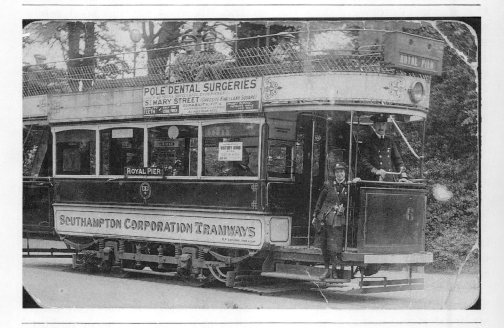

b) *Daniel Carter, Joy Udell's father, at the controls of a tramcar with his 'clippie' on the platform.*

110

During the first years of their marriage my father had several jobs; he was a tram-driver, a baker's roundsman and then a steward on board ship. On one trip he "jumped ship" and sent my mother a glowing account of life in America, saying he would be sending for her. There was just me at the time so my mother had our passport photo taken and patiently waited. Meanwhile my father had met up with his sister, who had moved from Canada to New York and for one week they had a glorious time, spending all his money. Alas, without a permit he was unable to obtain work in the U.S.A. and had to return to England the way he had left, as a steward on board ship. Very disappointing for mother. Then came the slump of 1926 and he was out of work for many months, patiently waiting in all weathers in the long queues down at the Docks, hoping for a days work. No Social Security in those days; my mother had to borrow money off her brother, who was a milk roundsman, in order to exist.

Then when my sister was born a brother-in-law who worked in the Ordnance Survey heard of a job going there, in the Plate Store.

He recommended my father and Dad remain there for the rest of his working life. His starting wage was £1.10.0d per week, poor even for those days. Later on, when I grew of an age to be company for my mother, he took evening jobs, mainly so that he could have some pocket money. He smoked a pipe and loved to have a "flutter" on a horse. He worked as a Commissionaire, in turn at Gatti's, The Gaiety Cinema, The Palace Theatre and, finally, the Picture House. He loved wearing a uniform; it made him feel important. In reality he was a hen-pecked husband. He adored my mother but she had only married him (at twenty-eight) for marrying's sake, having lost her true love in the First World War.

My mother was the only member of her family who spoke nicely and used the correct grammar. She had modelled herself on a schoolteacher she had greatly admired and for whom she worked diligently. She always aimed to be "genteel". Unfortunately her father died when she was ten and her mother was forced to take in washing. She used to tell me that she nearly died of shame when she had to take the finished laundry back to the customers. In addition she had to work before she went to school each day. Her job was to clear out the fires and re-lay them in a big Victorian house in London Road, Southampton.

During my time I worked in one of those houses, then used as offices by a Coal Merchant, and I used to think how hard it must have been for a small ten year old, carrying heavy buckets of coal up those endless stairs and along those cold, dark passages.

To return to our house. Our front door was only locked at night.

During the day one could pull a string which was visible through the letter-box, and this would spring the latch. Everyone either had this arrangment or a key on a string which one pulled through the letter-box.

We didn't have a holiday until I was eleven years of age. Until then we just had days out. Once a year we would go by train to Bournemouth, and once to the Isle of Wight by paddle-boat. The boat went from Southampton to Ryde. We took all our food and drink for the day, plus buckets and spades, swimwear, towels etc. That particular day was marred really by the long walk from the Royal Pier to our house, a slow upward climb, on tired legs, of some two miles or more. No money for trams. For the rest we would either have a picnic on the Common or a day on Netley beach, always accompanied by an aunt and uncle and three cousins — two girls and a boy of similar ages to ourselves. We had to walk there and back, carrying all we needed for the day. I used to feel so tired dragging homeward, I could have laid in the gutter and slept, and the tops of my arms would be all goose-pimply because we couldn't carry coats as well as everything else and I didn't possess a cardigan.

Southampton before the War was a totally different town from the city it now is. The Stores kept open until 9 p.m. Fridays and Saturdays and the fish shops, butchers and the market until 10 p.m. on a Saturday. There was very little traffic and the jostling crowds on the pavements spilled over on to the road. The many cinemas and theatres were brightly lit and coster mongers and buskers abounded. The floors in the Stores were just bare boards. Woolworths sold nothing over 6d and in the photographer's next door you could have your photo taken for 1/6d, with three postcard sized copies. When I was twelve I took the young ones there and we had our photo's taken for the parents' Christmas gift. We went again the next Christmas and this time the photo was finished in sepia! I obtained the money by doing a lone carol-sing at the biggest houses I could find. Our pocket money was ½d each on Saturday with 1d each on a pay-day (once a month).

When we were young the whole family would go to Kingsland Square on a Saturday night for the "selling-off" of fruit and vegetables, there being no refrigeration. Bananas would be as cheap as eight for one penny and oranges four for one penny. I didn't like the Square. The hissing, roaring flare lights over the stalls, which cast strange shadows, frightened me and there was so much noise. There was a monument in the centre, with drinking fountains, around which loitered ragamuffins. Straw was placed on the ground during wet weather to protect the feet.

On one side of the Square was the Kingsland Theatre, or the "flea-pit" as it was commonly called. Later an auctioneering butchers, Gillet's,

c) Joy Udell (née Carter) started school at five years of age. In this school photograph she is fourth from the left in the back row.

opened on the other side of the Square and we would go there for our weekly joint. the butcher walked up and down a high cat-walk displaying the piece of meat, stating the price and called for bidders. My mother used to take an endless time making up her mind.

By the time I was seven I was able to read and do "double-writing". I read anything I could lay hands on. Our daily paper was "The News Chronicle". My first complete book was Peter Pan and from there I progressed to "Little Women" and books by Gene Stratton-Porter and Ethel M. Dell. This exhausted my mother's collection so she enrolled me at the local library and there I would joyfully go on my own each week. The streets were safe for little children in those days.

Life passed happily, and uneventfully, it seems to me. There was, of course, the death of George V, then the abdication of the Prince of Wales followed by the Coronation of George VI, but by this time I was fourteen and clothes, make-up, films and the opposite sex were of a paramount importance to me. I do remember that murders were few and far between and those that did occur made sensational headlines. I recall the face of the acid-bath murderer, Haigh, who was convicted because his victim's false teeth hadn't been dissolved by the acid. There was also

113

the murder of a blond two year old boy in Bournemouth; I believe it was called the Red Tricycle murder.

My ambition had been to be a hairdresser but my mother couldn't afford the money for the apprenticeship. I remember my first-ever perm, which cost five shillings. The hair was rolled in strands on to steel rods, which had on one end a flex and connector. When the hair was all wound, the connectors were plugged into some sort of electric supply and the hair was baked for a few minutes. The resultant perm (if the hair was not cut) would last for at least a year. When home perms appeared on the market I looked after my own and my mother's hair.

d) Joy Udell (née Carter) aged twelve and three-quarters in her conformation dress.

My mother wanted me to be a secretary and on leaving school I was sent to a small private commerical school to learn shorthand and typing. The course was for one year, but with the other two children growing fast, my parents couldn't afford the fees after six months. Therefore I started work at Barrel's, a firm which specialised in office equipment, and finished my education at evening classes, which were paid for out of my 7/6d wage.

I went from there to a typing pool at Toogood's the seed merchants. It was a five-and-a-half day week, and the office staff had to clock on and off. I enjoyed the company of the other girls, and chatting over the fence to the soldiers in the barracks next door in the lunch hour. The pool was supervised by a very masculine lady, who reeked of Phul-Nana perfume, and who would cross-examine you if you dared to go to the toilet more than once during the morning or once during the afternoon. The wage was 14/- a week and I stayed ten months.

During all my single working years my mother claimed eighty per cent of my wages to "repay for my training" and I never once complained. With so little pocket money I had very few clothes, but I did have a lot of fun. When I was thirteen an aunt (my father's youngest sister) had taken me to British Legion Socials, admission sixpence, where I learned the art of ballroom dancing. I then started going to dances on my own or in the company of one of my female cousins. Three cousins lived nearby, all about my own age, and we considered ourselves very up-to-date with our Tangee lipstick and latest film star hair style. We drooled over movie magazines and annuals, yearned for "romance" but knew very little about sex. Even on my wedding night, when I was twenty-one, I went to bed not really knowing what was going to happen. We were, in a way, "protected" by the many prostitutes who walked the streets. Not that I knew what the word "prostitute" really meant, but I recall two in particular. They were tall and slim, one fair and the other brunette, and they wore the most beautiful tailored costumes (suits) with double fox furs slung over their shoulders, and high-heeled court shoes.

In the spring of 1937 the young sons of neighbours started to wear black shirts and, indeed, called themselves "Blackshirts". One Sunday afternoon I went to "Monkey Walk". This was a section of path on the Common running from "The Cowherds" to just past the Boating Lake. The young girls in their Sunday finery would stroll up and down, whilst the lads watched and whistled. My mother, not knowing where I was going, except for a "walk" told me not to be late for tea and placed my father's pocket-watch in my pocket so that I should have no excuse. I

115

looked at this watch whilst being chatted to by a boy and found I was already late, so started to hurry home. Turning a corner I saw a large crowd surrounding a van. A man was attempting to climb on to the top of this van but half-way up somebody pulled his trousers and they came off. I heard people in the crowd say it was Moseley. He eventually gained the roof of the van, where he stood talking, but by this time the crowd had built up, were pressing around me and I grew frightened. I pushed my way through and hurried home. When I reached there I really was in trouble, not only because I was late but because my father's watch had gone, stolen by a thief in the crowd. I had to confess where I had been and save up for another watch. I was seventeen years and six weeks when the Second World War started. My sister and brother were evacuated to West Parley in Dorset and life was never again the same.

"A fully-blown stone-mason."

R. Wollage

Isle of Portland

The first Robert Wollage came to the village of Weston on the Isle of Portland in 1806 and there has been an unbroken sequence of the family living there ever since. I am the fifth Robert Wollage of that family and I was born on January 28th 1912; I have lived the whole of my 75 years on the Isle of Portland. The first of the family were seamen, but the last three generations have worked in stone — for which the Island is renowned.

I was the first son and child of William Elliott Wollage and Lillian Bathsheba (Elliott) Wollage. Dad by trade was a quarryman, and Mother was the daughter of Williams White Elliott, Cheyne House, Water Works, Southwell; the first and only pumping station on the island at that time. The Waterworks were built by convict labour to convey water to the Dockyards.

My earliest memories are, of course, of the First World War. Dad, as did thousands of men, joined the Navy; I can remember waving goodbye to him as he returned to his ship dressed in his sailor's uniform; I remember, too, Mother taking my young brother and me on the train to Portsmouth in 1917 to stay for a time while Dad was in training at the barracks. I went to school there for a few weeks and then back to Portland to the Infants' Class of Dorset County Council School of East Portland, and, from there, in time, I graduated; the headmaster, Mr. William (Nemo) Edwards, retained that post from 1893 to 1924.

I remember well those early school days, we had to walk from the village of Southwell, about two miles away in all weathers, often arriving wet through, nowhere to dry your clothes, having to eat your dinner in the cloakroom, standing up or sitting on the hot water pipes, or on a fine day sitting in the park opposite, until the school bell rang.

Then you fell into a long line stretched across the road, and filed into the class room. If you were late you reported straight to Mr. Edwards, whose room was part of the girls' cloakroom, and without any argument, had the cane. I remember one lad refused to go, and ran off home leaving his boots on the floor. Mr. Edwards was one of the old timers who did not spare the cane.

I can remember the rope on the church bell being broken when Armistice was declared in 1918. About the same time the lads from school used to visit the German prisoners when they were building a road at Wide Street, Portland, during our dinner hour. They would give us a few coppers to go down to Easton to buy bread for them, and give us a little memento for our trouble.

Our out-of-school activities were mainly organised by the village chapels at Weston and Southwell. Mother and Father were long-serving members (as all the family had been before them), so our Sundays were fully taken up in the chapel; I would hasten to add — led, not forced, to come with them. We would go to the chapel with our mates of our own choice — as long as we went somewhere.

The build-up towards Christmas was full of excitement in our early days. The Co-op van that delivered the weekly groceries would call with fruit, boxes of sweets, nuts and many other things now forgotten which whetted our ardour so much that we couldn't do enough to please Mother. We were there at her call, ready and willing to do her bidding. We sat at the table night after night peeling the fruit, taking the skin off the almonds, turning the handle of the mincer, making the paper chains and other decorations. And when we came in from school and smelt the Christmas puddings cooking in the copper (that Mother normally boiled the washing in every Monday morning) we were nearly frantic with excitement and anticipation. We knew the great day was coming closer.

We also knew that many of these goodies, oranges, nuts etc. would be the last we would see until next Christmas, and this applied to our toys and other gifts as well. One of Dad's brothers always gave us 2/-, and that carried us well into the New Year for our weekly outing to the silent pictures at Easton — twopence to go in and a pennyworth of sweets and that was our only weekly treat. Another highlight at Christmas, when we were a little older, was to go out mummering to each others houses, we would dress ourselves up and black our faces and visit each others homes, boys and girls, and have a good old sing-song around the piano.

What wonderful days they were, how our parents managed it I do not know. There were never any holidays as the youngsters know today. On our school summer holidays Mother would load the pram with the baby and the food and off we would walk to Portland Bill for the whole

a) School photograph with Robert Woollage standing next to the headmaster, back row, right.

day — we nippers would scramble around the rocks fishing or bathing, and she would sit by keeping an eye on us, and send us up to the Lighthouse for a jug of water which we boiled up under the rocks for a cup of tea. We did this every day during the holidays if the weather was fine enough, and looking back I can never remember a wet day — it was sunshine all the way, marvellous days, never to be forgotten.

But what a grounding in life we had. And how useful it proved in later years. We gained so much knowledge when we were young. In those days we knew the ledges like the backs of our hands, and we would bring home fish, crabs, a lobster now and again, and enough to feed the neighbours as well. That is lost today, our fishing grounds are over fished; in my day fish were caught in their thousands, today they are lucky to reach the hundred.

Looking back at those brand new days and comparing them with the present, what a difference I can see. Today everything is laid on for the children to help and interest them in all aspects of their lives — the telly, radio, records, computers and dozen of games of every kind, motor bikes, cars, you name it, they have it. And yet our days were full to brimming over with the activities we loved. And we made nearly all our

119

amusements by ourselves. I daresay when some of the younger generation read this they will wonder what it was all about.

We had games for different times of the year. Our marbles season was usually in the autumn, when out would come the "Gertallys" and others from the lemonade bottles that we would smash to retrieve the "alley". Then Jimmy's father, a neighbour, would make most of us lead cocks to fire the marbles at, or we would throw them at the lid of an Oxo tin. I remember having hundreds of small coloured marbles that I had won from the other lads; in fact I had them for years afterwards. Mother would pull them out from under the cupboard and give them to my own youngsters.

"Ducky Stones" was another favourite game. So were "Whip the Tin", "Snickety Snack", "Lucky Hole", "Plant the Parcel", "Hopscotch" — a girl's game mainly — "Whip the Top" and "Jack the Lantern" during the winter months. These games were played all over our village and beyond, many in the middle of the road (with only a farm cart to disturb us and occasionally a thundering traction engine hauling it's load away to some large city).

We used the worked-out quarries to build our cabins where we met and cooked potatoes over a stinking grass fire; that usually got us into trouble when we arrived home. There were mushrooms to find and pick, blackberries in profusion covered the quarry workings, for tarts and wine. Birds in their hundreds built their nests in among the alders and ivy, and birds-nesting was always a fascinating pastime among the lads of our day.

We watched the sheep going through the "dip" and being sheared, and when 'Reg" made the rounds of the small household farms with his threshing machine, it was the highlight of the year, with all the lads of the village willing and ready when help was needed, even catching by hand the dozens of mice and rats that flew in every direction when the sheaves were moved. They were happy carefree days.

I am reminded of an unwritten rule of those times. Not one person would enter into a cut field of corn until the farmer had picked up the bundles of corn, and then returned to rake the ears that had been missed. Then all the village would gather in what ears there were left — and I can assure you there were very few. When a pig was killed in the village or a cow calved, the whole village shared in the yellow milk free, and the "chidlings" from the pig. We would get a few coppers from "George the Ragman" if we could manage to collect a few bones or rags or if Father killed a rabbit. One of the treats that Dad usually bought us of a Saturday night was a drink called "Iskey Stout" or "Kops Ale". It was a non-alcoholic drink that I have not heard of since.

120

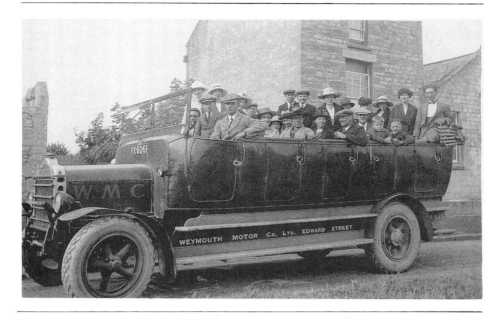

b) An outing to the sea in 1920.

But these marvellous invigorating hours slipped on into the past times of memory, never to be forgotten, and we move on into a completely different mood or road of life. On April 17th, 1926, just turned fourteen years of age I started work at the Masonry, Wide Street, Portand for J.F. Barnes Ltd.

Building work was recovering from the effects of the War very slowly. Quarries were opening and men were going into the masonry trade because it was the only work available. (There were a few jobs in the Dockyard but they did not pay anywhere near as well.)

I was apprenticed for five years at a Starting wage of 7/6d weekly, 44 hours per week — I believe the hourly rate was about 1/8d for the men. No holidays with pay; if you were just two minutes late at any time you lost half an hour's pay, and sat on your box awaiting the next time to start, whenever that might be.

If you did it too often you would have the foreman after you, and a right dressing down you would get, any back answers and you were on the carpet, in the Manager's Office, and if you were unlucky, up the road you would go — just one hour's notice — and never a chance of a job there again, you were a marked man for life.

I was put under a man who undertook to teach me the art of working

121

stone. There were at that time about a hundred men and boys at
different stages of their five years apprenticeship. And among them
were some of the finest stone masons in the country, men that could
turn their hands to any work that was given them to do, first class
workmen in every respect. They were founder members of the Building
Trade Union and fought for better wages and conditions for their
workmates.

In their early days the bosses paid different rates to all the men they
employed; the "Bell Boss" was paid top rate, and he set the pace and if
you didn't keep up you were again out.

The Union gained one good concession from the employers for the
apprentices. We were released one day a week during the first two years
to go back to school, and during the winter months, night school two
evenings a week. I did not think much of it at the time — but reflecting
back — it did not harm me.

If someone tells you that working stone is an easy life — then let them
go and have a try. It is hard, often boring, sometimes exciting,
sometimes gives great satisfaction in a good job well done, but it will
knock skin off your hands and sweat out of your body, and no-one will
thank you for it — and it's well under-paid.

Dad's job as a quarryman was like that. There were just three men and
a boy to a crew, all working under a hand crane, which meant that every
piece of stone needed all of them on the crane to heave it up and put it in
its position. All quarry work was "piece work", they drew from the
"Gaffer" a "sub" of 30/- weekly. Sometimes, if they did not earn their
"sub", it went on for years, until they were out of debt.

Father worked 5½ days a week in the quarry. He had about an acre of
land which he rented, where he grew his potatoes, greens, beans, peas
and everything that was needed in the garden. . . . It kept the family all
the year round; then he had rabbits, chicken. . . , a goat which kept us in
milk half a year, in fact we were nearly self-supported. . . .No work was
done on the Sunday, only to feed the animals. . . .Then I often gathered
the gulls eggs from the cliffs in spring time, which helped out at
breakfast time. So it can be seen that although we did not have much
money, we lived on the best of the land.

Generally speaking I enjoyed learning my trade as a stone mason and
was now coming towards the end of my five year period. Most of the
lads were a very happy crowd, and we have remained good friends right
down through the years. Some of us spent all our working lives together
and we developed many other interests in common outside our work.
By 1931 I had completed my apprenticeship and was now a fully blown
stone mason — being paid the full rate (which was still about £3 for a 44

hour week). The next year helped not only me but my family as well; there were four of us all told, my younger brother had also been out to an apprenticeship at the same yard as myself, so he was earning a few shillings. The quarry work was fairly brisk, so father was doing very well. I paid mother £1. 5 shillings out of my wages, which left me with a few shillings to spend on what I fancied — so things looked bright.

I had also found a young lady — or she had found me, we are not quite sure, and in the August of 1932 had decided to go to Bristol to stay with some friends who had invited us to their home. So we booked on the bus and away we went. And had a never-to-be-forgotten week exploring this thriving wonderland — it was the first time we had been to a city of that size and we enjoyed every minute of it. Arriving home Mother greeted me with "there's a letter for you, Sky brought'n in". Opening the envelope out fell my "cards". I was sacked without warning. Fortunately in the fullness of time I found I was not the only one, there had been about thirty all told, mainly the lads who had finished their "time" as I had done. But it didn't stop there, in the following weeks two more bunches of men were sacked, making about a hundred all told, leaving just about a half a dozen men and a few boys who were still under their apprenticeship contract, my brother was one of them. I was never to return to work for J.F.Barnes again.

So what did the future hold? Of this I had no idea. At that time it looked very bleak, and it was, make no mistake — bleak; not only for me but the whole country, and Portland was no different. Within a very short time nearly all the quarries closed and the few that were left went on three days a week. Whenever there was a job mentioned there were twenty men after it. Every Monday morning I would get on my bicycle and do the rounds (I didn't need Norman Tebbit to tell me what to do) but the answer was the same, day in, week out, year out. Some employers would talk to you like a Dutch Uncle, and you would think they were going to give you the world — others wouldn't listen to you — they simply slammed the door in your face.

When, through my young lady who had spoken to her boss, I finally got a job, it was the hardest labour I have ever known, before or since. But I did it. Six of us unloaded a sailing barge down at Castleton which had brought two hundred tons of granite for the Portland Urban District Council, for road-making. It took two days to unload. They put me down in the hold with my brother-in-law-to-be, filling up the baskets; my arms and legs were covered in blisters, I couldn't eat, only drink, and it was very hot — mid-summer. When eventually we finished I went up the road with £2, less 1/8d for the stamp, and that was the last work I did for the next twelve months.

The next opportunity finally came, on a building site, about twelve miles from my home. Of course I had to find my own way there and back, so I borrowed an old bike. I worked eleven hours a day — if it didn't rain — then back to my young lady's home for an hour or two, then back on my bike and home by ten o'clock and start the whole process all over again at six the next morning.

The rate at that time, 1934, was 11½d per hour for labourers. But we were only paid 10d per hour and told if we didn't like it, there's plenty waiting for your job. We worked 59½ hours per week and lost all wet times. I often sat in the hut when it was raining until it was time to go home, and then got soaked to the skin before I got there. And I can assure you — the southwest gales which frequently visit us were no help, it's very barren with no shelter between Weymouth and Portland.

In 1935 I heard there was work going in London and with great reluctance — I was leaving my girl behind — I caught the train to Waterloo. I had fixed up a job with the building firm of Trollope & Collis. But before I go on with our work there, I would like to reflect on the past a little, as I can now do from a distance. A man's attitude to so many things changes so much with his circumstances, especially when things are tight. The lore we had learnt as children stood us in good stead — we reverted to the natural instincts of our forefathers and became hunters. We made full use of the resources available to us in our time of need. And things were very tight money-wise, although Father and Mother never mentioned it at the time. . . . I know they had to borrow money from the better-off members of the family to keep their heads above water. (But I would hasten to add every penny was paid back in full when life got a little better.)

Anyway, looking back, those first two years of unemployment were in fact, wonderful days. I was free — free as the birds that I hunted — no worries, no cares, no money. I could do as I liked. My mother gave me the odd shilling for a smoke — which I used to enjoy, though no longer. So to help out with the one thing which really mattered, my pal Henry and I bought a second-hand gun. We made up our own cartridges, and with dogs, ferrets, nets, and Henry's considerable knowledge, we tramped our island night and day. Our best ever catch was five — bunnies, I mean, Portlanders never call them r-----s — but we nearly always had two or three. If, during our daytime roaming, we got within range of birds of any species — one more for the pot. (Even starlings.)

Some of the lads collected limpets from the sea shore, I expect there are many middens in and around the village of Southwell. And with the

124

abundance of fish and crabs around our whole coastline, there was no need to go hungry — and we didn't — and it was fun catching them. I also rented a piece of ground and reared chickens and ducks; I bought an incubator and sold the young chicks and the eggs to our neighbours. Henry and I sent for "clap net" and caught goldfinches to sell, the top birds fetched 2/- or more, the not so good 6d or 1/-; yes, when you are hard pushed, men will find a way to make a shilling.

I also know that some of those activities that we took for granted are today against the law and can be severely punished, and rightly so.

In our spare time there was always football, and we formed a team among ourselves which we called "The Portland Unemployed". Our pitch was on the Common Ground at Portland Bill, by permission of the Royal Manor of Portland Court Leet, which has been in being for hundreds of years — and still is.

It gives me great sadness to think about those early days now, for the lads of today will never again be able to enjoy those freedoms that we knew in our youth. Much of there land has been built over, there are new laws regarding guns, restrictions everywhere, even to many parts of the coast that we took for granted for fishing. Even swimming is restricted today. In many ways now we are like that vast Metropolis of London, thousands of people swarming around you — and you don't know a soul — and nobody wants to know you.

This was the first of the contrasts that hit me in the early days in London. At home we knew nearly everyone on the Island, and they us, or at least who our family was, and who we were related to, and it was very rare to pass in the street and not speak to each other. But in London, what a difference; most of us at that time had had a good sound bringing-up, and there was no doubt we all knew right from wrong; so we sat back and watched, in London, often with amazement at the way people were literally robbed and often without a word of protest. I found it amazing; it fascinated me. There were cheap-jacks of every kind, selling everything under the sun — ready to have you, even for a shilling. We were in and among the very people that we had read about all our lives — at home — with never a hope of actually seeing them in the flesh. Famous footballers — we saw them every weekend — I certainly did, stars of the screen and stage. I spent my last night in London up the West End listening to Gracie Fields, who was a big star in the 'thirties. It cost me 6/-, a lot of money in those days.

Then during the summer months I spent most of my Saturday afternoons at the Oval, watching the cricket, or at Lords for a Test match (South Africa was touring in England in 1935). I saw King George V shake their hands at the Test on the Lords pitch. We were also able to

c) Moving blocks of cut stone at Portland around 1920.

take part in the Jubilee of George V, when thousands of people made merry in the streets and stopped all traffic. Marie, my young lady, came up with a friend on that day, and we had to hurry to catch the train that left Waterloo at twelve midnight — and we just did it. But the one place I spent as much time as I could was at Hyde Park Corner. My curiosity and inquisitiveness burned like a fire, and I was always loath to leave that seething mass of humanity — it held me spellbound. There were speakers on every subject under the sun, that swung you to tears or laughter — booing or singing. There was nothing I enjoyed more than singing with the Salvation Army Songsters at Hyde Park Corner, or booing with the crowd that good-naturedly tried to take the "mickey" out of poor old "Charlie", a nutcase that got upon his box and went through the same talk word-for-word every weekend. The crowd knew it off by heart. Scenes such as this were repeated over and over again. I remember on one occasion doing a "pub crawl" just to sit and listen to the characters that frequent those sort of places. Both men and women. Women were very rarely seen in the pubs at home, I am not saying they did not go but when they did they kept it very quiet, it certainly wasn't the thing to be seen to do in Portland in those pre-war days — but of course the coming war altered all that.

Down in Trollope & Collis masonry works the Portland lads and men were doing well. They put us to work on Portland stone to start with, but when they saw how we shaped we were transfered to the job we were really taken on for — the stone a dull brown coarse-grained, came from the Midlands and was known as "Clipsham". It was used for the Houses of Parliament when a section was renewed. Some of the lads worked on the Houses knocking the old stone out to make way for the new. One thing soon became very apparent, and that was the Portlanders could hold their own with the best in the yards as workmen, and in many instances were far better. I think it showed that with schooling and training we had had a much better grounding in masonry than other lads who did not come from Portland.

Not that it made any difference. After about six months in London there was a war scare and all building work was stopped, almost at a minutes notice, certainly it was only an hour on the Friday. I decided to have one last day in London and go home on the Sunday, and the thought of getting the sack didn't worry me a bit. I almost jumped for joy, I was going home — to the people and the place I had always loved — and always will — those that want London or any other place can have it for me — I had seen all I wanted to see, and it didn't come up to Portland.

So, away I went, down Camberwell Green, the Vauxhall Road, past the Oval, over Vauxhall Bridge, across the grey-green Thames (water was never that colour in our surrounding sea), down the Wandsworth Road, stop one last time at the "Dorset Arms" next door to the stone works which were never to see me again — thank goodness.

Back to Portland with no job, wondering if I should to go through the same indignities as I had gone through after six months on the "dole" in 1933. I refer, of course, to the "means test". That humiliating and degrading experience which left a scar for life — and which we, the young, strong and willing had to endure from the indifferent, uncaring Government of that unhappy period. A Government who, within a few years, were finding all the millions needed to fight the war, yet at that time literally starved its people. I knew of several young married men who had been caught doing a bit of fishing to help out the meagre allowance. Their dole money was cut off completely, and some of them didn't have a penny coming in from any direction, only what their friends gave to keep them and their families alive, or what they were able to grow in their gardens. Most of them did have gardens — it was their standby.

But, provided you didn't mind what you did, there were a few more jobs about. Within weeks I was working again in Wyke as a mason's labourer building a large stone house. I still had about eight miles there and back on my bike across that windswept causeway that separates

Portland from the mainland. The boss on the job promised me a return to the stone yard when it was finished — but I didn't get it, so back on the "dole" for a few more weeks. Then another builders labouring job turned up — at 11d an hour. After doing a few months general house repairs and digging a "cess" pit on my own, I was sent to work on a housing site with a number of other men. In the course of conversation I found that the boss was paying them 1/- per hour and when he came down to see how the work was progressing I told him about it. He didn't know what to say, but on the Friday payday he gave me all the money that was due to me and said "if you insist on wanting the 1/- same as everyone else", which I did, "well, here's your cards". And that was that I was out again.

What trying times those must have been for Father and Mother — another mouth to feed, more work and more expense. But they took it for granted — it was as if you had never been away, your bed was ever-waiting.

Work in Portland began to look up and eventually the news filtered through that stone firms on the Island were taking on more men. I did the usual rounds but there was nothing doing for me. However I made another start at a labouring job, this time on the rebuilding of the Portland Gas Works, which was being done in two sections. Having completed the first part all the labouring staff were laid off, bar me and the wall masons. But by then the thing that I wanted was the sack so I might get a chance to return to my own trade — if you had a job of any kind no employer would consider you. So, after a few weeks, I approached the foreman, explained the position and he quietly gave me the "sack" and I rejoined the Labour Exchange and the "dole". Then, after six weeks or so, a message was sent over to me to report to the general foreman at the Bath & Portland Stone Works in Easton Portland — which I did without a moments hesitation, with a hope and a longing in my heart that I should at last get back to the job that I was born into and really loved — and did for the remainder of my working life.

It was now the first days of 1937, I was back to a life that I had not known for at least five years, a pound to spend and a few in my pocket and home. Work was consistent and steady for the next two years, so I was able to put a few pounds aside. So with about £100 in the bank Marie and I decided to fix the day and get married. She had been my constant companion, sharing my troubles and disappointments, my goings and comings, with no rewards, only a trip to the "pictures" or a night in the 9d's to see "Murder in the Red Barn" and other such plays, for the last seven years. So October 8th 1938 became our red letter day for the rest of our lives. The outlook for us at that period looked very bright — perhaps we didn't want to see the gathering storm clouds, and hoped they would go away.

Marie and I were settling down to married bliss very well — but — there's always a 'but' isn't there? We had two unfurnished rooms in a house of a widow in Easton and we had to share the kitchen. Now as most of us that has had much married experience know — two women in a kitchen, to put it mildly — is just not on.

Then a house became vacant in Weston Road — our present home — and we had the chance to rent it at 8/- per week plus rates. We jumped at it. If ever we made a wise choice, it was on that far off day. So again on the 1st July 1939 — we took over our own nest and have lived in it very happily ever since — and sincerely hope to go on doing so until the end of our days.

But what ever happiness that we felt at that time was very quickly removed in no uncertain manner. September 3rd 1939, war was declared with Germany and a decade of time was ahead of us that would make our last ten years seem like a holiday.

I have been blessed with a wife and partner that thousands of men would have liked to have had but never did. I am in her thoughts constantly, in sickness and health, and her in mine. As we both see the gap closing in years on our lives, so we have come closer, even more so than when we had our family around us. Perhaps it's because we had nothing to start with. We have had to wait patiently for the few material things that surroud us. We have each other — and that's all that matters. Our faith tells us that this is just one road we have to walk on, that it will continue when we leave this world — onto the next, together.

I realise that I have been a very fortunate man, from my birth to the present day, and with all it's fears, tears, hope and laughter — I thank God over and over again for the opportunity to have lived through it all. The world is a wonderful place, with plenty for everyone, the trouble is the greed of man. But I have great hope for the future — I can see that the world is gradually, but ever so slowly, moving towards the main law that God gave us — "Love thy neighbour as thyself". What an exciting world that would be.

"Nanny gave her secret smile, Clare shivered"...

Mary Freeman

The plain Ham Hill stone Georgian house came as no surprise at the end of the twisty laurel drive, for it was partly visible from the surrounding hills nestling as it did, in a hollow.

On the south side were the grounds which Clare's* grandfather had laid out with outstanding taste and imagination. He had spent much of his life in tropical countries. The damp mild climate had produced an abundance of shrubs and trees, some exotic, all fine specimens, some abnormally tall. From a wide sweep of gravel bounded by a balustrade, a wrought iron gate led across lawns to the first lake: here swans glided and moorhens nested undisturbed. There was a flat-bottomed boat which slopped about among the rushes and marigolds.

Yew and rhododendron walks carpeted with moss led to surprise places: a sudden burst of pink pearls, a greenish old Bacchus drinking his cup, a balustraded terrace with a sandpit for the children, a waterfall crashing into the second lake, silent glades, thick bushes and always the tall trees.

Clare and her brother Giles, younger by a year, were inseparable; little Joe lying in his pram hardly existed for them, and Frances and Robin spent most of the year at school. It was exciting when they came home, though Frances patronised 'little Clare' and Robin showed off for Giles' benefit, for they had new ideas, a different way of talking and fascinating stories to tell. They dropped all this, however, after the first week or so of holidays and ran with Clare and Giles tearing after them into all the secret places of the grounds to make camps, build wigwams, look for birds nests, chase the peacocks and catch perch in the muddy river. Sometimes Daddy would appear from behind a bush, wave his stick and walk rapidly away. Not so Mummy — she was everywhere. She nearly always carried a large straw basket filled with flowers. These she would

130

breathing. Her bulbous eyes swivelled frequently in Clare's direction, noticing with growing indignation the little girl's happiness and exhilaration ever since the injection episode of the morning, to which Mummy referred affectionately several times. On fine evenings like this one the children were allowed out to play for as long as the light lasted. Throughout the grounds, at this time of year, there was the scent of bonfires. In the potting shed were rakes and besoms with which to make the fires grow higher and brighter. They were joined by others, including Clare's special friend, Rory, and the gardeners kept watch, irritably reminding the children that they were not allowed in the potting shed. Summoned at last to come in, they chased each other through the hall, up the three flights of stairs, resting briefly by sitting on the old oak chest in the middle landing. From here seemingly miles of lawn stretched out to where rhododendron trees and bushes began, the huge Wellingtonia dominating all. The happy children were chilled by the note in Nanny's voice as she called them down. Giles ran down at once, leaping the stairs two at a time but Clare lingered — she stood up on the chest and glimpsed briefly at the pale sickly sun going down behind the Wellingtonia. She suddenly felt an unreasoning sense of doom, not dispelled by the sight of the cowed nursery maid standing self consciously by Joe's cot. Did she flash a warning at Clare? "That bonfire" said Nanny, "its got into your hair, we can't have dirty little girls, can we, Clare?" Clare stared steadily at Nanny. She was determined not to show the terror which was begining to grip her. "Run along to your room and get undressed and I"ll get the bath ready", said Nanny. She gave a quick smile and walked briskly in the direction of the far bathroom, away at the end of the back landing — "miles from everywhere" thought Clare. In seconds she was in her room. Automatically she tossed off her shoes. For an instant she stood stock still in the middle of the faded white carpet: terrified, bracing herself, then thinking hard. The intellectual exercise brought her a kind of peace. She knew now she would NOT go to the bathroom; she would NOT be drowned again. Noislessly she ran from the room and hugging the wall she tiptoed to the foot of the stairs which led to the top of the house. Here she paused momentarily, there was no sound. As she crept up the stairs in her bare feet, she knew what she would do. She stopped in the middle landing by the old oak chest. The lid was heavy and had to be pushed up with both hands and the chest was completely empty. Clare took off her cardigan and threw it in at one end. Near the wall there was a long slit in the wood and at the other end there was a considerable gash. Then a harsh calling note rent the silence — "Clare" — insistently. Clare climbed in quickly. She lay back, lifted her right arm and pulled the lid slowly towards her.

135

Just in time her arm went limp, she ducked and the lid fell into place. At first there was a feeling of having gone on a long journey, to a far distant land, dark and unfamiliar. Clare lay quite still, her hands clenched. Nanny and the hair wash, even Mummy and Giles were all forgotten. Suddenly and rather to her relief there was a glimmer of light near her feet. She moved a toe near the crack and felt the torn wood. A minute later she lifted a hand and clutched the familiar cardigan behind her head. There was another crack in the side and she pointed her nose towards it and breathed in — there was plenty of air. She lay back, limp and quite still now. The complete silence outside made no impact on her; she was in a far land and beginning to feel sleepy. In fact she did sleep for quite a long time, worn out by the intensity of her emotions.

When she woke it was quite dark. Before she had time to panic the landing light was switched on, making a faint glimmer, but someone must be near. Clare's forehead was damp but she managed to keep still. There was a confused murmer of voices, distant and mostly female. Then quite clearly she distinguished the deep burring tones of P.C. White; she couldn't hear what he was saying but she had a clear vision of his round red face and thick neck bursting over his uniform collar. Another man's voice: P.C. White was talking to Daddy. Clare felt suddenly comforted; surely they would understand. The voices dropped, there was only mumbling and no-one came up the stairs. Perhaps they had searched the whole house and the grounds, perhaps they had passed the chest while she was asleep. She wasn't sleepy any more, just restless and shivering. She wanted Mummy more than anyone. Flattening her head back as far as it would go she tried to push the thought of Nanny, floating and bobbing to the forefront, far, far down into the depths of her being. Driven by a feeling, quite new to her, of desperate loneliness Clare knew that she must get out of the chest quickly and find someone before screaming aloud. She hunched her shoulders and bent her outstretched legs. Then slowly raising her arms she pushed against the lid of the chest. Nothing happened. She pushed a tiny bit harder keeping her real strength in reserve. After relaxing for a moment she bent her head towards the long crack in the side and breathed in "I'll try again in a moment" — she was conscious of muttering to herself now. Then — she almost sat up and pushed with all her might. The lid didn't give an inch. Clare began to panic, real or imagined voices seemed to get louder, her head began to swim. Automatically she slipped half way down the chest, her feet pressed against the bottom, her hands splayed over her head, her arms rigid, pressing with all her might. She started to shout — "Mummy, Mummy" she screamed as the lid suddenly flew open and plopped against the wall. Clare literally rose up and fell out of the chest on to the floor beside it. She lay there panting and dripping, quite faint and not caring whether her screams had been heard or not. When she "came to" she was cold as ice. She sat up, remembering everything in a flash. A great wave of relief swept over her. For a long time she sat staring in front of her, her head lowered, her hands loosely covering her knees. She had a vague feeling, hardly "spelt out" in thoughts or words that she was somehow damaged, diminished by her expericence. She felt spiritless — perhaps she was hungry. At last she pulled herself to her feet and without touching the dreaded chest, took out her cardigan and slowly put it on. It took a little time to grope her way down from the landing to the head of the main staircase. The voices were still purring below: Daddy's and Mummy's dear and familiar; Nanny's soft and cajolling. P.C. White was still there. Clare gripped the banister. She controlled her sudden longing to rush down — she would go on thinking and not hurry. Nanny could still frighten her but she felt stronger now — like her admired friend Rory who would stare boldly at Nanny with his huge blue eyes. The steps down seemed endless but before she reached the bottom Clare knew that somehow, someday, perhaps after aeons of time, the damage done to her would be repaired.

*Clare's in this fictionalised fragment of autobiography, is the author herself. Mrs. Freeman was born in 1909: the period referred to is Circa 1919. Ed.

"Father was a doctor"

Houghton-Brown

Witheridge, Devon

I spent my childhood at Witheridge, a small village in Devonshire, about half way between Dartmoor and Exmoor, and ten miles from any station or town.

I had a brother, Christopher, two years younger than myself and two step-sisters, Enid and Cecily (the latter known as Bobby). Father was a Doctor with a large practice nearly twenty miles across, which he ran entirely on horseback or in a trap, greatly despising the modern method of travel — the motor car.

No children could have had a happier upbringing. Mother, who was also born in the country, taught us everything.

The garden was a large one, with a useful "Paddock" behind it. Almost as soon as we could toddle we learnt the knack of birds nesting, butterfly collecting, the building of wigwams and "houses" in the shrubbery, and generally "mucking it". One of our greatest friends was Mr. Leech, the gardener, who we knew quite definitely was one of the great men of the world. He never stopped working from daylight till dark and, so long as we behaved ourselves, was always kind and helpful to us boys. On occasions he was very severe and used to work himself into a great temper if we dared walk across his newly dug ground, or broke off the branches of fruit trees in our efforts to get at a chaffinch's nest, or some other careless mischief which upset the tidiness of his lovely garden.

Mother was always very keen on our keeping pets and looking after them ourselves — the idea being to make us think of things other than our own pleasures. Thus, at an early date, I remember looking after our tame rabbits in hutches at the bottom of the garden. We used to go into the hedges to pull dandelions and cow-parsley and return with our arms full to feed our hungry pets. They bred fast. We thought the mating act was a very interesting entertainment. In fact on one occasion in the winter, when my Mother had some rather fine friends in for tea, we boys were told to go into the Hall to play and amuse ourselves. Later, when our elders came out to collect their coats, they found us both on all fours, me chasing my brother up and down stairs. When I caught him I would jump on top of him and make peculiar noises. We were then asked what was the new game we were playing, and in all innocence I replied: "Oh, just buck and doe rabbit". I remember to this day the look of horror on the faces of our guests, and never understanding why Mother suggested quietly afterwards that we had better think of a new game, and quickly producing some cards we finished the evening by playing "Happy Families"!

If we thought Leech was a "great man", we knew Brent, the groom, was a sort of God. The stables had two loose boxes and two stalls, all of which were always full of some sort of useful horse flesh. Above the stables was a loft stuffed with hay and straw, and at one corner of the building was a Saddle Room — the "mecca" of it all. A blue stone stable yard led up to the Harness Room door, and outside it there was a "mounting block", a stone about two feet high which enabled my Father to get up quickly onto some of his bigger horses. On the other side of the Yard was a Carriage House (later turned into a Garage) in which stood our Pony Trap, a Gig and other horse-drawn conveyances.

Brent was rather fond of the bottle, and thus at times had a sour temper, but we boys loved him and rightly so, for he really was a first-class groom of the old school.

For six months of the year the Saddle Room always had a roaring fire and was a model of orderly tidiness. Above the stove was a big glass case in which hung all sorts of bits and chains, all beautifully burnished and shown off from a background of green baize. Then on one wall were the saddles and, hanging underneath, the clean single and double bridles, perfectly polished and soaped. On the other wall hung the driving harness with the "double" and "tandem" gear as a separate display in the middle. Over all this Brent was complete master. We had to sit very still each side of the fire if we were to be admitted to this "holy of holies". The little old groom used to hiss perpetually through his teeth as he polished a bit or rubbed saddle soap into a long "leather". In the corner, in a neat box, the tortoise-shell cat lived, usually with half-a-dozen kittens sucking her ever swollen teats.

On hunting days, Brent used to stir the horses' linseed gruel on the stove, being very careful that none of the mixture stuck to the bottom of the saucepan. When he had finished he would shout "Teats, Teats", and the old cat would creep out of her corner and lick the linseed off the stick that stirred the gruel.

Today our modern theory of horse management is to give the horse plenty of fresh air, however cold the weather, keeping the windows and stable doors open all the time. Not so Mr. Brent — every ventilation was filled up with straw, windows tightly shut, and the penalty was a string of oaths to anyone who was careless enough to leave the stable door open, even for a moment. However wrong it may sound to the modern ear, old Brent kept his four hunters as fit and as well turned out as any in Devonshire at that time. In fact the horses were the pride not only of Father and Brent but of the entire household.

Father's pocket was not deep, in fact very much the reverse, and so he used to buy horses "under the hammer" at Collins Repository in Exeter. These horses seldom cost more than £30-£40, but owing to the hard work of the practice they soon got knocked into shape and usually in the end turned out satisfactorily. Father generally rode on his rounds, but sometimes he would drive. His chief delight was to drive two horses as a pair or in a tandem. This, as can be imagined, was a fairly hazardous performance, especially as the horses had always been bought as "Hunters", and had had little or no training either in the "shafts" or to a "pole". However, as both my parents had "good hands with the ribbons" there was remarkably little trouble, especially as in Devon there was still little sign of the combustion engine, which later drove the horse off the road.

As we grew older we were sometimes privileged to drive out with Father on his rounds. This was grand fun up to a point, as Father took great pains to show us all the finer points of driving, harnessing and turn out. In fact sometimes, going up a hill, one of us would even hold the reins but the trouble would come when we arrived at some small Farm or cottage and the "Doctor" would put on his professional air and go inside to attend to his patients, leaving us boys to hold the horse or horses, whichever it might be. This was alright in summer when they would nibble the fresh grass on the high banks, but in winter it would almost reduce us to tears. The horses were always clipped out, in fact almost shaved, and although we would throw a rug over their quarters they would be so cold that they could not stand still. They would fidget, paw the ground, prance, kick, bite, throw up their heads, and do everything except bolt, which we always expected them to do at any moment. Father seemed to spend interminable hours in these cottages but in the end he would come out, smoking his old pipe, looking as pleased as punch and not at all understanding why it was that we looked so forlorn and miserable! He would pull off the rug, gather up the reins, and then off we would go at a good spanking trot, perhaps not stopping for another hour, so scattered was the district.

Looking back it is difficult to understand how Father made a living at all in that vast sparsely populated practice. Often he would ride or drive all day and only see half-a-dozen patients. The majority of them were poor farm labourers and could only be charged a minimum fee. In fact, I know hundreds never paid at all. Even the farmers themselves held their shillings very tightly. I believe in the end, after ten years hard work, Father left the practice very little better off than when he took it. Anyway I know he had no regrets. He reared a happy family, worked hard but lived like a lord, hunted at least once a week, and never knew what it was to be called up on a telephone!

We always knew he was going to be called out at night, by the "plod, plod, plod" of a Farm horse being ridden up the drive. Then the peal of the nightbell, followed by the lifting of the parents' large latch window, then Father's voice: "what the devil do you want at this time of the night?". "Oh, Sir. Mother fell down stairs this arternoon and Dad says he thinks she is going to have a baby a bit sudden-like", or "Our young Tom has been feeling main queer the last two days and then this morning he came out in red spots all over him, and Father says will you please come immediately". "Why the Hell didn't you come before?". "Oh, Doctor, we didn't want to be abothering of you".

Anyway, when all was over we would hear Father mumbling and cursing in his dressing room and eventually his step down to the stables to ride off into the dark to some little farm house, perhaps eight or nine miles away, not getting back till five or six hours later.

Our greatest sport, then as now, was hunting, and during the Great War Father helped run the local pack of stag hounds. These hounds were kept by a sporting old Farmer, who fed them entirely on "Knacker meat" which he kept fresh in the streams below the Farm. The hounds saw no meal at all, but kept very fit and showed wonderful sport, although at times they got almost too fierce to handle.

Father's chief delight was, on returning early in the morning from some maternity case, to "harbour" a good stag. He would then canter home, throw his tired horse to the groom and order two fresh horses to be ready in a couple of hours time. Then there would be such a rushing of early breakfast, changing into hunting clothes, Leech bringing violets for Mother's button-hole, and hurried mixing of medicines for patients who had been told to call during the day. We would go to see them off from the drive gates — Mother looking so smart in her trim habit and polished side-saddle, with Father behaving for all the world as if he had not seen a horse for a week. Long after nightfall the two tired parents would return, plastered in mud from head to foot, but with faces lit with animation. Then we would rush to feel in Father's pockets to draw out eventually a "slot"* all wrapped up in a clean handkerchief, especially taken out for the purpose. We would then help them both pull off their muddy boots as they lay back in big chairs, sipping hot whisky in which had been dropped two fat white lumps of sugar. As the years went on, ponies gradually appeared on the scene, when we would accompany Father both on his rounds and out hunting. The trouble in those days was that ponies were not broken with much skill, and as far as I can remember all our ponies had mouths like iron. We would gallop down the steep tracks in the woods, quite out of control, and could only pull up when the pony became exhausted half way up the next precipice. In fact I do not remember ever having a mount that I could control until I grew up and got my first hunter. We used to enjoy riding round with Father, especially as he used to appear a great man in the village, the women curtseying as we passed and the men touching their caps. There was no "mansion" in the neighbourhood so Father used to take the part of Squire, Parson, Confessor, Doctor and general family adviser. He may not have had a very remunerative practice but he certainly led a man's life, and did a power of good amongst the people every hour of his existence.

Every day to us was full of fun and laughter, but somehow Sunday in particular was a day of bliss. To start with, breakfast was later. We were allowed to go into our parents' bed for half-an-hour before dressing. This was a great privilege and we used to discuss the plans for the next week and play riotous games under the eiderdown. Then we got dressed in smart sailor suits, and at half-past ten walked off sedately to Church. We did not really understand the Service but enjoyed trying to sing the Hymns. During the sermon we cuddled close into Mother and held her hands tightly, admiring the beautiful rings she wore on her fingers.

Then, after Church, a parade to the stables where we found Brent in his smartest clothes and the horses in their best rugs, H.B. marked on the corners. Brent used to make a great show of this and had special plaitings of straw round the stalls and boxes. On a clean plate he produced scrubbed yellow carrots which we took in turn to each Hunter. Father inspected each horse minutely, feeling their legs for suspicious "splints" or "spavins", and decided how the horses would be worked during the coming week.

On other days we usually had our meals in the Nursery but on Sundays we always had lunch in the Dining Room with the "grown-

* For the benefit of our town cousin, a "slot" is a deer's hoof.

ups". Father was very particular about table manners and would constantly remark: "Sit up straight there, boy", or "Hold your knife properly", and so on. This did not worry us much as we looked forward to the dessert afterwards, sitting on Father's knee and sipping his vintage Port.

After tea we went into the Drawing Room, where Mother read us extracts from the Bible and tried to teach us to sing hymns. My favourites then, as now, were "There is a green hill far away", "Once in Royal David's City" and "Onward Christian Soldiers". Anyhow, we just loved Sundays. Even to this day I look forward all the week for the good day to arrive, and never feel it has been complete unless I have attended some form of Church Service.

My younger step-sister, Bobby, went to a School in Tiverton, ten miles away. Under the same Headmistress was a small Prep. School of about 15 boys of ages up to ten years. In 1913, when I was 7 and a half, my parents wisely thought it was time for me to leave my Governess and go to School. Owing to our isolated position they decided to let me start as a weekly boarder at the Prep. School in Tiverton. This might have been quite successful if there had been a number of boy boarders but, as it turned out, only one other boy and myself "lived in", the rest being day boys. We were in the extraordinary position of being the only two boys boarding in the same school as 50 girls!

I must admit my first year was a very unhappy one. Never having played with other children before (with the exception of my younger brother) I was naturally unlike other children, and no doubt was a very smug, umpleasant, horrid little boy. Anyhow, the other children thought I was and they made quite certain that I knew it.

Small boys can be devils. I must admit I was bullied from morn till night, and on one occasion I was hung up by my hands in the Bicycle Shed and had lime flung at me. Why I was not blinded I do not know. I was kicked, hit, had my books torn up and was generally treated like a worm. To make matters worse, the other boy with whom I shared a room in the Girls' School was two years older than me. He bullied me even worse than others, never giving me a moment's peace. The girls also thought it all rather funny and delighted in continually putting me in "Coventry", not speaking to me for days at a time. The trouble was I dare not admit to my parents how unhappy I was, because I thought it would make then miserable too. Somehow I stuck it out for a year and then things suddenly changed. My younger brother started to come with me to School and as a result I quickly became a boy instead of a child. I started the next term by hitting the first three boys I met, and nearly killed the other lad who was boarding with me. From that day all my troubles ceased and I became quite a figure in the School.

We continued as weekly boarders and the three of us used to drive backwards and forwards. We left home early on Monday morning on our two hours drive, and turned the pony out in the School playing fields for the week. Then, on Friday evening, the great hour would come and we would catch up the pony and drive back to Witheridge, getting home in summer just in time to see our rabbits before supper. It was a beautiful drive through some lovely country, and even in those days we thoroughly enjoyed it, discussing the change in the appearance of the country as the season advanced.

In winter Brent would drive us in on Monday mornings. We would then come home by the village bus, all jammed up with the buxom farmer's wives, fish, harness oil and other weekly purchases. Usually, about half way, we would have to stop for my brother to get out to be sick, but even so we would get home in time to eat hot potato scones (a new war-time dish) in front of a roaring fire in the Drawing Room.

I know I did not learn much in those days. A smattering of English Grammar, one Scripture lesson a week, some geography, history and a mist of French, Latin and Mathematics. I admit that to the end of my schooling Algebra was entire nonsense, and languages a sort of nightmare. To make things worse, at this Prep. School they tried to teach us the "old pronunciation" in Latin, whereas later, when I went to a Public School, I had to start again, as they taught the "new pronunciation". Anyhow, I do not think I ever got much further than "Amo, Amas, Amat"!

We were handicapped in those days by having only women to teach us, all the men having gone to the War. This did not matter so much in our lessons, but of course it meant that we got no "grounding" at all in our Games and in fact really got no organised sport at all. The Games Mistress, a fearsome woman, spent all her time putting brawn and muscle onto the legs and arms of the already angular girls, thus having no time for us "little boys". However, there was one great redeeming feature — there was a local parson, the Rev. Carter, who came over two afternoons a week to initiate us in the art of scouting. As he was such a fine personality I think, on reflection, that we got more value out of this than we would have done by learning how to play a straight bat at Cricket. He got uniforms for us, and organised us into patrols, which made us thorough Boy Scout enthusiasts. It became popular later on to laugh at Boy Scouts, in the same fashion as the ridiculing of Territorial Soldiers. Nevertheless, I still maintain that if these two organisations had been properly backed by the State and the People, then this second World War would never have taken place.

Mr. Carter ran our Scouts with an almost military precision, great trouble being taken over "turn-outs", "discipline" and "morale". Not only did we spend hours in the country learning woodcraft, camp cooking, bivouacking and tracking, but we also had long talks on wet afternoons on citizenship, religion and other quite serious subjects. Looking back it all seems rather smug, but somehow at that time it was very real. Carter instilled in us such enthusiasm that our scouting afternoons became the peaks of the week. I am afraid in the end I spent more time in studying my "Scout Guide" than I did my "Latin Grammar". I became so keen that eventually they promoted me to "Patrol Leader", and so for the first time I felt the thrill of leadership. At this stage I spent all my spare time in scouting and in training the younger "cubs", and although we were only children I felt I had the power of a man!

This was my first taste of success and from that day onwards the craving to lead never left me. I was only happy when I was at the top, and the "bug" of ambition having so early entered my blood I have had to spend the rest of my life trying to curb its ever-jealous nature. We are told by the wise that a healthy ambition is an admirable quality and is, in fact, the key to successful people. So it may be, but unless it is carefully trained and governed it can become so unquenchable in its desires that in the end it can only bring misery and disaster to an otherwise contented heart.

Having "bossed" the scouts to my satisfaction I then "set about" the little School, and the next term saw me as Head Boy. With a 12" ruler in my stocking to smite offenders I domineered the School with an iron rod and held such sway over my little army that the mistress unwisely seemed to leave me almost free to administer dicipline, as I felt necessary!

All this may have been alright up to a point, but my parents wisely thought that the time had come for me to go to a Public School. After much discussion it was agreed that next term, at the age of twelve, I should go to Berkhamsted.

145

*"My father employed fifty men and
had thirty carthorses in the stables"*

Richard Stratton

Kingston Deverill,
Wiltshire

Manor Farmhouse, Kingston Deverill

By Wiltshire standards, Kingston Deverill is a nicely isolated village where people are pleased to live. It was not always so. In the 1920s the cultural and physical gap between town and country was probably wider than it has ever been. In time, probably a fifty year lag. Partly this was due to the large labour force needed to live in the village to work the farms and partly through lack of motor transport.

Nowadays the car is an extension of one's legs. Then it was a temperamental enemy to be, with an element of luck, mastered. The road up the valley to Mere had a tarmac surface but the Maiden Bradley road was still chalk from the Whitepits quarry on top and flint, also quarried in the village or collected in the sheep fold, underneath. For the Sunday afternoon run over Mere Down to my Grandparents at Charnage an hour was allowed for the five miles. My father would have ridden there direct in half that time. We had an open four seater Sunbeam Tourer and quarter of an hour was likely for cranking it into life. Many the wrists that were broken due to backfires. We would then attack the hill from this side until my father stalled the engine. Thereupon Mother would leap out and put a log of wood behind a rear wheel. There followed two alternatives: either my father located first gear and juddered on or he reversed down the straight to the church, found bottom gear and charged the hill. By the time Mother was passed with her block of wood, the car was boiling and she had to abandon her post on the corner and catch up where the gradient eased.

The return journey involved the far steeper Warminster Hollow, from whose banks fifty years previously, the radical burghers of Mere had stoned Grandfather's coach after a rowdy political meeting in the town. One could not get up steam (literally) at this hill. At the bottom, we four children were put out to walk to the top while our parents wrestled with the infernal machine. If all else failed, they would eventually arrive in reverse gear. My father never, ever looked in a rear mirror and, uphill, would move his body backwards and forwards as when urging his horse.

The Newbury family were the carriers to Warminster, the Carpenters maintained the roads. Great was the glee on the frequent occasions when the carters were sent to tow home our abandoned car. The horses were hitched off and the car was ignominiously winched into the garage using the pulley in the roof recently used for a coach.

Hence the isolation. The village was, perforce, a community on its own. We worked and played together and life centred on the farm. My father employed fifty men and thirty carthorses were in three stables. Rent from the Glebe land supported the Rector, who also had the cure of Monkton Deverill. To miss church in Grandfather's day would have been to put job and dwelling at risk. By the 1920s the congregation had voted with its feet. The scene at Matins every Sunday never varied. Parson Henderson, a bachelor who lived in the adjacent, enormous and recently extended rectory, was stone deaf. His stipend was £260 a year. Mrs. Carey played the organ fortissimo, assuming that Mabel, the village idiot, stopped peering around long enough to pump enough air. Two adult Strattons (Mother seething!) and four children filled the front pew. There remained only the sexton at the back, George Carpenter, who said "Aw-men" in a stentorious voice. The bells were always rung for evening service. At Harvest Festival, the place was packed and I still remember the soft light of the oil lamps. The church was always marvellously warm in all weathers.

Two schoolteachers occupied estate cottages and some fifty children

147

did their schooling here. My father was fond of exercising his right to check the register, probably to sum up his future prospect for labour. When Jim Newbury reached the leaving age of 14, Father addressed him thus: "You look a strongish lad. Be up at the top of the road to start next Monday". Children walked up from Brixton Deverill in all weather. Once a year there was an outing to the sea.

The three villages combined to form a flourishing Womens' Institute. Also football and cricket teams. The New Inn at Monkton was a great boon to the men. Functions such as socials and whist drives in the club room there or in the school were massively supported. Everybody knew everybody and we just had to shake down together.

Although the farm had a wonderful water supply, pumped by a windmill soon to be fortified by an oil engine, domestic water was all pumped by hand or drawn up from the wells. We were encouraged to restrain our flushing of the lavatory. The hatches were maintained all up the valley and the river never dried up. I suspect that the water table was then 8 feet higher anyway. At Monkton, a water wheel powered a working grist mill. At the farmhouse, apart from oil lamps, we "enjoyed" petrol gas for lighting. For some reason the gas pressure was deficient. During adult or childrens' parties Ernest Raynes, the gardener, would be commissioned to lie in the tin shed at the end of the house; having unscrewed an access to the main gas supply pipe, he was then required to blow into it regularly. The light indoors oscillated accordingly and one learnt to count one's trump when they were visible. This plant gave way to a second-hand battery set only slightly better. The cooking range yielded to a second-hand Aga which did sterling service for another 50 years.

Mention of second-hand indicates a shortage of money — there just wasn't any. This fact alone was enough to deter anyone with brains from working in the country, which might have eased our plight. I remember only one implement being bought for the farm, an additional hay elevator from Titts of Warminster which had the advantage of being driven by its own oil engine rather than by a reluctant horse on a circular gearing. There was little machinery to break. Occasionally wheels would be sent to the Maidments at Burton to be re-bonded.

Before the arrival of the telephone my father had to ride to Mere in an emergency to summon help. Both the Doctor and the horse drawn fire brigade often arrived too late to be of use.

Our letters came from Bath to Maiden Bradley by horse-drawn conveyance. A cheerful hero, Charles Newbury, then did a bicycle delivery (previously on foot) down the valley six days a week arriving at the farmhouse at 8.00 am sharp. After resting in a shed provided at

Longbridge Deverill, Charlie did a reverse collection run leaving our Post Office at 6.45pm. Weather never stopped him. His wage was 5/- per week.

War against pests was unremitting and almost round the clock. There were so many birds about. Rooks demolished the corn ricks from outside while the rats flourished on the grain from within. Corn fields were proportionately scarce and rooks played havoc with germinating corn and at harvest. In early May local farmers visited the rookeries in turn and hundreds of young rooks were shot. Rook pie was considered a delicacy as were lambs tails which often coincided.

One of our family ploys in winter was to go sparrow catching round the dwellings and barns after dark. Father held the clap-net between long bamboos while I tapped the ivy or prodded under the thatch eaves with a long hazel. My sister worked the torch and the two youngest had a basket each. Many birds eluded the net but we would sometimes achieve a bag of 75 sparrows and starlings, some having lost their heads in the process! A starling once drove its beak straight into my brother's ear. No warning to householders of this activity was deemed necessary and startled heads would appear from bedroom windows.

Foxes were controlled by the hunt. My father set off at 9.00 am every day to ride round the farm all morning. At an early age each child was put on a pony and just expected to ride with him and this soon progressed to the hunting field. We thought nothing of riding on the first day of the school holiday to meets as far distant as Shaftesbury or Upton Noble returning at about 6 o'clock in the evening. This merited a boiled egg for tea.

The hill country of Wiltshire, most of it then covered with enormous patches of gorse midst virgin downland, was literally crawling with rabbits. Several thousand a year were killed at Kingston. In open crates they went to Whitbread and Co in Smithfield market via Warminster passenger and 9d each was considered a good sale. Every corn field was attacked by rabbits. Sometimes a fifth of the crop could be lost. Each winters' day at least two men would drive away in a pony and trap ferreting. Lunch was half a fresh cottage loaf each and a huge chunk of cheese. At the end of a good day one hundred rabbits would be collected up and paunched while the pony was harnessed into the trap. A favourite maxim was — "Never put a ferret in after 4 o'clock." Crazed with cold the pony would depart at a gallop all over the myriad ant heaps with men, spades, ferrets and rabbits flung about in a motley.

Dogs of all kinds were used for shooting in the gorse. Elsewhere guns and beaters were deployed like armies to manoeuvre rabbits into a killing-ground. This was often combined with a number of hare drives and another great slaughter. The great thrill for a boy was to help run out the long nets under the woods at night stealthily when the rabbits were already out feeding. Then cars with headlights would drive about the pastures and the fun began. Not a bad training for "Night Ops" ! Sometimes the Frome Coursing Club came up for a day's coursing.

Richard Stratton (1978)

Working hours on the farm were 7.00 am-5.00 pm with a half day on Saturday. Milkers and stockmen worked a seven day week without question; more-over, at hay and corn harvest they were expected to appear in the evening "having done nothing all day". The carters got the horses in at 5.45 am and went home for breakfast. At 6.45 they were back for orders and to harness up ready. Some 25 men faced the foreman at the top of the road at 7.00 am. Years later when I had been dancing all night, overslept and emerged into a dark dawn teeming with rain, the urge to tell them all to go back to bed was nearly irresistable.

We had a pair of enormous steam engines for ploughing and cultivating on a cable and a smaller engine to drive the threshing machine. Their water was barrelled from the river and the terrified horse often bolted. Three horses abreast were needed to pull each binder at harvest. Hay was the staple stock food in winter. No fertiliser was given to grass land so enormous acreages were set apart for two months haymaking. Later on, the only commendation I ever received was to overhear my father telling a friend that I had achieved twelve hay ricks in one week. In the autumn the barns were stuffed with imported animal food at rock bottom prices — rice meal, flaked maize, ground nut and cotton cakes. This was made up into production rations which could not be matched by costs of home grown.

In a wet season hay and corn harvest were sheer Hell. The farm staff had low morale and were understandably disgruntled by long hours of hard, manual work for poor pay allied to primitive housing. They took every chance to depart to the towns and who can blame them? Many rows were occasioned by exhausted men. After a day with a pair of horses on the hay sweeps, a carter leaving for the stable at 8.00 pm was bound to be on a short fuse. Farm prices after the repeal of the Corn Production Act in 1922 were desperately low and were accentuated by the low productivity of farm labour. One man could only hand milk eleven cows. It took a whole day to haul 30 cwts of wheat to Warminster and load back with engine coal. A gang of ten men only saw 70 to 100 sacks of corn from a day's threshing.

As the men steadily departed, the situation was eased by an influx of small petrol/paraffin stationary engines — Listers and Petters. There were three hand milked herds of Shorthorn cows, cheese being made at Bradley Road, pigs fattened there on the whey. The sows ran wild at Dee Barn building. They disappeared into the gorse to farrow. Arthur Day, the stockman, took up his horse and float daily to throw out whole maize. On one occasion he was accompained by Gertie Cook, the bailiff's little daughter. She played in the sow building and had to tear off her knickers because they were black with fleas! Jack Pearce, shepherd of the arable flock, was once persuaded to attend Wilton Sheep Fair. He returned to find that the sows had eaten alive one of his ewes running out on the down which had become cast on its back. He never left again! A feature of this hurdled flock was the elaborate straw and thatched lambing pen erected near the winter root field following Christmas. The shepherd would stay there and sleep in his hut-on-wheels without a break for several weeks.

151

In the autumn truckloads of lambs to run the downs arrived from Scotland by train. Etched on my memory is helping the shepherds home up through the woods and tracks from Witham Station and the sun breaking through the early morning mist. Store cattle arrived at Warminster station and one man, Fred Orchard, prided himself on fetching them home alone. There was never a mishap.

In 1920 my father bought the Manor Farm at £13 per acre. In 1930 he could have bought it for £10 per acre at most, but by then tractors and better cars were coming on the scene and the worst was over. None-the-less, Kingston Deverill did not really join the 20th century until 3rd September 1939, but that is another story.

My life-style pre-war days; concerning Longleat
and the local surroundings
"A Worm's Eye View"

Kenneth Doel

Although nearing my 65th birthday, memories of my boyhood days are still very clear and dear to me, and sometimes it seems that happenings of fifty and sixty years ago occurred only yesterday.

As a small boy during 1923 I was transported in a ramshackle old motor-cycle combination (with the rest of the family), my elder brother and parents, from a small village in Gloucestershire, to a small gamekeeper's cottage in Horningsham on the Longleat Estate. My father had accepted a post as a gamekeeper to the late Lord Bath. During my early childhood I saw little of Dad; during the summer months from dawn until dark the keepers spent most of their time on the 'rearing fields'. In those days thousands of young pheasants were reared in order that the gentlemen of the day could hold their 'Shoots' around the Christmas period; and the duties beforehand of the gamekeepers were many and varied. Keeping vermin at bay — hawks, foxes etc., who are very partial to a feed of nice young pheasants. Feeding them two or three times daily with boiled rabbits and chicken eggs chopped finely. Opening the coops, closing them at nightfall and looking after any sick birds, these were just a few of the summer-time duties. Dad was on the field long before we were up in the mornings and we were in bed long before he came home in the evenings.

During the winter his nights were often occupied trying to catch the gentlemen who used to raid the coverts with their catapults and shotguns, (assisted by the lurcher dogs and a nice bright torch). A pheasant's life is NOT a happy one!

Life was hard in those days in the cottage — an old stone sink, no electricity, hot water or flush toilet. Washing of clothes in a boiler in the draughty out-house (providing one could successfully keep the fire burning under the boiler). Putting the clothes through the mangle in order to dispel any excess water required the energy and stamina of a horse — to be followed by the heating of flat irons — which one duly spat on in order to ascertain the correct temperature. If the spittle sizzled and dispersed into minute globules one fired away. Yes, happy hard days, especially for the poor housewife.

Early school-days proved to be rather a hazard for a five year old — the school being one and a half miles away. No transport and during the winter months I well remember traversing the country lanes in deep snow, again no snowploughs — arriving when it was really gloomy — to my home in the woods, sometimes wet through — but looking forward to nice hot rounds of toast with dripping, which mother had cooked over the open range.

Although not a brilliant scholar (my place in class usually varied between 4th and 10th at the end of each term in a class of 36) I developed a great flair for Art and usually held the first or second place in this particular subject. Although now retired I spend many enjoyable days during the winter with my oil-paints. It is a great hobby. I find it stimulates the mind and also helps one to see far deeper into the wonders of our lovely surroundings.

After leaving school at Christmas 1935 (a month after my 14th birthday) my father said "I have spoken to Mr. Collins", the butler at Longleat House in those days. "There is a vacancy. Mr. Collins has offered you this position and you may start on Monday as the Hall Boy". No argument on my part — times were hard with very few jobs available in the '30s, and the respect for one's parents' wishes over-rode objections anyway. On the Monday I presented myself with my little tin trunk full of almost new clothes as mother had spent her all on me in order to look presentable for the forthcoming ordeal.

For the uninitiated, the Hall Boy holds the very lowest position possible in the line of male staff. Roughly, one is expected to wait upon the other Junior Staff at table, wash dishes (and in my own case, the Servants' Hall, stone floor and some of the very long stone floors in the passages downstairs). In fact, any menial tasks that are simply beneath the dignity of those in any position higher than his own are allocated to him.

For the first few days I was completely over-awed and trembled at the thought of my new lifestyle and indeed what the final outcome would be. My wages were to be £18 a year to be paid quarterly, with a suit (made to measure) every 6 months, plus of course my food, as I was now "living-in" and sharing a bedroom with two slightly older lads who were my seniors — the Stewards' Room Boy and the Pantry Boy. These gentlemen in turn ranked below the 2nd Footman, the 1st Footman, and finally, Top of the line — the Butler, Mr. Collins, whom I found to be a very fair man, quite jovial but strict in his duties.

Although £18 a year now seems a pitiful sum, it must be remembered that in those days I could buy a shirt for four shillings and sixpence, a pair of grey flannel trousers for seven shillings and sixpence and a nice pair of leather shoes around eight shillings. I well remember the 1st Footman's salary was only £80 a year, incidently he tried to raise his income by having 6d bets each way on horseracing. Of course this form of mad investment was far beyond the reach of his juniors, including myself. The two footmen when on duty were very smartly dressed in long black jackets with a velvet collar, black trousers and lovely bright orange waistcoats — with lots of lovely silver buttons. The Butler's attire was of course the traditional dark coat with pin-striped trousers and grey tie. The three boys, i.e. Pantry, Steward's Room and Halls wore the measured blue serge (with NO fancy buttons or pin-stripes.)

The house-keeper — Mrs. Parker, controlled the assorted division of 6 housemaids. In her better moods Mrs. Parker had a rather irritating habit of addressing all and sundry (even His Lordship) as "Dearie". Her intentions were good, as she tried to control the staff but the methods rather hopeless, as her temper would rise for very little cause — although to coin a phrase — her bark was worse than her bite. Her constant companions were, one Marty, a short-haired, very fat terrier whose disposition matched that of his mistress (the difference being that the *dog's* bite was worse than it's bark) two, a grey African parrot, it's age unknown, but believed to be nearly 70. The parrot rejoiced in the unlikely name of 'Cardi' and would spend most of it's time throwing empty pea-nut shells from it's cage, and for some peculiar reason, shouting "Yes Mam, yes Mam" over and over again. The third member of her pets was a cockatoo, which tried to hold far more lucid conversation to anyone who would care to listen — often slipping in an occasional swear-word. I wonder if perhaps he had picked up this choice phrase from the house-carpenters or Steward's Room Boy whose duty was to clean the cage out.

Mrs. Strickland — the cook — controlled the kitchen staff, consisting of four kitchen maids and two scullery maids with quite a firm hand. She was of a different disposition from Mrs. Parker. Mrs. Strickland was a very portly lady, short but of colossal dimensions around the waist. Whether the assumptions were ever proved we know not, but the general opinions ranged anywhere between 16 and 20 stones. The cook was not the only big feature in the kitchen. Her pet was an enormous black cat which weighed in around 24lbs. It rolled around the kitchen on little stumpy legs, tummy almost touching the ground; with a self-satisfied smug look on it's face (one could just see the eyes half-hidden

155

under folds of skin and fat). It was in the appropriate quarters to be fattened up, but one could really feel for it as it resembled a huge rather fat, shapeless black-pudding waddling all over the place.

Miss Dunning — head laundry-maid — and four others worked very hard in the laundry — but we were not on quite such intimate terms with these ladies as their department was, at that time, situated in the stable-yard — although we met at lunch-time in the Servant's Hall. Finally, two still-room-maids; an odd job man who used to keep the fire systems in order and transport all the coal and huge logs to the Front Hall; the night watchman and the house carpenter accounted for the full complement regarding indoor staff — at that time a total of 28.

Although few week-end parties were held in the summer months, we were always very busy over the Christmas period when the pheasant shooting was in progress for a few weeks. The official party always included the Viscount Weymouth, the Ladies Kathleen Stanley, Numburnholme and Northampton plus their families, lady's maids, chauffeurs, etc., etc., and the house was quite noisy and ringing with children's laughter — a very different atmosphere for his Lordship, as most of the time he just enjoyed his own solitary company. In some respects he was a very frugal (although lovable), old gentleman. The suits he wore on shooting days were invariably of vintage age and design and the butler had to be extremely careful as the knees and elbows were actually darned and almost threadbare and the boots were always very worn at the heel. Indeed the brush had to be used very carefully in order to avoid further damage on His Lordship's clothes. I will not enlarge upon or even discuss the activities of the gentry further — it would not be fair and indeed I do not feel qualified to do so. More, I believe are my qualifications to gaze upon the other servants — from a worm's eye view so to speak.

A few days after my entry into a private service one of the greatest errors — or should it be an element of sheer bad luck, befell me, and I prayed for a huge hole in the ground to appear in order to swallow me up, as even unto this day I cannot forget the embarassment and havoc which was created. At noon all the under servants descended upon the servant's hall for their lunch. The footman sat at the head of a very long table in order to carve the joint, with the female staff on one side and the lads opposite them. My task was to set the table beforehand and then transport the meals with the plates from the kitchen, each course as required. Then return the dishes to the kitchen and wash the plates in my own little scullery which was joined to the servant's hall. On this occasion — all had gone well — with the meat course, and the sweet course was ready to be brought from the kitchen — in this particular case two very large rice puddings in enamel dishes, plus the plates. There was about a score in two neat piles, stacked on my large wooden carrying tray, which I had tucked well into my tummy so that the weight should be evenly distributed. Altogether it was quite a heavy load.

I had washed the stone floor earlier (another of my regular Thursday morning chores) and the floor had not yet dried completely. A trestle was opened out near the head of the table on which my tray was to be placed as always. Horror of horrors, when placing the tray on the trestle I slipped, nearly looping the loop on the wet flagstones. The two rice puddings and plates catapulted over the front end of the tray and with a terrible crash ended upside down on the floor, the plates in a thousand pieces and the pudding splattered everywhere — including over the 1st footman's smart uniform (he wasn't very happy at all as he was expected to serve lunch in the dining room within the hour). My humiliation was far from over; not only was I given a dressing down from the footman, but everyone else was most irate having lost their sweet course. I then had to face the wrath of Cook (she also wasn't very happy after putting her all into the lunch) — and humbly ask her if there was anything else available as a substitute.

After a year, I was duly promoted (just one rung up the ladder) to the position of the Steward's Room Boy — and my salary was increased by a further £8 a year for which I was very grateful, as, if spent all at once, it would allow me a further pair of shoes or two shirts. Oh, I really could go mad with this incentive.

One of the great highlights of the Season was the wonderful Servants' Ball His Lordship used to give after Christmas. That really was the never-to-be-forgotten occasion, and how the servants revelled in it. One of the large dining rooms was cleared of furniture, the floors highly polished, fairy-lights set. A local dance-band of seven, lead by one Les Whitmarsh (who in private life was a butcher, but nevertheless an excellent musician — the master of both piano and accordion) was engaged to supply the music. The Ball commenced at 8 o'clock, when Lord Bath would open this session with the Housekeeper. After one complete revolution of the ballroom, the Lord Weymouth (the present Lord Bath) would partner the Cook (by this time Mrs. Strickland had left and was replaced by a Miss Bell).

Then — it was a free for all and everyone joined in. Each of the girls was given an invitation to present to a male of their choice and each male could invite a female — so everyone had partners. The complete staff were also invited for this occasion from the London house, 29

Grosvenor Square. After 10 o'clock the society gentlemen and ladies would leave us to our own devices (and what devices). The butler would then release the drinks — to everyone's complete satisfaction, and it was the case of dance, drink, eat and be merry. We had the most wonderful cold supper laid out in the Steward's Room. Half the dancers and half of the band would eat at the first sitting, while the others danced, and the other half at the second sitting. So the music and dancing continued non-stop until about 5 o'clock in the morning. Although the drink was plentiful and varied, no one abused his Lordship's generosity — but eveyone was extremely happy. Wonderful times, never to be forgotten. I had the privilege of attending on three occasions, twice whilst a servant and once as a visitor.

During late March or early April the male staff from Longleat including (with the exception of the Hall Boy) the cook and the kitchen-maids would be moved en-bloc to 20 Grosvenor Square, for a period of about 6-8 weeks during "The Season". During this time an army of ladies would move into Longleat in order to do all the house cleaning, repairing, washing and dusting. The windows outside had the annual clean and polish, (during this operation the fire ladders were used in order to reach the upper floors.) Unfortunately for me — being only the Hall Boy — I had to forfeit this unknown pleasure in my first year. I had never visited London in my life. The others went and I was left behind doing odd jobs and helping the Housekeeper when visitors arrived to view. Mrs. Parker in those days was the only guide and the house was opened I believe in order to raise money for a babies' sunshine fund — my duties were to follow behind the queue to see that nothing was touched or stolen.

However, during the next season — as I had then been promoted to the Steward's Room — my dream was realised and finally I went to London with the crowd. I have never forgotten the excitement of the train journey to the City and the times we had. I was just 15 years old.

Longleat was responsible for my greatest achievement; the shy little fair-haired girl who followed my footsteps through junior then senior school was one of the gardener's daughters — Leonard Gould, who later became Head Gardener to Lord Bath — she finally married me after I was de-mobilised from the R.A.F. in 1949.

"Father was a very skilled gardener"

E.L. Davis

Rushmore Park,
Wilts/Dorset

On old age one realises that memory plays tricks and that it is possible to forget or be unable to pronounce the name of a well known person to remember something that happened a few hours earlier, while incidents of years and years before come flooding into the memory with absolutely startling clarity.

I was born on the 16th January 1905 at The Lodge, Frimley Hall, Camberley, Surrey. My father was Head Gardener at Frimley Hall, and in May 1912 we moved to Rushmore Park on the borders of Wilts and Dorset, the seat of the Pitt Rivers family, where my father was to be Head Gardener.

I can remember nothing of the journey except that we were met at Salisbury Station by the estate luggage brake, a large vehicle which I afterwards knew to be a 112 h.p. Mercedes. I had never ridden in a motor car before and it made a great impression on me.

We, my mother and father and my sister Dorothy, stayed at the big house for a few days until our furniture arrived. We had our meals in the very grand surroundings of the Housekeeper's Room. We went to the Gardens on May 4th 1912 — all the red peonies were in full bloom — and I never saw them so again on that date.

The kitchen gardens at Rushmore were really something, they were laid out by General Pitt Rivers in the 1880s. There were four acres inside the walls with a tower, used for storage, at each corner, and another three acres of orchard, frame ground etc., outside the wall. The wall facing south held a range of greenhouses and the gardener's cottage was in the centre by the large iron entry gate.

My mother was most unhappy at the change. She had used to be able to walk into Camberley for shopping and now, at Rushmore, the nearest shops of any account were at Blandford, ten miles away and no means of getting to them. But a butcher called twice a week, and a baker three times. The Park at that time housed quite a number of estate employees and was in effect, a very scattered village. Grocery came from the old firm of Stratton, Sons and Mead from Shaftesbury. Their traveller "Outride" as he was called locally, came on the first Tuesday of the month and arrived in time to share our midday meal. I remember him as a small smart man, with a ginger moustache. Out came his book and my mother ordered for a month. The goods arrived on the following Friday in a large covered wagon drawn by two horses. A fishmonger called, not very regularly, with a very smart box trap. He rejoiced in the name of "Dutcher" Gray, took bets and in season collected some game from the Game Larder.

A large number of gardeners were needed, as all cultivation was by fork and spade. The kitchen gardeners were paid 14 shillings a week, plus a house on the estate if married. They worked from 7 a.m. to 5 p.m. in the summer and from 8 a.m. to 4 p.m. in the winter. My father rang a bell which was housed in a little tower to announce times of work. In wet weather there was always plenty of work under cover in the potting sheds and store towers.

Three or four men were permanently stationed at the House, which was about three quarters of a mile away across the Park, for mowing and attending to a very elaborate rose garden and Miss Marcia's garden (the daughter — later Lady Astley Corbett). There were about three acres of lawn inside the Ha-Ha.*

The range of greenhouses in the kitchen garden included a large vinery. The roots of the vines came through a wall into a patch of ground that was enclosed by a low wall and kept religiously clean... nothing was ever grown there.... I can picture my father now, standing on steps in the vinery, sweat pouring down his face, thinning out the grapes to obtain the perfect shape required for the dinner table. After fruiting the vines were cut down from their wires, scraped carefully, removing all old bark and then dressed with a mixture of several mysterious ingredients made up in a bucket.

There was a large peach house with a specially shaped metal framework for the training of the trees. The rear wall of the peach house housed several large fig bushes. There were two houses for pot plants and tomatoes and a very large conservatory with palms in very large wooden tubs. The four acres inside the walls were accessible by drives gravelled and wide enough to take a carriage and pair and motor vehicles. These drives surrounded and quartered the garden. The

* Ditch with wall on inner side forming boundary to park or garden without interrupting the view — Oxf Ref.

quarters were further enclosed by yew hedges 8 feet high and three feet wide, taking two men three months to clip, all by hand of course.

The greenhouses were heated from two large boilers and a Saturday evening and Sunday rota was kept to keep the boilers going. The "PITS" was a sunken greenhouse, like a huge garden frame in which melons and cucumbers were grown in intense heat.

Then there was the Frame Ground, an open expanse in front of the Bothy, with large brick frames used mostly for growing second early potatoes and the raising of cuttings. All covered, when necessary, by large woven raffia covers. There were also two large hot beds, made up of rotting beech leaves and fresh manure. The frame ground was surfaced with boiler ashes, raked level. The hundreds of chrysanthemums were potted and staked out to overhead wires while getting ready for their winter quarters. At the end of each row was a small wooden mallet on a cane handle, with which the man doing the watering would tap each pot as he walked along the row; a nearby tank contained water in which sacks of sheep droppings and soot were always soaking. This odorous mixture, very much diluted, was the fertiliser for the flowers. Artificial fertilisers and insecticides were unknown. Soapy water was the weapon against aphids. Unhealthy plants were quickly rooted out and destroyed. One or more of the single gardeners were housed in the Bothy, looked after by Mrs. Bastable, the widow of a former headkeeper.

My father was a very skilled gardener, indeed he had to be to deal with the wide variety of horticultural tasks that came his way, and which included room and table decoration. I understood that he had been apprenticed on a big estate at Ightam, in Kent. He had a Latin name for all his plants and for the many ornamental trees which had been so lavishly planted by the late General. His great gardening friend was Mr. Usher, from the Ismay estate at Iwerne Minster. Mr. Usher was a great exhibitor of the day and is often quoted in gardening books of the period. He often came over to Rushmore in his pony trap, especially when there was a big show in the offing.

I can remember some of the gardeners — the foreman under my father was Albert Kempshall. He spent all his time in the greenhouses. He lived in the Bothy. He once had a very badly poisoned thumb and came in every day to my mother to have it dressed. He was called up and went down with a troopship in the Mediterranean. The senior outside man was one Kelly, an old man with a beard. He lived in the Park, and was reputed to have money. His son John, a little man drove the garden horse, Tom, did the mowing around the House and made occasional trips to Tisbury Station. There was a Frank Buttch, who lived

161

with his very old father in the village of Tollard Royal. He was an avid reader of boys papers and cowboy stories. I think he was called up, but I cannot remember hearing his fate.

I must say something about the gardening set up which was quite normal for the times although perhaps a little on the grand side, but which people today would have difficulty in understanding.

Nothing was bought in the way of horticultural produce for use in the House. The gardens had to produce vegetables, fruit and flowers for the family and house guests and for a large servants hall and Housekeepers Room. In the summer vegetables were gathered in the early morning and taken to shed adjoining the potting shed where the root vegatables were trimmed and washed under the pump. At 9 a.m. all was loaded on to a sort of wide wooden stretcher with a leg at each corner and short shafts front and rear. Flowers and fruits went as well and the whole was taken by two men across the Park to the House, about three quarters of a mile away. My father met them there and saw that the vegetables went to the kitchen and the fruit and flowers to their appropriate spots. When there were guests an early evening visit for table decoration was also required, but potted plants such as arum lilies or chrysanths, etc were changed pretty early in the morning.

When the family were in London for the season at 4, Grosvenor Gardens, vegetables, fruit and flowers were packed into a large wicker hampers and taken to Tisbury Station by the garden wagonette and old Tom, driven by John Kelly. This happened once a week.

The Park was entirely enclosed by a high wooden deer fence, there being, it was said, some four hundred deer in the park. There were the native roe deer, a few red deer, a lot of fallows, and quite a few very dark coated deer — which we learned to call Japanese. In the Autumn the air was hideous with the roars of the rutting stags and until we became used to it we children were very frightened by the tossing heads and the menacing steps in our direction. There was also a flock of brown St. Kilda sheep, which would suddenly emerge at full gallop from a wood. The rams had been killed off before our time, but the flock of ewes lived on for many years.

The Park contained parkland as usually thought of and also considerable woodlands. Some of the woodland was hazel coppice and this was periodically cut and made up into faggots, bean rods, pea sticks etc. The pieces of wood so cut would then be fenced in with a high wire fence until the new growth was safe from the deer. This work was done by the estate woodmen and was for estate use only, but in the woods around the Park, the Cranbourne Chase etc., there the pieces of coppice were sold off at an annual wood sale and bought up by the local hurdle makers and woodmen. In these days of electricity for cooking and heating it is difficult to realise what a large part these woods played in the local life, providing lighting and burning wood and very important, the "baffins", the large bundles of twiggy branches used in the bakers ovens to produce that crusty bread, which is, alas, no more.

Passing the stable yard was a terrifying experience for small boys because of the huge Newfoundland dog kept there. I believe his official name was Neptune, but he was known as "Ben". His bark was worse than his bite, but he certainly frightened all strangers. The dog and the large stable clock were the great features. The carriage house contained all the old carriages, not used. There were no carriage horses, but three or four hunters kept for "Mr. George" who was with the 1st Royal Dragons.

There was very little restriction placed upon the movement of the estate children, as long as they didn't disturb the cricket. It was the keeper's job to see that children were kept under control. The Head keeper, Mr. Sweeting, was a tall man with a fair moustache. He lived in a large house in the park surrounded by kennels and animal quarters which in the General's day had housed many exotic animals. He had two sons, Tom and Leslie with whom I played endless games of cricket. Mr. Sweeting was called up fairly early in the war and was killed in France.

The second keeper was Mr. Pitman. He lived in the cottage and kennels at Badger's Glory in a corner of the Park adjoining the Chase; here the wild rabbits snared were brought in. I believe any park employee could have a brace each week free and another brace for sixpence. Rabbit and home cured bacon were the main items of diet for all country folk any other form of meat was known as "butchers meat". One of the other keepers was a young man — Sid Stacey — and we children used to say "Knock 'em down Sweeting — pick 'em up Pitman and carry them on Sid". A cat who strayed from any cottage had very short shrift, but they never appeared on the keeper's "trophy" pole!

The Park was not "shot" much, because of the deer, but the pheasantry was in the same place every year. No incubators in those days, but dozens of coops and broody hens. A shepherd's hut was brought in for the duty keeper and small boys were not welcome.

The birds were later distributed all over the Estate. Most of the shoots took place in the covers near the borders of the Park, or in the woods on the edge of the Estate. On shooting days, when there was no school, we boys went as "stops". This meant being taken to the fringe of a wood early in the morning and staying there tapping the fence or trees until that wood was "driven". The reward was a shilling "Big Money"! The men got half a crown. There was a good lunch for all; for the men a rough brown paper parcel with half a loaf, a lump of cheese, and another lump of red salt beef. For the boys, a slightly smaller parcel was brought out. Most of the beaters produced onions and large pocket knives — the keeper produced bottles of Badger beer and a good meal was soon underway, the remains being carefully stowed away in the poacher pockets before the next drive. The game larder was in the shrubbery close to the stable yard and was a wooden framed building with sides of perforated zinc, standing on staddle stones. There the birds remained until really ripe and one heard stories of the young scullery maids whose task was to dress the birds and were violently ill in the process.

Leaving the Park by the South Lodge on the way to Farnham village on Minchington Down was the golf course, constructed for the use of Mr. Pitt Rivers; a professional was employed to look after the links and to give Mr. Rivers a game when required. Very rarely indeed, other guests had a round of golf, and then all boys were rounded up to act as caddies and earn some small change. At the outbreak of war, the golf professional disappeared and the links slowly reverted to nature.

All the park children went to the Church School in Tollard Royal, which meant walking about two and a half miles across the park and fields, or in very wet weather, a walk around the roads of about three miles. In practice every child arrived at the school with wet shoes, from the heavy dew in the summer and rain in the winter. Very rarely, in very bad weather, the garden wagonette came into service.

The mistress was an elderly lady, Mrs. Mildred Penny — I have occasion to be grateful to her — she was very strict indeed but we could not have had a better teacher. The subjects taught were limited and, by modern standards, the supply of books and other teaching aids was pathetic, but when a child left the school at the age of twelve or thirteen, that child could read and write, do arithmetic to advanced fractions and decimals and knew the difference between right and wrong. Not that the children were a lot of angels by any means — they spoke English in school and when outside they relapsed into a dialect that was almost another language. The Biblical "thee" and "thou" were used all the time.

The playground was rough grass and mud on a steep slope — there were no organized games. "Rounders" was the only game played if someone had a ball. I'm afraid most of the village children were very poorly dressed; large families seemed to be the order of the day among the farm workers who at that time earned twelve shillings a week with a few pounds at Michaelmas. Overtime as paid today was unknown, although at haymaking and harvest times they worked long hours.

The Park and the Estate maintained their own football and cricket teams. The Pitt Rivers colours were yellow and mid blue — and they could be seen from miles around on all the farm gate posts. (The footmen's livery was made up of the same two colours.) Both pitches were in the Park and were roped off to keep out deer and cattle. In summer the whole male population of the park turned out every evening for cricket practice, even the footmen after dinner had been cleared away. And on Saturdays, matches were arranged with the local villages. Teas for all were provided by the House.

My father was a very good bat and a very tricky medium paced bowler. He was a great follower of the fortunes of Kent, having had, I believe, a trial for the County in his younger days. In the evening practices all the boys were given a short turn at the wicket and it was quite common for one of us boys to be called on the field, usually at long stop or go in last wicket down at one of the Saturday matches.

Even at Rushmore, so remote from the world, the war (1914-18) had an immediate effect. The heir to the estate was at once actively involved; very shortly after fighting started the House was turned into a small hospital and the first wounded arrived, Belgians and French, direct from the firing line. The Army and Navy reservists were called up at once and many of the younger employees volunteered for service.

But it was the transformation of the House into a hospital and the arrival of the wounded that really brought things home. I think the men brought were walking wounded, certainly within a few days they were to be seen in the park. They had come straight from the front and the local doctor from Sixpenny Handley, Dr. Atkins was called in to do the dressings. All the park wives, including my mother, were called upon to do two days a week ward duties and formed a Voluntary Aid Detachment.

We boys were very busy trying to persuade the soldiers who came out into the park to part with the large brass numbered buttons that held their tattered uniforms together. One very large coloured man named Felix excited our curiosity, as he was the first coloured person we had ever seen.

The war made things very difficult for my father. With all his able bodied men gone he had to supply vegetables in ever increasing quantities for the hospital.

All this was over seventy years ago. I sometimes wonder if it can really have been true — because today it is so difficult to imagine a community so completely concentrated around, and dependant upon, just one grand family.

165

Milkmaids Fair

Mrs. M. Jellett

My family, the Jestys, lived in Yetminster for generations, having reputedly arrived from the Continent in the 17th century, named Just.

At an early age I was told the story of our illustrious forbear, Benjamin Jesty. He had lived at Upbury Farm, which still stands, at the time when the dreaded smallpox was raging, and causing widespread death and disfigurement. It wasn't "dabbling in the dew" that made the milkmaid fair, but rather that they were free of pockmarks. Most of them had contracted cowpox early in their milking careers, and this gave them immunity from the more virulent smallpox. Not everyone, however, associated cause and effect, but Benjamin did so, and carried his convictions a stage further by performing a crude vaccination on his wife and two small sons, using pus from an infected cow. This aroused a storm of local criticism, and had very umpleasant side effects in Mrs. Jesty's case, but enabled the family to survive the current, and future, smallpox epidemics unscathed. This was more than 20 years before the practice was scientifically approved. All that Benjamin received apart from the health of his family, was a signed testimonial from the "Vaccine Pock Institute" in London, where he had his portrait painted.

I was born in a cottage on the Ryme road, next to the old cattle pound. I can dimly remember being taken to the celebrations to mark the end of the First World War.

The Jesty's were both prolific and long-lived, so that when I was young the village seemed full of my distant cousins, all claiming hopeful, if tenuous, descent from Benjamin. The milkmaids, too, were still in evidence.

Families hand-milked in the pastures, often with a babe-in-pram parked in the gateway, in preference to the mayhem which resulted when cows were brought home to be milked. Several herds of rather wild Shorthorns would get mixed up in the main street, accompanied by

166

yelping mudcaked dogs and swearing would-be milkers. This chaos was multiplied a hundred-fold at the annual Cattle Fair, held in an orchard beside the High Street. I remember standing on a gate viewing the scene with a mixture of fright and excitement.

a) Benjamin Jesty, who noticed that the milk maids were free of smallpox.

Every morning and evening the procession of milk carts, each with a load of churns, buckets and strainers, passed to and fro, their silent occupants swaying to the gait of the pony, "pinners" tucked round their waists.

167

I knew all the local people and the various conveyances they used to bring in their milk yields. There was Miss Williams from Higher Clifton, seated on a pony wagon, rug draped primly over her knees, Jack Partridge (Sen.) standing on his high-sided pig-cart, and Charlie Hillier with one churn on a wheelbarrow. Fred Wills, from Knighton, was experimenting with home-made crystal wireless sets, and would describe his results when he brought his milk. So the tales went round, "Poor young chap. Up there in that shed, thinking he can hear music and voices."

I loved the village with fierce and proprietorial pride. It seemed like the centre of the Universe to me.

Mornings reverberated with clanging metal and hissing steam. We often gazed into the roaring furnace which heated the factory boilers, or watched the men splashing about on the metal platforms. One woman, Fan Lane, worked alongside them. She had a cleft palate, wore heavy boots, a sacking apron and a flat cap. The manager, Mr. "Paddy" Hewson, frightened us with his nearly unintelligible Irish accent. My sister did housework for his wife after school for which she was paid 6d. (2½p.) a week.

I remember the heady excitement I felt, running down the street on summer mornings, the orchard a sea of blossom, the crumbling stone walls festooned with "Kiss-me-quick", (valerian), and over-hanging flowering shrubs, watching the milk being unloaded at the United Dairies milk factory.

We were told that "Yetminster" means "Church at the Gate", (of the New Forest). It had been an important centre since mediaeval times, and it still was in the 1920s. Besides the factory, right in the middle of highly fertile dairying country, there was the Great Western Railway Station. It was unnecessary to carry a watch out in the fields, the trains acted as a reliable time-keeper. We had "the milk", "the twenty past eight", "the fast", "the quarter to five motor", and "the twenty past seven", among others. The early milk train took away the churns, until the construction of a special siding into the factory and the advent of glass-lined bulk tankers. They were viewed with much head-shaking and dire prophecies of the milk going "wrong".

In winter, when the flood water descended from the hills, and the river was "up", our only connection with the outside world was via the line. Milking herds would get marooned out in the fields for days, with regrettable consequences to their health and to their owner's pockets.

My grandfather, Robert Jesty, and my father Thomas James, carried on a haulage business, using horse-drawn wagons and timber carriages.

Sometimes I went "out stable" when the horses were "done up" for the night, chomping steadily through their mangolds and chaff in the glow of the hurricane lantern. Great was the excitement when a new mare was bought at the Dorchester Sale, and greater was the depression when she developed "big leg". The (amateur) vet cycled from Bradford Abbas, having been alerted through the grape-vine — no phones in those days. He carried his physics and instruments in a little black bag on his carrier.

The haulage area included all the surrounding villages. Hills like Bailey Ridge, Totnel, and High Stoy, "up round the rocks", often required the use of a trace horse. A gripping adventure occurred when the bond came off a wheel some distance from home, necessitating complicated logistics with borrowed wagon and off-loaded goods. We had harness for ceremonial occasions, brass hames, ornate "housens", hoops of bells and top knots.

I was terrified when we descended steep hills, drug shoe under the wheel, the horse sitting back in the breeching, shoes slithering on the greasy road. Nearly as frightening was the sight of his straining flanks as he struggled up the "knaps", with a roller behind the back wheel to prevent running back.

Of course, had no water supply, and drinking water had to be fetched from the pump-house up the road. Further up lived Mrs. Annie Warren and her daughter, Nellie. They eked out a precarious living (in common with many other women) by "gloving" for one of the Yeovil factories, "sitting at it" for long hours, sustained by tea kept brewing on the hob.

In the same row of cottages were Mark and Sally Bartlett. Mark, a cripple, made spars for rick-thatching, usually seated in a barn in front of the giant cider barrel, cup at the ready. We would watch, fascinated, as he skilfully split the hazel stems on his leather-clad knee, and being illiterate, chalked up the score on a board.

Towards Ryme Intrinsica was Briar Thickett, whose owner, Mrs. Fownes, would send soup to my mother when babies arrived — soup which we children usually drank! (My mother paid into the "Nursing" for attendance on such events.) We were taken along the Ryme road to inhale the smell of the sheep, supposedly good for whooping cough and similar complaints — it was probably the Stockholm Tar.

One of our annual excitements was watching the flocks of sheep on their way, on foot, to Sherbourne Pack Monday Fair. They would usually rest overnight at Thornford. Another spectacle was the steam lorry from Brutton's Brewery in Yeovil, belching sparks, and on one occasion setting fire to a thatched roof. There was also the "entire", the

b) Upbury Farm, Yetminster, the home of the Jestys.

travelling stallion, bedecked in straw and coloured ribbons.

The lovely creeper-clad mellow stone farmhouses, with their mullioned windows, and solid barton gates, on one side of the village street, date back to the 17th and 18th centuries. Most of them had a cow-yard, rick (barn), and garden, with orchard and calf-paddock beyond, all at right angles to the road. Charles Bugler lived at Higher Farm, and I spent many hours sitting on the stone seat beside the huge open hearth, feeding the fire with twigs, whilst he held forth on "Queen Anne's Bounty" and the "Sub-Sidney."

The family farms employed little outside labour, except at haymaking, the busiest time of the year. The hay was hauled or "swept" loose into the rick, to be cut out with a hay-knife, (a solid triangular blade), or sometimes "trussed", in the winter. The team was reinforced in the evenings by "strappers", mainly men employed on the line, and hay-hauling went on until dark, supported by the ubiquitous cider-jar. Very little grain grown, was used for home consumption by the stock. I remember sitting in the hedge all day, waiting for Mr. Bugler to start off with his horse-drawn binder, whilst he mended the knotter.

My father never ate meat, and we grew quantities of vegetables in garden and 'lotment, especially potatoes and mangolds, the latter for the horses, our own and other people's. All this was hand-cultivated after work, Easter weekend being a popular time for such activity. A sack of potatoes was always given to the church Harvest Festival, destined for Sherbourne's Yeatman Hospital. I adored the "Harvest" service, it seemed so personal, and when we all sang lustily "Oh summer land of harvest", I would be nearly bursting with emotions.

There were several very welcome charities in operation in our village, the "Boots", the "Gurt-coat", the "Bread" amongst them. The Bread charity took the form of loaves to be collected from the front pew of church on Sunday mornings. When I did this, armed with a clean red handkerchief in which to carry it, I scooped out the soft end of the cottage loaf and ate it on the way home.

Clem Vowles' bakehouse was kept open on Sunday mornings so that cottagers who had no reliable oven could roast their weekend joints, and at midday mouth-watering dishes would be carried about the street.

A number of businesses ancillary to farming flourished in Yetminster — the saddler and harness-maker, the rake-maker, the blacksmith, the miller, in addition to the carpenter, masons, and Bradford & Sons, (coal and timber merchants), who had a depot close to the station. At least two lime-kilns were working when I was young, and I would peer into the glowing depths, while the night-watchman entertained us with his melodeon. Some of the younger men worked in Westland's in Yeovil, and the girls went off to the gloving factories.

The old chalk-pits were favourite repositories for rubbish, there being no refuse collection, and provided happy hunting grounds for us children. I found the doctor's old ledgers there, with fascinating personal details, only dimly understood, relating to prominent villagers.

There was no mains water, sewage system or electricity, and apart from the trains and the "carrier", transport was by "shank's pony". My father and I would walk to Longburton on Sundays to see my sister, who was in service there, some 6 miles each way. And we would go for long walks in the fields, viewing crops and animals. I knew the names of all the fields; Frylake, Ryelands, 'Erbury, Dippits Way, Chestie Furlands (phonetic spelling!).

The village school taught girls up to 14 years, but boys gravitated from "infants" to the endowed "Boyle's" School at the top end of the street. It had quite a large catchment area, and transport was not provided, so bicycles and ponies were much in evidence. Children from Beer Hackett and Knighton would often arrive at school with wet feet, having traversed the sodden footpath's: (No wellies then.) There were no school meals either, but cocoa was produced in the winter.

171

The quality of the teaching was superb. We received splendid grounding in the three R's, in Christian precepts, and in an understanding of country matters, which have lasted a lifetime. No-one was classed as hopeless, and even the dimmest child benefitted.

On weekdays, old Charlie Brand, who was very deaf and crippled, delivered the bread from a high horse-drawn trap. It is surprising the number of disabled people who led an active part in the community. I especially remember Mr. Forcey, who, in spite of appallingly deformed hands, fashioned beautiful wooden hay-rakes.

The Post Office was kept by the Wrights. Mr. Wright, a pillar of the Wesleyan Chapel, did a post round of seven miles, partly on foot, every weekday, taking in Whitfield, Knighton, Beer Hackett and Trill. We also had two pubs, several shops and a number of craftsmen, masons, painters, a cobbler, in fact all that a village needed.

Dr. Stevens lived next door to the Vicarage. He held surgeries in a hut in the garden. We had a District Nurse, who cycled round. Most families paid into the "nursing", and various neighbours acted as unofficial midwives.

In the past 60 years there have been changes in Yetminster. The milk factory has closed, and the railway has been reduced to a single track. But the faceless church clock still chimes the National Anthem at three-hourly intervals, the ancient creeper-covered mullioned farmhouses stand beside the High Street, families still "chase after the cow's tail", now armed with quotas and machines. And there is still a deceptive air of lethargy and somnolence almost tangible.

"Better than television"

Mrs. Roberts

St. Denis, Nr Southampton, Hampshire

Before the 1914-1918 war, English people were very loyal and patriotic — great flag-wavers. We had a big flag pole in our garden, my Dad used to hoist a big Union Jack before going to work, and draw it down at sunset. It was left flying proudly all through the War. Eventually the wood rotted and it fell down never to be replaced, for nothing was the same as before the War, people were disillusioned.

I must have been 7-8 years of age at the start of hostilities, with two elder brothers. However, I remember as though it were yesterday how life changed. We were an average family, just a little better than working class. My paternal grandfather was a Senior Magistrate in Southampton. He was held over our heads, a threat to our peace of mind should we ever transgress. My father was a ship's blacksmith, my mother an experienced tailoress. Her earnings from work, done at home, combined with Dad's wages, gave us that little extra status. Our parents were devoted, caring people and we loved them dearly.

We children were devastated when War finally broke out. Suddenly all shopping, food and provisions, became a nightmare. Nearly all shops were closed, unable to buy goods because of the deadly losses of ships at sea. If there was a consignment of food, a notice would be put in the shop window saying what time what goods would be available. The children were allowed off school to queue — which meant standing for hours — for sugar, marge or meat and bones. In any case we had the choice of only one commodity each time; and sometimes we would just get to the top of the queue and a notice would go up saying 'Finished'; and so were we. My mother would make us thank God for a few bones.

At home our biggest problem was coal. At this time it was rationed at one hundred-weight a week costing two shillings. Old Roger, our coalman, bent the rules a little, but not often. My mother tore down every bit of wooden fence and saved anything burnable for when Dad

173

was home. Us kids went out with an old pram gathering wood. The rest of the time it was shivering between blankets.

Everybody had plenty of money with nothing to buy.

The things I was most frightened of during the War were the mules. We lived near a camp and remount. The camp was built on the Common — a huge tract of land — given by some big bug to Southampton people for posterity. Here, men, horses, and those horrible big-eared mules, were sent to recuperate after fighting in the front line in France. Twelve o'clock each day, just as I left school, along came these monsters, line upon line, bucking and rearing all over the pavement, sweating, foaming at the mouth, tails and ears flapping — four mules to a man — such a very young man, hardly able to contain them — and they were on my route home from school. Should I chance the mules, or dive behind someone's gate? Trespass, a dire crime in my day and age, and my Dad was very heavy handed with his slipper.

I had a dread of "Zepplins coming over", tho' I hadn't a clue what that meant. My father had been classed unfit for military service (and given a copper badge to wear, proving he wasn't a shirker) and worked in a munitions factory. My mother was petrified at being alone at night in the house without Dad. One particular night he came back and I heard him saying to Mum "They are over, Dot; got as far as London".

Then there was the sewing — oh how I hated it. Everyone had to do war-work. A laundry across the road was compelled to undertake so much of the troop's washing and mending. As my mother sewed, she was asked (ordered) to take two baskets of mending — but at least she was paid. Huge baskets, containing socks, some with hardly any feet, shirts, pants etc., etc. My mother said every one must help the war effort, and as I had been taught by my maternal grandparents how to sew at a very early age, I got the prize (with no pay), sewing on the buttons. I had had enough with my brothers, where do boys buttons go? The troops were nearly as bad, and shirts, such rough, harsh, tickly flannel. Oh well, press on!

My grandparents lived in a house directly opposite us and I am sure more of our time was spent there then at home. They held the key to any child's heart, a great long garden that ran down to the river. My feet were always itching to get back to Gran's garden. Such a long, long garden. Winding down to meet the river Itchen. Heaven to us kids. It was wild and unplanted for the spring tides carried the river right up to Gran's back door. Nothing but grass could grow because it was salt water. It was soft and lovely for paddling and skylarking about, with two tides a day, what more could we ask?

All sorts of annual events happened on this river. Like carnivals, well organized, every type of boat competing in events. Dressed all over in a holiday mood, rowing, motor and sailing boats. I remember one motor boat called "The Scarlet Runner" won year after year. The bank at the end of the garden was slap in the middle of the course and we had a fine view. There were diving and swimming events, acrobats, with lots of boats inshore selling ices and goodies. Larger boats had bands aboard, playing the same tune to bring out the volume. Cobden Bridge crowded with people, all traffic stopped, and as evening approached, everybody danced, even policemen waltzed. Oh, happy, happy days, never to return.

a) Mrs. Roberts, husband with his sister and parents during World War One.

My grandparents and two of their sons, with two girl apprentices, carried on a home tailoring business. The big workroom was a source of wonder and joy to us children. That kind of tailoring was not the wishy-washy kind of today — but Bond Street style, with canvas, stay tape, silks, thread and the buttons of yesteryear, pretty linings and jockey's silks. A poem to see cloth laid on a counter — measurements made, then a small cross on the material made with (pipe clay) tailor's chalk. Crosses lined up — then the magic moment — the master cutter comes in with his big, big shears, and away they go, snip and cut, and behold, a garment emerges — ready for the machine.

In fact the tailoring business took up quite a lot of us children's time as well — because Gran and Mum were 'out-door' hands. We went every day, before or after tea, to fetch or deliver the various garments. Trousers for Gran, vest (waistcoats) for Mum. These unmade garments were rolled up with the trimmings inside — which included linings, stay tape, buttons, canvas, tailor's marking chalk, thread and Silko. The prices paid for the work, 5/6d for trousers, 4/6d for vests. Extra if it was a mourning order — which had to be made quickly to agree with the funeral.

Sometimes the wares were quite numerous so my two brothers and I all went together. It was a tram journey between 2-3 miles costing 1d from our home. We had to return the made-up garments so were fully occupied. Other kids envied us always having plenty of pocket money and a tram journey which was a bit of a lark. Sometimes we got 'perks' from the shop, but kept it dark — Gran paid us very well. And we could always earn a bit of money from Dyers Boat Yard, where if the tide was out the hired boats were put on a set of wheels and run down to the water's edge on a wooden track. This was about six gardens away from Gran's. Nifty for us.

Life was very much a pattern in those days — chores started early — and as my Mum used to say "if the grate is done, and the fire lit, the room looks tidy". The actual grate, kept ebony black and shiny with the use of blacklead, brushes and lots of 'elbow grease'; the hearth, spotlessly white; wash the hearth, rub in a product called hearth-stone, a big square block like chalk, then smooth over with a damp cloth and leave to dry to lily perfection. The same proceedure on the front door step. What pride and hard work, also competition, among housewives to get things shipshape and Bristol fashion.

Then away with buckets and out came brooms. The bit housewives loved, the whole pavement in front of the house swept "clean as a whistle". Time here for their little chat and it was chat and not gossip. Something like this — Mrs. A., "Has Mrs. Harris had her 'bargain' yet?

Saw Nurse Jones (the midwife) hurry in when I was seeing Ken (husband) off to work last night." Mrs. B., "Oh yes, Tom Harris came over to tell us — seven and a half pounds boy — he's over the moon — but Letty had a very bad time — laying straw this morning (in the street)." This was a custom to deaden the noise of traffic in case of illness. The actual house would have the door knocker muffled as well. The housewives, now disinclined to talk, would go slowly home. You could bet your sweet life, before an hour had passed a whole campaign had been launched. Mrs. A. — washing, Mrs. B. — cooking, Mrs. C. — looking after the patient. No problem of older children to look after — this was a first baby. A little extra work for Mrs. C. — but she'd love that, being childless herself.

The Vicar and the doctor would call, but there was one certainty, the Harris family would want for nothing, the whole terrace bending over backwards to help. The Police were very active in situations like that, one would patrol every hour to see that nothing was allowed to harass the patient. No doubt the patient or her husband had been approached about hospital, but hospitals weren't very popular with that generation. The pivot in their world — *home*. People didn't run to doctors or hospitals for every little fiddle-faddle as today. Home remedies and commonsense usually worked wonders, plus good neighbours who were the salt of the earth in every way.

The Police in those days were tactful and understanding. And they were permitted to give "Billy" a cuff in the ear for misbehaviour — while the Dads added their quota as back up. We got up to mischief and were no little angels, but we had to consider our position very carefully before setting off for a lark. Would it be worth it — if we got caught?

We were brought up with the understanding that children should be seen and not heard which meant that there was no common ground between the generations — and so we rarely asked questions and we did as we were told.

Ooh-la-la, it's Monday — washing day. As immovable as the Rock of Gibraltar or the Pyramids.

The stage was set on Saturday night, when the big copper in the corner was filled with a short piece of hose attached to the tap over the sink. Why, even Dad left his armchair to lay and set the fire under the copper ready for the big off on Monday morning. Wash-day was a big job and seemed to bring the family together. What could we do to help?

Monday, 5 a.m. Now we kids had to shift for ourselves. "Eat, wash up, clear away, don't forget the breadcrumbs" said Mum. She was very meticulous about her damask tablecloth. So the brush and crumb tray

177

was brought out. A dainty piece of bric-a-brac, bone, something like a dust-pan only rounded top with a scythe-shaped brush to match, at that time used to dispose of crumbs on the cloth (long since redundant).

Now battle begins. Mum had lit the copper fire to heat the water. Gathers up equipment. A big bath balanced over the sink beside the copper. Ladling water with her big dipper — a sort of cast iron bowl with a short handle. Soap, soda, scrubbing board and brush, labelled for linen only. Bed linen first, having been scrubbed, rubbed and thrown into the copper, there to boil with oddments of soap collected through the week, plus a handful of soda. The clothes meanwhile being poked and tantalized with a copper stick. Washing products on the market then were Bisadol and Oxydal. Mum scorned them both. A ten minute boil then she emptied the bath water. The clothes hauled out of the copper and rinsed twice in the deep earthen sink — then, we mustn't forget the blue-bag skimmed around in the final rinse, to make the water blue and the clothes whiter — strange but true. A second copper full of white linen had exactly the same treatment, with socks and woollies done by hand afterwards.

This was not the end, oh dear no! Not for the clothes line yet. There, all sedate and beautiful in the garden, stood the housewife's friend on it's sturdy iron legs, the mangle. In case anyone doesn't know, it's two big heavy wooden rollers, a piece of wood fore and aft, supports for the clothes, with a big wheel to turn, propelling the clothes through and wringing the water out. Clothes all ready for the clothes line to be pegged firmly with hand-carved gypsy pegs.

Gypsies often called selling pegs, lace, pearl and linen buttons, also telling a good fortune for sixpence. They lived in bright caravans, their horses their pride and joy. Good, colourful, clean honest people making a living which often included basket-making, skilfully done, sold at a reasonable price.

Home from school, clothes blowing dry — what's for dinner. Ninety-nine guesses out of a hundred, it's bubble and squeak, with the remains of Sunday's joint followed by a milk pudding. All through the years this meal went hand in hand with wash-day. Sometimes a little sniff, then Dad would say "You don't know how lucky you are with three or four daily meals, you should see the little bare-foot children outside the dock gates as the men leave work, hear them pleading 'any bread mister? Just a crust guv'nor', it's pitiful."

Then it was back to school, Mum cheerfully carrying on. Still not finished yet, the routine had to be kept up. I helped with the small linen, nappies and socks. Washing all brought into the house to be sorted into two piles. One for dry mangling, one for ironing, the latter having to be damped down. A basin of thin starch water sprinkled over the washing with the fingers, rolled up and put away for ironing on Tuesday. Still the mangling. What a joy mangles were, saving a lot of ironing — where did they go? They were a real gift to anyone with cotton sheets.

Sometimes we went gathering blackberries. Armed with basket, crook and a day's food we would set off in the coolness of the morning, fresh with dew, silver spider's webs hanging on the bushes like Christmas decorations. It was good to be alive. Each of our baskets held roughly 4lbs. We wouldn't stop until they were full. Mum would now start her jams and preserves using lots of fruit from the garden, to be followed by the making of pickles, piccalilli, beetroot and sauces. All housewives vied with each other in this field. A bottle of everything would be set aside to be given to the Harvest Festival.

We had all been brought up with a reasonable religious background, attending a small Chapel near our home. This meant morning service and afternoon Sunday School. On the first Sunday of each month the whole family of us and Dad's own family attended a church service in the High Street, Southampton. A church called the Church of Christ. We had a family pew there.

Churches and chapels were much more patronised and then, loyally supported. I think the Vicar and curate, with a very small stipend, were the most hard working people of our time. Their duties endless. Amongst them, births, marriages and deaths, several choir practices, the boys and girls Life Brigade, each with their own bands, to name just a few. A bugle call on Sunday morning would bring people to their doors to see the procession march by in their uniforms, with a wave to Billy or Sally as the case might be. Just a little thing, but an event to those concerned.

Now the time was soon dawning for our Harvest Festival — a time to thank God for everything grown and created. Saturday would be spent decorating the church. Done so willingly and happily by volunteers. Flowers from gardens, greenery from the woods, with a corner left for the children — with sweet-smelling herbs, clover, daises, buttercups, cowslips, to be arranged in tiers in the space left vacant for them. Then came the gifts to be set out on display. First the huge harvest loaf, a big plait, across the top, to be laid on an already prepared altar on top of which lay sheaves of corn, wheat and barley. Spread everywhere around the church the people's gifts to God; a thanksgiving; fruit, vegetables, preserves, pickles and sauces, nothing forgotten. The next morning, Sunday, with the congregation and organist in place, the Pastor would enter, followed by the choir boys, every one in their spotless white surplices. The Pastor in the pulpit as the organ rang out. The hymns "Now thank we all our God", "We plough the fields and scatter the good seed on the ground", "Oh God our help" and the sailor's hymn "Eternal Father" were some of the chosen hymns, sung with great gusto, with descants from the men. A short address from the Pastor, a collection and handshake as the congregation left the church.

On the following day, Monday, everything was sent to the hospitals, including the collection.

Personally I couldn't even bear the word 'hospital' having lost a dearly loved sister in the 'Isolation Hospital' with diptheria. I think hospitals were considered only as a last resort, to be avoided if possible. True, people did died and there was grief and sorrowing for a long, long time. But you can't win them all, seemed to be the general attitude.

Schooldays grew nearer as the fall (autumn) advanced. We began to think ahead as the weather cooled a little. For new pursuits our shared scooter would come out of the shed; whips and tops went speeding along the then very well cared for smooth pavements. Two kinds of tops, ordinary and the 'window breaker' which speaks for itself. The whip a stick with a hole bored through the top to which the string was attached. The string drawn through a lump of bees wax. Hey presto! Ready for the off, to see who kept the tops spinning longest. Great competition here on our way to school. The ordinary top, squat and bulky, grooved to receive the string — the 'window breaker' light, with a long slim body, sometimes when whipped would take off into the air with disasterous results — hence the name.

Leap frog, another popular game. It starts, all the gang in a line — one had to be 'bender'. The rest behind him, hands on back and leap up over the bender. OK, thats easy for one but the next man over has to put the same distance as between bender and first man, not easy I can assure you. Sometimes a dozen men, strung down the road — bender gets up and makes as assessment of positions, giving out lots of really nasty forfeits. No, leap frog wasn't one man over another and finish.

Touch the road — you must go over — a team game. One in the middle of the road has to see that nobody gets across to the other side. If even so much as a toe touches the road you must go over and the centre man has to catch you if he can. A game where the art of dodging can cause a lot of fun. The road was a safe enough playground then.

Football was allowed in the street too, with an understanding that the team paid for any windows broken. Same rule in our house — our kitchen window was broken so often we nearly had a standing order with 'Daddle Smith' the carpenter. Cost about 2/6d, although they were big sash windows with big sheets of glass. Cricket, boys and girls all enjoyed the game. The girls, mostly wearing navy blue bloomers, tucked in their petticoats and let themselves go.

Quieter, naughty games like 'tinkle button', an arrangement with string and buttons, to tap windows. Parents knew of the game, and woe betide the offenders if caught. My father confessed to playing that himself years before. We tied convenient letter boxes together, knocked on the two doors, then off. A burst of applause as we heard the doors slam — happy days!

At home, so many games to play during dark winter evenings. Ludo, Snakes and Ladders, Happy Families, dealing the cards, playing them and exchanging them to make a family. Mr. Jones the baker, Mr. Black the undertaker, etc., etc. First one to complete a family was the winner, with a little special knick-knack from Mum. Playing cards provided Whist, Fish, Pairs, Spoof, Beat Jack and Cribbage. Chess, Draughts and Dominoes. Better still, Dad arranged Spelling Bees and General Knowledge questions.

We didn't do homework. According to Dad the hours at school should be sufficient for our needs. Such a difference in standards, today. We went to an elementary school. Infants first, then divided into Girls and Boys. Us girls went into classes 1-7, then 7 plus. A teacher took us in all subjects for one year, then up one class. Same proceedure for another year with a different teacher. And weren't they brilliant teachers. One I particularly remember, Miss Perrin. She was a typical looking old maid. Long black skirt, immaculate white blouse — but her hair — oh my God — never to be forgotten. Dragged back from her face so tight it might burst any minute, concluding in a flat bun. But as a teacher, none better.

I was supposed to be a brilliant scholar, up in the top class at 11 and a half years. A nuisance to myself and everyone else. Kept to the same subjects for 2 and a half years it wasn't surprising. My Dad's brother begged him to let me sit for a Grammar School scholarship, but Dad was adamant — NO. Service for girls — yes, he was one of those — they did exist.

Roger was really Gran's brother but she never admitted it because of the stigma which workhouses carried at that time. He was known to us as her house-boy. Roger had a terribly sad life. In his younger days he had been happily married. His wife had gone berserk after the birth of their son. She had fed the baby methylated spirits and no doubt caused it's death. She had also set the house on fire. So poor Roger, called from work, lost all he had cherished in a few short hours. My Gran fixed him up with a few clothes and he 'took to the road'. This meant he walked from town to town, putting up at the nearest workhouse. There was one in Southampton, in St. Mary's area. Roger said it was a fine life and if emulated today might simplify a lot of problems for folk who like to live free. He said they could enter a workhouse at 7.00 p.m., not before. They had to have a compulsory bath and their clothes taken to be washed in the laundry to be ready next morning. A meal, then a bed for the night. There was no charge, but they had to do a few hours work. So with the help of very few staff everything ran like a military campaign. The place in this way was kept clean and hygienic. They were given a substantial plain meal before departure to the next workhouse, probably miles away.

Years later when he left the road Gran took him in and he ran her home to perfection. All she did was the washing; carrying on with her tailoring business. To us he was always 'Mr. Fix-it'. His first job when we came on our annual school holiday was to build us a big tent. Here he served and we ate all our meals together at the bottom of Gran's garden. So, lazy holiday would pass, spent mostly by the river, with Roger. Both Mum and Gran were happy knowing we were in good hands. And their tailoring business thrived on both sides of the road.

I truly believe Roger was happy during his years of roaming. He described country ways, birds and wildlife, and said he had never felt nearer to God than at those times.

Gran paid him wages, Mum bought his tobacco — a happy solution all round.

Recently, thinking about elections, what fun days they were. A day off school and out came our Union Jacks to wave to anything or anybody. We would go to the Polling Booth and sing "Vote, vote, vote for Dr. Knowlton, knock old Balfour out the door, if we meet him with his wife, we'll stab him with a knife and won't vote for Balfour any more." Bloodthirsty, even in those days. Dad and his dad were staunch Liberals. Both spending years as members of the Liberal Club in Dorset Street. My grandfather, with great sorrow, retired when the Gaming Laws were changed and Sunday games were allowed to take place. He had opposed the recommendment.

September a beautiful month, a month's school holiday. All the time spent, except night, by the water. So much to do. At the shore, beach, pebbles and shells to collect, just like the real seaside. Crab catching (tiny ones) hidden under big stones.

Gran's neighbour owned a great big motor boat moored away from the shore. With a few friends we were allowed to swim out and play out our fantasies. Pirates, Ku Klux Klan, Cops and Robbers; with a good nosh in the tent every so often.

When the tide went we'd go ashore for grasshopper races. We'd put a tiny spot of different colour on their anatomy, put them in a ditch and start them off. If we were in funds there was a little gamble on the winner.

Everybody in those days owned a bow and arrow (made by themselves). We would set up a target and be off. Included in this category were our catapults which were fabulous fun. On these occasions we all took our kites as well. There was always just the right amount of wind off the river to make them a great success, the long garden ample for our needs.

The kites were real works of art, manufactured at home with brightly coloured paper, glue, a long piece of string for the tail, with strips of soft wood to manipulate into shapes. Dad versus kids for ideas and suggestions — then a test of nimble fingers. They were mostly made on winters' evenings in one person's shed, usually Toby John's, the biggest and warmest on offer.

After a few antics on shore the tide would be fast flowing back in. The rest of the day spent in diving and swimming. Out of the river Roger would hose us down with fresh tap water and towel us dry. I am sure we were his favourites of all things on God's earth and we loved him dearly too. A final nosh, then in to say "Goodnight, God Bless" to Gran and Gramp. Across the road and into home — warm and welcoming. Dad and Mum missed their 'Little Hoydens'.

Our home was lovely, warm and welcoming through the years. Into this life now and again came a dear old lady we called Granny Cull. She really came to help Mum if there was illness or stress of any kind. On a couple of her visits we noticed Mum ill in bed, and we first had a new brother and then a new sister. After a natter amongst ourselves we decided Granny Cull must bring babies in the big black bag, where else?

The lying-in, of ten days, after childbirth was a time when a woman was truly, truly spoilt. The nurse who came to help every morning of that period was very strict about this. She said "You can't heal the strains of nine months in a day".

Mum looked so lovely and happy on her frilled pillow slip which I had 'goffered' with special love. Her long black hair hung in two braids over her shoulders. Mum received her visitors and her presents with the air of a duchess. So many, bootees, matinee coats, vests, a pretty head shawl, all hand knitted. Then there were the petticoats and they were named, with deep lace frills, made to complement the beautiful cambric day gowns the baby ware. These were beautiful works of art. There was much love shown when a baby arrived and everyone was happy.

When Dad came home at night, I had seen so much love in that bedroom that I grew bold and asked him "What is love, Dad?". Quick as

183

shot he replied — "an itching of the heart — but you can't scratch it".

Then came the 'Churching' — a ceremony observed by all the wives at that time. A woman would never go outside the gate until she had been 'churched'. It was a little service arranged with the Vicar. Just the two parents and the new arrival, to thank God for a safe pregnancy, delivery and the gift of their child; also to renew their marriage vows which is perhaps why their marriages lasted. My Dad had a strong belief in this service. Not christening. He said it left the way open to choose our own religion if we wished when we were old enough to understand.

My brothers were only allowed one courtesy visit a day to see Mum and the new arrival. I, being a girl, had to save Granny Cull's legs — she was old. So I got quite bigheaded while my mother was lying-in (ten days). She had a sort of gruel called Robinson's Groats. I had tasted it and loved it. She had it morning and evening. And what did I do? I sat on the top stair and had a good old lapper out of the basin before Mum got her share. That wasn't all. My Dad, the proud father, sent my mother up so many delicious extras like ice cream, chocolates, her favourite sweets, grapes, brandy snaps, shrimps and prawns. I enjoyed every stolen mouthful and all said and done, I did have to run up and down stairs with the goodies.

We missed Mum at these times. She was perfection in every way. We missed the hum of her machine as she coped with her tailoring. Most people used Singer treadle machines. My mother used a Wheeler & Wilson hand machine with the cotton wound on a cob not a bobbin. I just don't know how she managed, ending up with six children, three girls and three boys. She did everything beside her tailoring and preserving. My Dad did nothing in the house, men didn't in those days. I once heard Mum say she hadn't been out of the house in seven years.

My mother paid into a Doctor's Club. One penny for children, two pence for adults. I think doctors were some of the most respected people and very much venerated by us working class.

Our doctor, Dr. Bacon was the only person we knew who owned a car. But then, we didn't go to the surgery as today. He called on us and called it his "rounds". Us kids found him quite pleasant, but hated him for one thing. Whether it was a broken limb or measles, his first words were "No potatoes". This hit us hard, especially in the summer months when Dad was digging his "earlies". He was in the habit of leaving all the little ones on the hams. This was our supper treat, with loads of butter, pepper and salt after they were cooked. They say butter is bad for one, today. I must have eaten enough to sink a battleship — and still do. It's lovely and I am eighty and no regrets.

184

Of course, in our house, any illness meant a fire in the room. What pictures and stories came from pictures made by the flickering firelight at night. My dad was a dab hand at it. He always called the doctor the 'Crocus', you can guess why, but no prizes for the answer.

One cupboard in our house was reserved for medicines. Nothing I can assure you that anyone would want to steal. Castor oil, magnesia, liquorice powder for stomach, also home-made diarrhoea mixture. For general aches and pains or chest trouble the most hated stinking muck called 'Russian Tallow'. Also thermagene wool, it kept everyone at bay but it was, I must admit, most effective. Where it came from I don't know, probably some of my Dad's sea-faring friends. When it was needed it was warmed in the oven in a stone gallipot (jar) and Dad advanced on the patient's back and chest. Rub, rub, thump, thump, up and over. I should imagine any germs there might have been had long since hopped it. Following this my mother would come forward with a piece of brown paper liberally smeared with this atrocity to bind round chest and back, but it was good and effective.

I am sure people laughed more in my youth, and strange as it might seem, enjoyed and took pleasure and pride in their work. Streets were gayer because of little things, eagerly looked forward to each week. The German, and Salvation Army Bands, a juggler and tho' perhaps not strictly legal, the 'Punch and Judy' man with his show. Then a little man with his organ. We called him 'Mr. Thursday' because he always called on that day.

Most tradesmen called for orders and delivered to the house. Butcher, baker, etc., etc. Big stores from town delivered anything. 'Edwin Jones', now called 'Debenhams' had elaborate horses and carts with uniformed driver and van man. They would deliver a packet of hairpins, price twopence.

Twelve noon, most deliveries ended. Loads of horse manure left behind, out came the kids with shovels and buckets — fourpence a bucket, cash, we could never meet the demand. Every man was a proud gardener, visiting neighbours, admiring, criticizing, praising or envying the produce, then off to the local for a pint and a chat.

We children were always too busy to be bored. Our biggest problem was to find time to do all the things we wanted to do. Everything was a challenge to our ingenuity, so we had to get the old grey follicules working overtime.

One of the nicest hobbies was collecting cigarette cards. Most of them were real works of art — not like the rubbishy ones that occasionally

185

crop up today. Sets of cards numbered 1-50 were put on the market by the tobacco firms. We made up our sets by swopping each others'. The pictures on the cards — unlimited. Birds, butterflies, flowers, soldiers, uniforms and steam trains, a great favourite with the men. Oh yes! they were as bad as the kids.

One firm was called B.D.V. Cigarette companies started giving away, instead of cards, silk flags, which later, much later, still in silk, turned to roses and flowers. These were much sought after by the ladies, sewing them together (5" x 5") to make the tops of cushion covers — the seams being hidden by lines of silken embroidery stitching. Albums were freely available at the newsagents to stick fifty cards in. They would hang little 'swop' notices in the window for half-penny.

Our parents must have got fed up with our collections, stamps match boxes, tins (most attractive then), jam jars which we sold, for a half-penny. small, 1d. big. Newspapers we hoarded to sell to the butcher and fishmonger, to overwrap the greaseproof ones. Rags and bones were sorted into bags, cotton and wollens, more cash for the woollens. Rag and bone men came with a horse and cart shouting "Rags — bring out your bones". They were weighed and paid for, or one could have a goldfish instead of cash — oh yes, it was all go!

We had marbles, we called them "mibbies", clay ones up to five different colours. Then the beautiful coloured glass ones, the myriads of colour, swirling and curling inside white glass. We played marbles all along the gutters going to school. Every kid had a marble bag with their name on it, a drawstring at the top. The other game of marbles was played in the garden. A hole three inches wide dug, two players to take turns, first deciding how many marbles to gamble. Standing 5-6ft away, the object was for each to throw their gambled marbles into the hole. Many went astray some distance. These had to be aimed and shot into the hole with the thumb. The final marble in decided the winner — he took all.

There was a cinema just round the corner from home called "The Scala", tickets two-pence. We had a rip roaring time there on Saturday morning matinees. A woman played suitable music to the film on a piano. The films would all be silent and the words and conversations printed on the screen — bad luck if you couldn't read well.

A commissionaire showed us to our seats — he was very grand in an ornate uniform with gold buttons, and a peaked cap. He carried a powerful torch. He was very jovial and didn't mind how much we shouted and stamped our feet while the house lights were on, but once they were off, we were expected to behave. If there was any noise the operator would switch all the house lights on, and then we couldn't see the film. About halfway through the show, the commissionaire would come down the aisles with a big spray to cool and freshen the atmosphere — squirt, squirt, very pleasant, something between scent and disinfectant. It would fall on us like a fine mist.

At the end of the film there was always a serial with a cliff hanger making us eager to see the next episode. Somebody would be tied to the rails, with a train coming, a house on fire, someone hanging from the window. And then — THE END would loom up on the screen to a disappointed "Oh no!". Happy memories of "The Clutching Hand", "The Mysteries of Myra", "The Perils of Pauline", "Tom Mix" and many others; Pearl White was our favourite actress.

So, the fall was closing in on us — the leaves all gold and brown, heralding winter. Summer days fleeting, sad, for it had been a gorgeous season. But we mustn't repine. Winter brought us many compensations. Reading in a big half circle round our cosy fire, lost to all around us. Winter meant a daily visit to the library, a fresh book for Dad. Amongst others he favoured Rider Haggard, Dickens and Baroness Orscy. Mum said we would all get 'noggle headed'.

Autumn had now said farewell. Dad had filled his little barrel for anyone who popped in. They dropped in our house like flies. Dad was popular and a good organiser. Our kitchen a happy rendezvous for friends and neighbours.

Winter started off with a big bang with a 'ring session' organised very similar to darts of today. A big round board, studded with hooks under which were numbers — a net below — to catch the rings which fell and didn't score. With four rubber rings, the object of the game was to hook the highest numbers, someone kept the scores. It was teriffic fun, and it suited all the company. Dads v kids, ladies v gents, neighbour v neighbour, girls v boys, would be the order of the day, everyone drawn into the game, a regular jamboree. We stayed up later, but no reading at the supper table. Not even Dad. Soon it would be the winter in earnest.

Now the time to start skipping, three different styles. Individual — just self and your own skipping rope. Long skipping — this meant a long rope with a 'triller' holding each end. 'Triller' meant the one who kept the rope turning. Anyone could join in. Anyone stopping the skip had to take the place of the triller. Then the game started all over again. The last kind was called 'French' skipping. What a shambles that was. Hard to learn, harder to accomplish. Boys better than girls, perhaps because of wearing knee breeches — free from skirts dangling around their knees. Two ropes need for the trillers, one in each hand, setting up a rhythm. A group of kids for this, one at a time, sort of leaping into the ropes and skipping to the rhythm. Then suddenly the trillers would start singing "All in together, this frosty weather, *this* one, *that* one, *out* goes *she!*".

Hopscotch was played at this time of the year, it was so warming. But now we were really warmly clad. I noticed Mum had hung the button — hook on the dresser, thinking of my knee-high button boots.

But back to the winter evenings. A sing-song, a winter favourite with everybody. I think everybody likes to sing — have you ever noticed? A person is pressed hard to sing, reluctantly agrees, and all hell to stop once they get going.

So later we begin at Mary's house, round her piano. Certain of a good crowd there, with Dad to wind them up. Plenty of songs and ballads to come. If popular, plenty of applause, with hand clapping, foot tapping and whistling. Tear-jerkers with their right quota of tears, a sort of "Oh, I had a wonderful evening — I cried all the time". The men piling on the agony. Always a solo singer, often Dad. By special request his "Drinking Song", maybe a tenor as well after. Lovely nights these — not a cloud in the sky. The finale? A patriotic "God Save the King" stood at full attention. Mary received a box of chocolates for her music. Some of the songs; "The Old Rustic Bridge", "Nellie Dean", "The Old Apple Tree", "Daisy" and "Dolly Gray". Pub songs; "Thora", "The Long Trail", "Red Sails", and "Marble Halls". Songs or ballads; "Beautiful Picture", "Vacant Chair", "If Those Lips Could Only Speak". Tear-jerkers; "Break The News to Mother" — weren't they just! These of course only a fraction of the songs — throats being often revived with 'neck oil', tea, lemonade or ale. Better than television.

"There were no driving tests in those days...."

A. Eastwood

Liss, Hampshire

I was born in Leeds on the fourteenth of July 1905 — a date easy to remember as I am a lover of France — and it is also the year in which the Automobile Association was formed and the first patrol put on duty on the London-Brighton road — a coincidence as my life for 45 years was to be bound up with the AA.

In the summer of 1912 we moved to Wetherby, into a quiet road, my mother said, but by the winter we were to realise that it was on the route from the station to the racecourse, and the rowdy and excited crowds passed our windows — on the return journey though, somewhat subdued and quieter.

My father was a commercial traveller in brushes and my early recollections of him were when saying goodnight he would rub my cheek with soft bristles which he told me had just arrived from Russia. Alas, he died of cancer aged 39 and left my mother with nothing but debts, so at nine I was bundled off to school as a boarder at the Royal Commercial Travellers School at Hatch End, Pinner. The headmaster constantly reminding me that I had not only got to earn my own living when I reached 15 but to provide also for my mother, although he failed to indicate to me what trade or profession would best suit me.

That was a really uneventful time — recollections of standing for hours in the basement corridors when the Zepplins came over and the thrill of seeing one come down in flames in the direction of Watford — of breakfast consisting of two slices of bread soaked in black treacle and of interminable stews for dinner. One afternoon a week we were allowed 'exeat' and with the other boys would go to Pinner and buy sweets to bring back and sell to other boys — two for a farthing — and so make a bit of pocket money.

In 1914 we moved south to Liss where my mother earned a little by teaching English at the local school and billeted Canadians in our

189

four-bedroomed cottage. She organised flag days and in the holidays I would go with her to the camps at Longmoor and Bramshott where she was always welcomed; she would sometimes collect £150 in one day.

*a) Mr. Eastwood as a boy with his mother
during the summer 1918.*

After leaving school I went to work in a garage learning to drive on an old gate-change Daimler, and in 1925 applied to the Automobile Association for employment — I was taken on as a patrol and told to find a push-cycle, for which I would be given one shilling a week for upkeep. I started work in June of that year, and was supplied with a holder containing pliers, screwdriver and spanners and a very smart uniform. I had not worn leggings before and of course put them on the wrong way which did not put me in the good books of my officer in charge. He impressed upon me that the AA Telephone Box should be kept in an immaculate condition as Senior Officials were likely to inspect it on their visits. I was advised to attend First Aid classes and if I passed the examination I would qualify for another shilling per week. This I did without much trouble.

My duties — 8.00 a.m. to sunset — were to act as relief for patrols on adjoining beats and to direct traffic at Cadnam crossroads; this latter duty filled me with apprehension as I had had no training and it often happened that some inexperienced motorist — there were then no driving tests — had difficulty in stopping at my signals and there were quite a few near misses. On days when my duties entailed cycling from Cadnam to Ringwood — eleven miles — I had to be in Ringwood shortly after 9.00 a.m. in case the Sergeant was awaiting me.

It seemed strange to salute all cars carrying the AA badge, and when I did not salute the driver would stop and ask me the reason; it usually meant that there was an obstruction in the road or perhaps police activity. The Road Manager from London occasionally passed through 'my beat' and once after I had saluted him he stopped and when I went up to him he said "Eastwood — I did not think much of your salute, I will turn round and come back and when I pass you again let me see a better example". He was not much liked by the patrols but one had to admire his desire for perfection in all matters relating to the service.

To show that one had been on duty we were instructed to enter all details of repair work etc. on our worksheet, or in the absence of this, the registration number of all cars that passed on our section of the road — in those days it sometimes happened that only a dozen or so cars passed throughout the whole morning. Part of the Cadnam-Ringwood road was still a gravel surface and punctured tyres were a daily occurrence.

Sir Conan Doyle lived near by at Bignell Wood and would stop for a chat, and his sons would consult me regarding mechanical problems with their sports cars. Earl Howe — the racing driver — was a regular weekend visitor to Bournemouth, driving a Bugatti, and as there was a sharp incline approaching the crossroads, where I was on point duty, he asked me to watch out for him and he would blow his horn on breasting the hill and I was to halt traffic so that he could cross the junction at speed.

Augustus John, who lived near Fordingbridge, was another frequent visitor and we had many interesting conversations.

I remember one incident in particular — I was approaching Cadnam at about 7.00 p.m. one evening in summer when I came across an elderly man standing by his car at the top of Ockley Hill — I stopped and asked him what was the matter, and he said the engine needed oil and would I get some, so I cycled to the Cadnam garage, strapped a can on the carrier of my bike and returned and started putting the oil in. When he asked what I was doing, I told him, and he said "Did I ask for oil? I meant water for the radiator!" I went to a nearby stream and filled his radiator, when entering details in my note-book I requested his name and he replied "Professor. . . ." After that I always checked to make sure what was wrong in the first place.

b) Mr. Eastwood was one of the very early AA Patrols.

Adjacent to the crossroads was the village bakery and the owner had a Model 'T' Ford, it broke down so often that I would call in each morning to test it before going on duty.

Pauncefoot Hill just out of Romsey was very steep and the local brewers — Strong — employed a number of steam lorries for deliveries, but they had difficulty in ascending the hill without 'tacking' across the road so the driver would whistle at the bottom and I would halt all traffic at the top until the steamer had reached the summit.

In 1926 I became the proud owner of a bull-nosed Morris Cowley, price £99 and it was licenced as OR 488, this was the first time that the letters 'OR' had been used for Hampshire-registered vehicles. On my day off I used to attend Brooklands and watch the racing, it was thrilling to see the cars come down the Railway Banking at about 130 mph. After racing one could take private cars onto the track for a fee of about £1 and try to emulate the professionals, but hardly ever achieving a speed in excess of 60 mph.

In 1927 the AA opened an office in Southampton and as I had realised by then that patrol work was hardly my metier I was able to obtain a transfer to the indoor staff. It was a great change and we held some 35,000 members' details, covering the whole of Hampshire. Many were the problems brought to us, particularly Insurance Cover for those over 70, and disputes arising from collisions. We were asked to supply routes — some hundreds for periods just before Bank Holidays etc., some literally for journeys from Southampton to Bournemouth, and some for extended tours of the British Isles avoiding all main roads. Later on I was to form what was called the 'Foreign Touring Section' and we prepared carnets and triptychs for members taking cars to France and beyond —a popular venue was the Irish Free State, particularly with the local priests.

Southampton was the port of call for many foreign shipping lines and it was common to see five or more Atlantic liners in port at the same time, amongst them such famous names as 'Mauretania', 'Bremen', 'Nieuw Amsterdam', 'Aquitania' etc. Some liners would anchor in Cowes Roads and be dealt with by tender and I would attend to see that passengers with cars had proper papers, and then return with those disembarking at Southampton and clear their cars through Customs. The German Line would always have a band playing on deck to welcome the passengers as the tender approached.

We dealt with the issue of International Driving Permits. America was not a signatory to the appropriate Convention but to obtain an IDP one had to have a British driving licence and, after 1934, pass a driving test. So, after instruction, I was empowered to test Overseas Visitors arriving at Southampton and I well remember testing Olivia de Haviland and Douglas Fairbanks Jnr.

193

Changes at Chargot

Sir Edward Malet, Bt.

a) Edward Malet on degree day at Oxford 1931.

My father, Sir Harry Malet, bought Chargot in 1926: today the manor has assumed much of its former extent, some 800 acres.

On a summer's day in 1925 my mother packed a sandwich lunch, and my father and I set off by train from our home in Wiltshire to reconnoitre Chargot. Newton Tony to Salisbury, Salisbury to Taunton, Taunton to Washford, where we were met by Mr. Linnell with a car (the last of the old agents for the Chargot estate).

On arrival we were entertained by the caretaker, Mr. and Mrs. Tom Howe, in the Chargot servant's hall (where I now write, it is the farm office) — tea with cut rounds, raspberry jam and Somerset cream. Mrs. Howe, a pretty demure little lady, poured tea out for us, she wore a smart black frock and white apron. Tom had a limp and a rosy face, as gardener his specialities were begonias. They lived in the lodge. After tea Mr. Linnell showed us round and introduced us to the Scotts, the Maddocks and the Ridlers, all local farmers.

Chargot House was then completely covered with thick ivy and surrounded by laurels, neatly trimmed by Tom Howe and his gardening aid Sid Coles. The house had been unoccupied for several years. It smelt damp, the shutters all closed had to be opened for our inspection. It was nonetheless in good order and roofed with huge Treborough slates.

My father and I duly reported back to my mother, who used to laugh when she recalled how my first comments on Chargot were to tell her how many varieties of water and other birds I had seen; but I still find this first impression well founded. Where else could one find such beautiful and varied surroundings, where indeed the birds or the profusion of ferns, rhododendrons, or the variety at that time of butterflies?

Back at school I received a telegram (I still have it). It reads, '21 Sept 1925, Have bought Chargot, Dad'. The reader can imagine the excitement of the first Christmas holiday. My father, having previously been Master of the Tedworth Hounds, lost no time in mounting us, and in joining the stalwarts of the West Somerset Hunt — Sir Dennis Boles, Mr. Frank Hancock, Mr. Thomas and his three sons, to mention only a few, with Charlie Back as huntsman and Harry Holt as whipper-in; it was a very different country for us, but we soon got used to the hills and the banks.

As a boy the ponds were a special attraction, as indeed they still are to small boys visiting Chargot. Parson James (the wizard fisherman who ate no fish) taught my father and me to fish. The Rev. Courtney Jenoure, our Vicar based on Cutcombe, spent weekends at Luxborough, slept at Chargot, made his H.Q. With Mr. and Mrs. Jim Stark (the gamekeeper) and fished the ponds between visits to parishioners. He had some good fishing stories to tell, some a little tall, but he was much respected and well read. He lived to be a very old man, so that he was not always able to take Luxborough services. His last few years in office were with one foot over Jordan and a glimpse of the promised land, which he shared with his small but faithful congregation.

There are other unforgetttable characters, whom I can still see in my mind's eye and who were an essential part of the place. Mr. and Mrs. John Venn lived in the new house, Pool Town. John was the village carter and took his horse and covered wagon back and forth to Washford station. He had his stable at Lower Ponds and owned the meadow at Kingsbridge which I now refer to as Venn's Meadow, and where we hold our annual church fete. He wore a 'Newgate frill' and was an expert at rough stone walling and until he died he prided himself he had never lost a tooth. Mrs. Venn was very neatly dressed with a tight little bun at the back of her head. She was a great friend of my mother's. We used to think her morose as she always seemed to frown as we passed, until we discovered that she was doing us the honour of a curtsey despite her rheumatics.

Mary Cording lived in Boubier's Cottage in the depths of Church Wood. She was there when we arrived at Chargot, and I first met her looking out of her front door as I rode down the path which passed her gate, quite unconscious of the picture she made, framed in the climbing roses over her doorway. For her cottage she paid half-a-crown yearly and came to present the half crown personally — this was quite a ceremony; she handed over her coin to my father, who gave it back to her with a glass of port and they had a long chat. Needless to say, after my father's death, I or my mother (in my absençe) carried on the little half-yearly ceremony. On one occasion my mother asked, "Marr, have you ever had an old age pension?" "No my lady, because I don't rightly know how old I be" she replied. My mother, who knew she was a good Christian, asked her if she had a Bible. "That I have" she replied, "but I can never read'un". Mary fetched her Bible. It was very ancient and sure enough on the fly leaf there were Mary's antecedents with their dates of birth, faithfully recorded, including Mary herself. My mother told her, "I believe you are 88, Mary". She got her pension.

Mrs. Dorcas White, Mary Cording's niece, lived in the New House, Pool, next to Mr. Venn. In those days if you lived in Luxborough you had no call to go far abroad, let alone as far as London. After all we had our stores, our smithy, our baker, our milk supply and all the essentials of life; but it so happened that Mrs. White did just that. She had gone with Mr. Venn's wagon to Washford to take the train to Taunton to call on relatives, but she never got there — 'leastways' she padded through Taunton because, never having been in a train before, she 'dursen' get

b) Sir Edward and Lady Malet on their wedding day.

out at Taunton and the GWR took her to Paddington. Here the kindly guard found her in her carriage and asked her where she wanted to go. Dorcas replied "To Taunton plaze, zur". "Very good, Madam, it's the train just over the platform" he told her, and escorted her there, where she sat patiently till she got out again at Washford. She never saw her relations in Taunton but she had been to London, which was more than a lot of us in Luxborough had done.

Visiting personalities included Dr. Mead King, who rode over from Dunster, often arriving in his hunting clothes, to see his patients. Mr. Beaver, with his very smart butcher's cart and pony. Mr. Bryant, equally well turned out, boasted a gold medal from Paris for the Roadwater Bakery. Mrs. Jeffreys, or one of her young volunteers from Roadwater Post Office, would deliver a telegram by bicycle or pony.

As to the law, we have always been under the watchful eye of Dunster Police, who have never failed us. Soon after my father arrived at Chargot, he put up a poultry house in the 'Park', but soon the hens started to disappear, each day there were one or two fewer. My father had his suspicions. The Dunster Constabulary, complete with bicycles, were seen in Luxborough. Someone had a bad conscience and by the end of the week all but one of the hens had returned to roost. My father remarked, "That's fair enough — we must have had that one for Sunday lunch".

The Changing Landscape

Which is responsible for the great changes — forestry or farming? I believe that the Forestry Commission has done more to alter the face of Exmoor than the much maligned farmer. For example, the coach drive from Chargot to the Brendon Hill road was a fairyland in 1926, carpeted with grass, lined with staghorn and sphagnum moss, crowned with rhododendrons and a background of well-grown beech and oak. Now of course the drive is metalled (a very good job done) and planted almost entirely with conifers. The denisons of Chargot Wood have also changed, the little red squirrel supplanted by the grey, most wood-loving birds have gone (fewer warbles, woodpeckers, and finches). In 1926 I picked up a dead pine marten but have never seen one alive.

I must plead quilty that Leather Barrow Common is now productive pasture land, no longer gorse, heather and bracken; but although we have lost these things, where once we had rabbits, badgers and curlew, we now have in addition hares, green and gold plover and a much increased lark population. That we have lost the very rarely seen grouse and blackcock also goes without saying. My Exmoor and Closewool sheep, and even our Red Devon herd to my mind give the Barrow land a look of purposeful awareness truely beautiful. True, one can no longer cut the bracken for bedding, but one can walk with ease to the top of the Barrow and marvel at the view. Could you do that 20 years ago?

Deer are perhaps fewer but it is a complete fallacy to imagine that they are being exterminated; and the Forestry Commission must be congratulated on establishing a number of deer lawns which will both contain the animals and prevent damage to crops.

What of the butterflies that have gone? In 1926 our woods and fields were gay with all varieties, many of them uncommon. Now we are left with Whites, the Meadow Browns, and the occasional Red Admiral, Peacock and Tortoiseshell. The dragon flies have gone too, and the pollinating bumble and honey bees decimated. Nobody has taken the trouble to assess the damage that farm sprays have done to our ecology.

The effect of the iron mining on the landscape can now only be recorded by a decreasing number of old scars. Mine buildings and pits have largely been assimilated by Nature. Kennisham chimney was quite recently blown up as being dangerous. The old Incline is still the focus of tourists on Brendon Hill, mainly on account of its fine view, but nothing to compare with the view from Leather Barrow. But, as one stands at the top of the Incline and half shuts one's eyes, one can imagine the full trucks going down and the empty ones returning. While the old relics have been disappearing from time to time, the ground has literally opened up on Brendon Hill to remind one of the workings beneath: as for instance happened to Jack Burton when he lived at Round House. He ran a cow in a small holding in which the Forestry Cottage now stand. One morning he went to bring her in to milk. Nowhere could she be seen though he could hear her 'boving'. Eventually she was located about 6 feet underground quite unhurt, was lifted out and the hole filled in.

The arrival of modern amenities completes the changing picture, nor is the new picture as pleasing as the old. New roads are certainly useful amenities but at what a cost? On the Hare Path (Heath Poult — Raleighs Cross road) we seem to lose a foot or two of the good grass verge every year; no longer easy to pause to admire the view or to gallop along. It is even less safe for droving as its increasing width encourages even faster traffic.

On Lype Common a wireless mast raises its ugly head. When the telephone posts and wire came up the Luxborough Valley we thought it the height of desecration, although, of course, we all needed the telephone, but the electric poles and wires followed almost unnoticed.

In 1931 the nearest telephone was at Roadwater. Medical emergencies could be given first aid by the village nurse, but other emergencies — fire, police, the doctor — could only be met by one car (my mother's) or by horse to Roadwater post office telephone. The Luxborough elders put their heads together, I was asked to ride round and get guarantors for a minimum sum of (I believe) £150 for a year's income. I got enough signatures to persuade the authority to put in our telephone system, but at the end of the year, alas, the minimum had not been spent in telephone calls (we were used to being without, was what I told the GPO); and so it looked as though the guarantors would have to pay — until my mother had the brilliant idea: "The Postmaster General is an old school friend of mine from Canterbury. I shall write to him and point out that the Post Office should be proud of including Luxborough on their map, and that in view of the year being the centenary of the 'Penny Post', the PMG in his wisdom should surely be content with payment for calls made and waive the guarantee." To our delight we received a charming reply and all was well.

Modern tarmac roads have certainly changed the landscape. There was not one into Luxborough in 1926, which meant clouds of dust in summer and good red mud in winter. The arrival of mains water in Luxborough had done little to change the scenery, though not all of us appreciated it as we should; and many prefer the natural springs, even though we have to pay to use them. The appearance of a freshwater shrimp from the tap fills me with confidence — if he can live it cannot be bad for me and — no chlorine. God's will be done and we are still a happy community in Luxborough, while I feel sure the ancients smile down on a relatively prosperous Manor of Pool and Langham.

*"It's best to keep off the moor when the
fog blows"*

Two Memories of Exmoor by

S. Vaulter, Dunkerton, and *R.J. Pearse*

S. Vaulter.

Exmoor is a very hard place to live in the winter, but one grows to love the place. I born at Spire Cottage, Liscombe, Dulverton on 12.11.03.

I was six years and five months when I started school and because of World War One I was allowed to leave school at the age of twelve to work on the farm. I worked on Liscombe Farm and lived with my father and mother at the cottage. My weekly wage was half a crown.

My father was known as a horseman or a wagoner. For this he received 13 shillings a week — one shilling more than an ordinary farm hand. He had three horses to work and look after and he worked six days a week from 5.30 a.m. Sundays he mucked the stable out, gave the horses their breakfast and let them drink, at mid-day fed them dinner, at 7 p.m. supper, out to drink, stable mucked out and finally bedded them down for the night. Day after day this went on, no holidays, the only days off was Christmas Day, Boxing Day, New Year's Day, and Old Christmas Day, the sixth January, now forgotten, and Good Friday.

Around 1930 I myself was paid thirty shillings and sixpence per week. This was the weekly income for my wife and me. I think we were as happy then as a good many are today. We had no big prices to pay, it was a struggle to pay small prices.

During my early life my great-grandfather and great grandmother lived in the cottage with us. It was either that or the workhouse for them. They received three shillings and tenpence per week Parish Relief. The Relieving Officer brought this to them each week. When my great-grandfather was too old to work on the farm he cracked stones by the roadside, 80 years old and over, but glad to earn a copper. My great-grandmother died when I was twenty, a few months short of 90 years; when she first received O.A.P. it was five shillings per week, twenty five pence today, and you had to be 70 years old to receive it.

When we were children we were told weird stories of pixies, and that you could be pixie-led on a dark night. My father's father lived two miles from us. He firmly believed in pixies. The only chance you had with them was to turn your pockets inside out, then you had nothing to fear.

We played cards, my parents taught us to play so that we could play with them. I cannot remember when I could not play Nap. I am very glad that I learnt, at the age of 83 I will still walk a mile for a game of Nap.

It is almost impossible to write about Exmoor and not mention the Red Deer, and men like Ernest Bawden who was considered by many to be the best Huntsman the Devon & Somerset Stag Hounds ever had.

The Red Deer lived all around us. I learnt from an early age how to tell which sex and size they were by the droppings. October was the rutting season and quite a number of people were scared to venture out at night, firmly believing that the stags would attack them. This I consider unfounded. The stags were much bolder during this period, and during the time I was a rabbit trapper I had a few close encounters with them.

On one occasion when trapping in the Barle Valley I saw a stag eating acorns at the top of a cover and thought I would see how close I could get to it, there was a small bush covered with ivy on the fence. I crept up behind this bush and looked over the fence. As he was eating with his head down I could see into his ear. When I spoke he leapt about ten feet in the air and dashed off down the cover. On another occasion I went around my traps, again in the Barle Valley. I was carrying the rabbits in a sack. I put the sack down underneath an oak tree, took a couple more rabbits out of the trap, picked up the sack, put it on my shoulder and as I straightened up a very big stag was looking at me through a gap in the fence from a distance of five feet. When I spoke to him he gave a couple of leaps back, turned, took another look at me and then made off.

Although one can live for years among deer there are things you see once in your life with them. One evening I saw a calf or fawn suck its mother, and one morning I was in a field adjoining a cover, I could hear something moving in the leaves in the cover so I climbed over the fence and there found a fawn which had just been born. It was staggering around quite weakly. I went up to it, then had a look to see what sex it was. When I put my hand on it its mother, which was lying in some bushes, barked at me. I put my hand on the calf a few times, every time I touched it she barked at me. I looked around in the bushes but never saw the mother. In the evening I went back to the spot but saw neither of them.

I was out with the gun one evening at Hawkridge, stalking rabbits, and five hinds came up across the field which I was in. They were going through a gap into the next field, the gap was quite close to me, the old hind which was leading them barked at me a few times, she was what Ernest Bawden the huntsman would descibe as a grey-faced old granny. She really was quite cheeky but did now know that I could have dropped her quite easily. There was no man who knew more about Exmoor and its paths than Ernest. When he retired he had a bungalow built at Rinham a mile from where I lived. There was nothing I liked better than to ramble through the woods with Ernest looking for sheep. He was so interesting, he could talk on any subject. One story he used to tell was about an old stag he hunted from the Barle Valley right out to the cliffs and lost him. A month later when hind hunting, he was drawing a cover near Marsh Bridge when he saw the same stag again. Ernest used to say he was such an old gentleman that he lifted his hat to him, one old gentleman to another.

a) Mr. S. Vaulter on a typical day out.

On Exmoor the seasons are often late getting there, but this never applies to winter. That's always on time. As regards the storms and deep snow and being frightened, I pride myself that an Exmoor man does not frighten very easy.

In my life the quarter days meant a good deal to us and most of us knew the dates of the quarters. 25th March was Lady Day, the most important day on the farms when the farmers changed farms and the labourers changed their jobs. Midsummer did not mean so much to us, it was a time when we expected nice weather but quite often did not get it. Michaelmas Day was when a few farmers and labourers changed their jobs. Christmas Day was the only time we had a few days off.

In the spring and autumn I cannot think of any sight that's better than looking down into the Barle Valley. All the different colours of the many kinds of trees when leaves come out in the spring, and in the autumn the changing colours as the leaves come to the end of their time.

Deep snow would frighten some people who have not lived with it. It's a time when you have to stop and think what is the best thing to do. 1916 was the deepest snow I saw. It was very late coming. February was a lovely month, plenty of sunshine, something out of the ordinary for Exmoor. March was a murderous month, snow day after day, until at the end you could walk for miles over the tops of farm gates and fences, really hard to believe what it was like. I was thirteen then. Our bread and groceries came from Dulverton, and there was no way they could reach us with a horse and trap, the nearest they could get was a farm called Highercombe. We had to fetch it from there on horseback and on foot (this was three miles). The drifts were several feet deep at Hawkridge. This is the highest village on Exmoor. A snow drift which they cut through by hand, no snowploughs in those days, was over thirty feet deep. They cut through to reach some sheep in another field and the same night it snowed and filled it in again.

It was impossible to plough the fields in April and many of the fields had a few acres ploughed in the middle. I had an uncle who lived in South Devon. He came to stay for a holiday and wrote back and told his family "Up here they unhang the gates for the snow to blow through and they have not been able to hang them up again." The gates had to be unhung as there was no way of opening them.

The frightening thing on the moors is the fog, it's quite easy for people who know the moors to get lost. I moved around as much as very many on account of my work at night, but was only lost once. That was in daylight on a moor which I knew very well. It's best to keep off the moors when the fog blows across especially when dark.

Rhyming weather. When I was young this was a lovely sight caused by raining and freezing at the same time. There were hundreds of beech trees on the farm fences, nearly all of them are now gone, the branches would get so heavy with ice that many of them would break off which meant tons of firewood. This was something which only happened once in ten or twelve years, or even longer periods.

I once saw where a large oak had been pulled out of the ground, taking away the road, down into the river which was about two or three hundred feet below. This was going from Hawkridge to Torr Stepps. When this tree was pulled out by its roots it was a very severe winter around 1937 or 8. The River Barle was frozen over and it snowed on the ice and rabbits, which were quite plentiful at that time, were crossing on the ice from one farm to the other. When the thaw came, thousands of tons of ice came down the River Barle. The weight of the ice took away a good deal of Torr Stepps and blocks of ice piled up at each end of the bridge to the height of around 20ft. When it's a very wet season the Barle will flood quite easily. On one occasion I saw a good size oak tree swimming down the middle of Ashway Ham with all its branches on. This was normally dry land. One of the worse floods in the Barle was at the time of the Lynton disaster. Many houses in Dulverton had water to the ceilings. A barrel of beer washed out of the Bridge Inn was found nearly at Tiverton, wedged in some bushes on the river bank.

I also trapped moles from the age of thirteen. This is not done now, they are poisoned instead. I caught the rats during the first war. I was paid 2d per tail, by the Government through the Parish Councils. The man whose job it was to count the tails hated handling them. He would ask the people who took the tails to him to dispose of them. I can only think that sometimes he paid twice. I learnt how to catch trout and eels with night hooks. I could buy six-penny worth of hooks and three-penny worth of line, these would last me for a couple of months. I put the hooks down in the evening with a worm threaded on, the bigger the worm the bigger the fish. Collect the fish in the morning, trout or eels for breakfast. I caught hundreds of eels, when they were skinned and fried straight away it was quite a job to keep some of them from jumping out of the pan when frying. I learnt to catch trout with my hand, this is known as groping. One Sunday afternoon two other young men and myself caught 50 trout in the River Danesbrook. The small ones we threw back. In the evening we took six of the very best to an old gentleman who at that time was the head magistrate at Dulverton. He told us we should not be doing things like that, gave us a couple jugs of cider and bread and cheese. I can only hope he enjoyed his breakfast the next morning as much as we enjoyed the cider.

When I was about thirty years old I started taking the odd salmon out of the river, thus becoming a poacher. This was something I never did in a big way, just one for a taste, a small piece for my friends, I never sold any. I spent many hours on the rivers. Sometimes you could get one very quickly, other times it took a while. It was a salmon that had been played around that took a bit of getting. We used the lamps off our bikes to shine on the water, this would draw the salmon. When we used the wire it meant that you had to get the salmon to hide, this it would do by putting it's head underneath a large stone or the river bank. Then you placed the wire over its tail which was sticking out, once the wire was on it would spread its tail and keep it spread so that the wire could not slip off. With the gaff it was much quicker. A quick strike with the gaff and that was it.

In the autumn quite a few Water Bailiffs were sent to Exmoor to watch the river, that was when the salmon came up to spawn. One old lady, now long gone, had a fairly large house. She would lodge three of these bailiffs. When they came in from the pub at night the old lady would place a small paraffin lamp in the window which shone up the river. If the bailiffs went back out the old lady would put the light out. One time this old lady had three bailiffs and three salmon hanging up in the house at the same time. (Only the salmon were hanging.)

When I was young the beech fences were allowed to grow to a large size and the wood used for heating and cooking. I never used any coal during the first half of my life. When one of these old fences was cut off, the foxgloves came up by the thousand. The seeds would be dormant for years. There were not that many wild flowers on the moor.

We also had plenty of yellow gorse flowers on the commons, and there was a small wild orchid which I found growing in sheltered coombes, but these were very rare. We had Marsh Marigolds growing in very wet ground but again not many. There was a pink flower which grew in the road hedges. We called them Campions, I don't know if this is the correct name. A good many words used by the old people on Exmoor were never in a dictionary. One thing could be found if you were lucky and knew where to look was what we called Stag's Horn Moss. Very scarce, it grew from a centre in three or four different directions for a length of eighteen inches or two feet with branching pieces coming off it, the moss looked like the velvet which grows on the stag's horn in July and August. I would think this is where its name came from. No doubt you know all about the stags loosing their horns each spring. When the new horns start to grow they are covered with what is known as velvet. This drops off in early September.

I must say something of the Exmoor ponies. They ran wild over much of Exmoor. The largest herd was the Acland Herd, branded with an anchor. They were kept at Old Ashway Farm. They had the run of the farm Ashway side, Winsford Hill, Southill, Summerway and the Allotment, a good many hundred acres. They were fed with a little hay in severe weather, but did not need much looking after being very hardy. Each year these ponies were rounded up and taken to Bampton Fair. The number of ponies have gone down so much that no ponies were sold at Bampton this last year. Bampton Fair is held on the last Thursday in October.

About five years ago it was considered that the true Exmoors were dying out so a part of Heddon Hill was enclosed and they are now bred there. Many of these ponies if bred from would have mixed blood and a true sign of an Exmoor is what is known as its mealy nose.

Long before my time the Acland family owned all of Exmoor. I read in one book that Thomas Dyke Acland bought the whole of Exmoor for £5,555. He was like Royalty, the only man, apart from the King, who had a right to kill a deer on Exmoor. He sold part of it to the Knight Family, who after several more sold it to Earl Fortescue who later sold the farms to the farmers. When I was young it was often said the Aclands could walk from Honlicote near Porlock very nearly to Exeter without going off their own land. Death Duties upset this kind of life. Their farms were sold to the farmers, Winsford Hill and a few other moors handed over to the National Trust and Sir Francis Acland also gave Killerton to the National Trust.

R.J Pearse

I was born in a small Somerset village. My parents were farming and we were a family of eight, six boys and two girls.

Jobs were extremely scarce and hard to come by, but I managed to get a job on a farm in the heart of Exmoor, "Hall Farm" on the edge of Brendon village. Very little adult labour, other than family, was employed on Exmoor farms. Labour was usually supplemented by boy labour known as 'Home Boys', from Doctor Barnardo's homes. Their wages in the early 'thirties were four shillings per week live in, all found. My wages were six shillings per week because I had farming experience having virtually cut my teeth on the farmyard gate.

I could already hand milk and tackle up and work horses, and ride of course. Work and conditions were very hard indeed, but the farmer and his wife were kindly people and worked very hard and long hours with little reward themselves. We had plenty to eat, and there was usually a bowl of clotted cream on the table.

The farm house had no piped water. This was pumped with a hand pump in an open shed opposite to the back door, where one completed ones ablutions. The toilet was situated at the end of the garden and consisted of a shed with a toilet seat fixed on a framework over a stream, not a place where one would linger on a dark and stormy night.

The day's work commenced at 6 a.m. and ended, well, depending on the time of year, and what had to be done. On dark winter evenings milking was done by the light of a hurricane lantern, there was of course no mains electricity, although some farms had their own generating sets and produced their own electricity.

The milk was scalded in big glazed earthenware pans to make clotted cream, and then put to cool on the dairy floor. The cream was sold to the cafe and hotels at Lynmouth, and the skimmed milk was fed (with additives) to calves and pigs.

My first job every morning during the summer months was to ride to Lynmouth with the cream, all in jam jars tied down neatly with greaseproof paper in a basket on my arm.

The route from Brendon village was up Combe Girt, along Countisbury Common to the Blue Ball Inn and down Coutisbury Hill where the pony would jump up onto the bank, not liking the slippery tarred road, and go down the bank at a sharp trot, jumping across the outlets made to let the water run off the road. The pots of cream would practically jump out of the basket and my heart would be in my mouth as I could see the almost sheer drop below me to the sea, but the Exmoor pony is famous for it's surefootedness so I need not have worried.

Coming home across the Common I would have to see that the sheep were alright. Lambing started at the end of March and then there would be many trips to the lambing pens at night, and it was a great relief when this was over. Cattle cabbage was grown to feed the ewes and lambs, and these had to be cut and hauled to the field and thrown off the cart to the sheep. It was always a source of wonder to me how "Bess" the old black mare would never step on a lamb although they would be all around the cart and running underneath her. I would be up in the cart throwing off the cabbage and she would be making her own way across the field.

Our nearest market was held at Blackmoor Gate. Messrs. Sanders & Son were the auctioneers. All animals would have to walk to and from market. We would drive as far as Paracombe on the Sunday and put them in a friendly farmer's field overnight, and go back early on Monday morning to drive into the market to pen sheep or cattle. Driving on the roads then you met very little, if any, traffic, and dogs played a very big part in moving livestock in those days.

Catering for the farmers was carried out by a lady known as Mrs.

Keats, in a Nissen-type hut (with a long trestle table up the centre) situated on the right of the road a few yards from the Market. (The Blackmoor Gate Hotel, which eventually burnt down, had not been built.) There must be a few Exmoor farmers left who can remember the delicious cold beef served up by Mrs. Keats, a large helping for sixpence and a cup of tea for a penny.

I remember well the sheep shearing parties when farmers went around to each farm in turn, shearing with hand shears, hot and thirsty work. A barrel of ale would be got for the occasion and a large joint of cold meat. There was considerable rivalry as to who could shear the most sheep in a day. The record at that time, of a hundred sheep, was held by my employer's brother, Mr. Albert French of East Lyn Farm, Lynton, quite an achievement. My job was to tie up the fleeces or catch sheep. A handful or so of pull wool used to find its way into some of the fleeces. Pull wool came from sheep which had died, they were left for a few days when the wool could be pulled out easily, not a job for the squeamish, no prize for guessing whose job this was.

"Trumps" merchants from Barnstaple, their buyer a Mr. Verney, would come and negotiate a price for the wool; in 1931 their offer was fourpence per pound for good quality wool. Some farmers, including my employer declined to sell as they considered the price was too low, so it was stored to 1932 when the price had dropped to threepence halfpenny. The breed of sheep kept was the hardy Exmoor Horn.

Some times during the hunting season the Devon & Somerset Staghounds under the Mastership of the late Colonel Wiggin would meet in Brendon village at the rear of the Staghunters Inn, whose very popular landlord was a Mr. Joe Totterdell. Usually one could expect at least two hundred riders, and many more when the meets were at Brendon Two Gates, Exford, Winsford or Cloutsam. Farmers would quickly join in when the hunt was around, many a working horse had its harness removed and was pressed into service as a hunter on such occasions.

Ploughing on this very steep and stoney farm meant first ploughing a few furrows along the bottom headland and hauling the soil to the top headland and spreading it, this laborious job was done with an implement working on the same system as the old-fashioned horse-drawn hay sweep, but shaped like a scoop, very effective but hard work for horses and man. One might see this implement in an agricultural museum now. Ploughing was of course one way, down over.

Haymaking took place at the end of June or when the weather permitted, cut and carried loose of course, and made into a rick. The rabbits saw to it that crop wasn't too heavy, and in those days little or no

209

Winsford Meet D. & S. Staghounds.

b) Winsford meet on Exmoor.

artificial manure was used, just basic slag.

The main winter feed for cattle was oat sheaves, fed with the oats unthreshed. They cut by reaper and tied by hand, they were cut before they were quite ripe. Herbicide sprays had not been invented, so there were always a liberal number of thistles in the crop to contend with and was pretty hard on your hands. The sheaves were tied with a handful of corn stalks and the sheaves stooked in fours with another straw band around the top to prevent them blowing over. When they were dry they were made into round ricks about twelve feet in diameter and thatched with rushes which were cut from some of the boggy places on the moor. These ricks were hauled in from the fields in the winter as they were needed. No straw was used for bedding the animals in winter, but bracken was cut ricked for that purpose, straw being too valuable for feeding.

The winters were long and hard and a hungry time for animals, especially the Exmoor ponies who would often come down from the moor at night when snow covered in the hope of finding something to eat. Deer too would wreak havoc in the root fields, but farmers would tolerate their activities because of the sport which they provided.

Many farmers would 'walk' hound puppies for the Hunt and a blind eye would be turned towards their wrong-doings. They were full of mischief. If you put down a bucket of milk outside the cowshed and turned your back for a moment their heads would be in it. Often enough you would find a boot or shoe chewed beyond recognition and used as plaything. However it was all overlooked in the interest of the Hunt.

In late Autumn or early Winter the rabbit trapper would arrive at the farm. He had no transport of his own so I would have to fetch his traps (gin traps in those days) from the farm where he had previously been trapping. He was quite a character. He hailed from Barnstaple, name of Charlie James and he had been travelling around the Exmoor farms for many years. He would stay at our farm for about a week and for that week I would have to follow him around with the horse and cart, shifting his traps to different parts of the farm and collecting the rabbits. He was paid so much per head for catching them, and rabbits in those days were a source of income, in fact it was often said of some farmers that they paid the rent of the farm from the sale of rabbits!

I learnt a lot from Charlie James, he was a very knowledgeable man in the ways of most wildlife. The Lynton to Barnstaple line was still in operation at that time, so the rabbits were crated up and taken to Lynton railway station en route for, I expect, the London market. The day before he was due to leave for his next farm all the traps would be collected and brought back to the farm. He would then put down about a hundred traps for rats. His methods never ceased to amaze me for he would set these traps in all sorts of odd places. He never bothered to cover them up or set them near holes or runs. I think he must have put something on the traps that attracted them, but that was a secret which he kept to himself. About 10 or 11 p.m. he would say to me "come on boy, and bring a wheelbarrow" and I would keep count of how many because he used to be paid, I think it was threepence a tail, for these, and I would end up with half a wheelbarrow full.

Fifty years on I went back to look at the old farm and I was disappointed. Gone were the avenue of beech trees reaching from the farm to the blacksmith's shop where Dick Squires and his son Charlie used to ply their trade, and where the sound of hammer on the anvil could be heard at the farm. This has long since closed and new houses have sprung up around the village, but I prefer to remember it as I knew it in the old days. Of the shearing parties and the Harvest Home Suppers and the Agricultural Shows held in the field at the back of the Staghunters Inn, and the pony races held afterwards in the field opposite, and the gathering of the Exmoor ponies prior to Bampton Fair.

Some of the old familiar names still remain. Farms now farmed by

211

sons and grandsons, of French, Piles, Burges, Woolacotts, Floyds etc., whom I knew.

Tough and honest, hard working Exmoor farmers of a bygone age, who wrested from the bleak and windswept farms a living.

The modern generation of farmers and farm workers, with their modern and sophisticated machinery have no conception of the hardships endured by their forefathers who farmed on Exmoor.

"A Good Clean Shave"

L. Grogan

"Next gentleman please". It was over 70 years ago that I remember hearing my late father call this out when his chair was vacated by the previous customer.

Quite recently I heard a lady say "It was just laziness that men used to go to a barber's to be shaved, my late father and grandfather always shaved themselves." On reflection I thought how little she knew, for there were many things in those days which contributed to going out to be shaved.

Then, shaving was the principal service given by the barber. He was an expert, for he could give a clean shave as he could get at the beard at most angles a person shaving themselves could not.* Secondly, he could set and strop a razor so that he always had several razors in tip top shaving condition, something the ordinary man fell down on. Next, he allowed sufficient time for the beard to be thoroughly lathered, also the price was only a penny halfpenny so it was better and cheaper to go out and get a clean comfortable shave. I've heard my late father say many times "You don't cut yourself with a sharp razor, you cut yourself with a dull one", which is quite true, for a good sharp razor used properly will scythe through the whiskers whilst with a dull razor you are pushing it and going over the same place to get it clean, besides in fact you are making your face sore and tender. My late father had such a light hand that I've known customers get up from the chair and feel their chins, for they had not felt the weight of the razor and could hardly believe they had been shaved clean. Of course there were some barbers quite the reverse, who were very heavy-handed, used wide one inch blades and great long strokes, so much so that they almost terrified their customers whilst in the chair.

*Mr. Grogan is, of course, referring to the old, open-blade, cut throat razors. The modern safety razor had not become in common use. Ed.

a) The Grogan hairdressing shop established in 1896 with his father & mother outside.

My mother was the youngest of five children (four girls and one boy) and she was only about 5 years when both parents died intestate, within a few months of each other. As the children were all under-age the law decreed that everything should be sold and the proceeds put in trust until they were of age. The children were then put out to various relatives to be brought up. The names of the children were Polly age 12, Martha age 10, Fanny age 8, Ernest 7 and my mother Minnie 5 years.

All children were determined that they would have to make their own way in the world. Polly, after one or two local jobs, married a Londoner and left the district. Martha more or less kept an eye on her two younger sisters until they were of school leaving age, and then she helped them to get into employment with a good Bristol family. Fanny went first as a junior cook and my mother was nursemaid.

The family — the Eberles — were a well-respected family and lived in Pembroke Road in quite a large house. The head of the family was Mr. James Fuller Eberle, and he owned a large carriage building concern in Deanery Road. As you will understand, this was in the days before the motor car, and all the gentry had their own carriage and horses, so carriage building was a prosperous industry. They had many servants who were well clothed in smart uniforms and well fed. The gentry *were* gentry in those days, and to get into their employment was good security, for although long hours were worked (which was the rule for all then), they did concern themselves with their servants' welfare.

My father was Edward Grogan, always called Ted or Teddie, and his particular pal was his cousin Fred Grogan, who lived in Totterdown, Bristol. They liked to walk on the Downs and of course the inevitable happened and boys met girls.

On my father's side, my grandfather, John Grogan, had a nice personality and was apprenticed to ship-building at the John Payne Co. at Bathurst Wharf; he was popular and a hard worker and finished up Foreman Plater. John Payne Co. were a good company who built mainly tug-boats, strong and sturdy, these being used locally to get the bigger vessels into position in the harbour, besides bringing boats up the twisting and winding River Avon. Grandfather was not a big man, grew a full beard and had bright blue eyes. He kept his beard to a nice shape and I always thought of him when I saw a Players Navy Cut cigarette packet, for he looked just like the sailor in the centre picture. Incidentally, the Players packet was the most expensive packet to litho, it being said that there were seven different colours used to produce the finished article.

As my father Teddie was not strong it was decided to put him to the Gents Hairdressing, and he was apprenticed at 116 East Street, Bedminster.

The shop was long and narrowish with 4 chairs along one wall, worked by two hairdressers and two apprentices, there being waiting seats along the other wall. About 85% of the male population went to the barbers to be shaved in those days.

My father was well trained and an excellent worker, but pay was poor and hours very long. Weekdays it was from 7.30am until 8.00pm, Fridays 9.00pm and Saturdays 11.00pm and some shops even opened on Sunday morning from 9.00am until 2.00pm. My father stayed on at the same shop after his apprenticeship finished, but soon after my grandfather developed rheumatism and was unable to go to work. In those days you just lost your job and there was no redress or help from anyone.

Something had to be done, and after the front parlour of No 20 Greenway Bush Lane was altered to become a Hairdressers and my father had to become the breadwinner for the family. My father was by now openly courting my mother; both he and my mother were now about 25 years old and were saving what little money they could with the ultimate aim of getting married and starting a business of their own. Premises were finally found at number 230 Gloucester Road, Bristol 7. This was beyond Pigstye Hill and was a small row of old cottages which had been converted by making a small addition to the front parlour and fitting double shop fronts, or building extra rooms at the back of the premises. This was more or less country, but development was taking place and Bristol was growing slowly. There were fields behind the shop. There had been several different tradesmen who had been in the premises before and had given up, unable to make a living.

It was finally settled to rent No 230 from January 1st 1926, for an annual rent of £26 plus rates. The shop was made with a small counter and front shop and then an inner door to enter the Hairdressing Salon. The front counter was to be used for tobacco and cigarette sales, and toilet goods sales.

There were not so many lines at first to stock, cigarettes being Cinderellas, Woodbines, Players Weights and Tabs, selling at five for 1d, and ten for 2d in cardboard slide cartons, with Gold Flake and Capstan and Players Medium Navy Cut being the better class lines and selling at ten for 3d. A few tobacco lines were popular such as Wills Westward Ho!, Wills Superfine, Odgen Coolie Cut and Players Navy Mixtures and Ringers Bell, all selling at from 3d to 4d per oz. Wilson's S.P. snuff was also sold and was about 6d per oz.

The business at Gloucester Road was quite a struggle and I know my father said that the first twelve months he didn't even earn enough to cover the rent. Of course, charges were very low, being only penny half-penny for shaving and twopence for haircutting. But at least other things, general expenses and living costs were low as well.

My father was not very tall and carried no weight. He was round-shouldered as he had had an accident when he was young and had some sort of rib injury; in common with other problems, there was no free hospital service or free doctors, so nothing was done about it at the time. He was of dark colouring, had a dark moustache and very dark kind eyes. He had a very nice even temperament, and was not given to swearing; liked a glass of stout, but was not one to go to pubs; and was a moderate pipe smoker.

My father had an English concertina which he could play fairly well. And I remember our first gramophone. A salesman came and brought the square box with a turntable on top and a large horn, and they were making a special offer of the machine and choice of any six records for £5. This was quite a large outlay to make, but how we enjoyed them. They were played over and over again. A ten inch record then cost about two shillings and sixpence and slowly we built up quite a fair sized library of records.

My father was good at his work and soon had a good trade. I had two brothers older than myself. Betram Edward born 1897 and Alex Ewart born 1900, myself 1903. Many a Saturday we would be put to bed about 9 o'clock and if we woke up we would come downstairs and sit in the salon to listen to the conversation. My father at this time would be busy in the salon and my mother serving tobacco and cigarettes at the small tobacco counter. Although they did not encourage us to come down, they were too busy to stop and deal with us. Also, unlike lots of other hairdressers, there was little bad language or story-telling.

In those days some hairdressers opened Sunday mornings but my father was dead against this from the start and was a prime mover in getting a by-law passed prohibiting Sunday work. Years of soliciting signatures and canvassing City Counsellors did get results. Then again there was no official half day closing, and at one time my father was the only one in the district of about a dozen hairdressers who was doing so.

Uncle George was a wild one — didn't get into trouble, but had no settled idea of what to take up. He tried one or two jobs, but did not seem to fit in, so ultimately as my father wanted more help he came to the shop to learn the trade from my father. He made the grade well and although not apprenticed was soon a good assistant; the trouble was he had a nice nature but was easily led and unfortunately made a friend of the publican's son who kept the Golden Lion Inn on the corner of Cambridge Road. This pub was kept by a widow, and her son about the same age as George, acted as Barman. So what happened was that Uncle George would be missing from the Hairdressing Salon and we knew where to find him. The hairdressing trade was very erratic in those days and my father was not one to quarrel with anyone. Many a time George had gone up to his friend's and the shop would get busy so one of us boys would be sent up to tap on the window. I don't think any of us ever went into the pub, but George got the message and in a minute or two was back at work.

August 4th 1914 saw the start of the First World War and Uncle George was among the first to go to Horfield Barracks and volunteer for army service. I well remember on the morning of August 5th my family standing on the doorstep to see the first batch of volunteers march down Gloucester Road. There were about 200 of them all in civilian clothes and going to Temple Meads Station en route for Salisbury Plain for training. Some training they got, but within three weeks they were out in France facing the Germans. The war lasted four years and Uncle George was in action in France all through.

I must explain that our shop was in the centre of a block of cottages converted into shops lying between Bishop Road and Cambridge Road — in all about 14 premises. In those days there was very little change in shop ownership and all had the ambition to become known as "Old Established". The only multiple shops were in grocery: The Co-op, Lipton, Home & Colonial and Maypole. There were no multiple tailors. Of big stores there was Baker & Jones in town, Cordeaux's in the Queens Road and the Barton Warehouses in the Barton. A Chinese Laundry was opened along the road and run by Alfie Lam, who after a few years became a Christian and was sent back to China as a missionary.

b) Mr. L. Grogan in 1917.

226 Gloucester Road was Harry Loney's butcher's shop and they had one long window and a side door with a passage to get out to the kitchen and garden and at the bottom of their garden they had a stable. In those days shop-keepers had regular rounds of customers in the district and had to have transport, so Mr. Loney had a cart which he kept in the yard of the Golden Lion Hotel, which was on the end of the rank of shops. But the horse was taken out of the shafts there and then brought down to the shop and led right through the passage, kitchen and scullery out into the garden and put into his stables until the next day, when the proceedings were done in reverse.

The next shop, No 228, was then a faggots and peas shop kept by two old maids, Miss Wyatt and Miss Rundall; Miss Wyatt being a very large lady and Miss Rundall the reverse and quite small. They used to make the faggots and kept them hot on a heated container on the counter. People would bring basins and containers and buy what they required for dinner or supper to take home and eat whilst still hot. On the other side of the shop there were tables and chairs where people could sit and eat on the premises.

Then came our shop, which had a small vestibule and counter, very much like the kiosks of today, and another glass panelled door opening out into the hairdressing salon. There were three basins and chairs along one wall, and on the other two were long rexine covered settees for customers to use whilst waiting their turn for service. Up in the window we had a big fly wheel complete with shafting running along the level of the ceiling, from which we could suspend a rubber band which was attached to a rotary brush. The operator used this to give the customer's hair what was called "machine brushing". These machines after a few years were condemned as being un-hygienic and were taken out of most establishments.

From the corner of Cambridge Road one could look up and see the main entrance to Horfield Prison with the clock tower over it. Between Cambridge Road and Longmead Avenue there were only first, Prison Officer's quarters and the National Provincial Bank. Incidentally, my father was one of the Bank's first customers soon after the Bank was opened. My father also attended at the Prison on request to shave the men on remand. He used to go there at 8.45am when the officers paraded and one of them would be detailed by the Principal to be with my father all the time he was at the Prison. He would possibly shave four or five men who were that day due to go into Court. The charge, which had to be privately paid, was fixed by the Home Office and was more than four times the charge outside. I have heard my father say he had earned more money by going to prison for half an hour than he could earn all the rest of the morning in the salon. Competition among barbers was very keen in those days; many salons were poorly fitted up and were not kept clean and tidy. They would consist of one half of a shop, or a room behind or up and over another type of business. My parents were always keen to keep a good clean and tidy salon and it paid off in the end.

Mr. Partridge, the chemist, was a daily customer of ours for he had a very thin skin and could not shave himself without drawing blood, and as his veins were very close to the surface, once blood was drawn it was a job to stop it flowing. Mr. Linton was also a daily shaving customer of ours. He was a single man then and lodged in, Wellington Hill, ran a car and had a big Alsatian dog called "Leo". Our shop used to open at 7.45am and Mr. Linton always came in about 8.15am; that gave him time to be shaved and open up the chemist shop at 8.30am.

The next shop up was the Co-op. They used two shop sites for the Grocery Department and next door again was the Drapery Department. All the staff in the Grocery were male; they were customers of ours and were quite a good crowd. This was in the days when shops opened long hours — approximately twelve hours daily. No dinner hour closing, and if you were lucky you were given a week's hoilday after twelve months service. Wages were very low. There were leisure chairs being provided for customer use, and an assistant called round the neighbourhood for grocery orders once a week. The goods were delivered free.

One of the row of houses was used by W. Crawford for newspapers and tobacco, but his biggest trade was of paper rounds. He employed many boys both before and after school hours to deliver to all parts locally, paying just two or three shillings a week, for papers in those days were only a half penny each and delivery charges were unheard of.

The rest of the houses, before you came to the Bishopston Methodist Church on the corner of Wesley Road, were used privately. In the first one next to the dairy lived a Mr. and Mrs. Lawler and they had two sons younger than me. Mrs. Lawler was a milliner and employed a couple of assistants, so had quite a reasonable business. In those days no lady went out without wearing a hat.

Then there was Hopkins Grocery Store — Mr. Hopkins was a real old - fashioned man. He packed all his own goods such as sugar, currants, rice etc., and his own cheese, butter and bacon. He was very methodical, everything had its place, and after weighing had to be returned there, before he would go on with the next item. He was slow but the shop was kept spotlessly clean.

On August 4th 1914 when the Kaiser declared war on us, Uncle George went straight up to Horfield Barracks and enlisted, thinking like many more that the war would not last long and the boys would soon be back home. But England was not prepared for war, and time went on and things got worse with us at home.

Ration cards for each person were needed and coupons had to be cut out to get supplies *if* these were available. I don't know what the people of today would have thought of it. One week's ration per person was as follows:

1oz Butter, 2oz Margarine, 3oz Bacon,
2oz Sweets, 3oz Sugar, 4oz Meat, 2oz Cheese

My brother was six years my senior so when conscription was introduced he was called up. He was passed Al but never served in H M Forces and was sent back to his usual work. His papers were endorsed with something like "This man must NOT be enlisted. His work is essential and is of National Importance". Lots of people could not understand why , but at that time for security reasons alone, he could not explain. He was an analytical chemist at Christopher Thomas Soap Works, on Broad Plain, making soap. But it was not the soap they wanted, but the by-product of glycerine to make nitro-glycerine.

By this time my father, who had never been a strong man, was in poor health, due to the food rationing and overwork as more hairdressers were being called up, and their businesses closed for the unknown duration of the war. He would not take advantage by increasing his charges, so customers used to queue for the shop to open. We had to close to get something to eat ourselves, and as many people were themselves working long hours, we kept open during the normal dinner closing hour — 1pm-2pm — and closed from 2pm until 3pm. At 2pm we would bolt the door and would still have customers inside to deal with. Sometimes it would be 2.40pm when we would let the last morning customer out, and by then other men would be waiting outside ready to be let in at 3pm.

I agreed to leave school and come into the business to help my father. In this way we could keep two chairs working for there were many jobs I could soon learn. Shaving; I could get the customer into his suit and then tuck a towel around the neck; then draw the hot water from a large urn, which was kept hot all the time by a gas ring, very few salons had tapped hot water. I would then lather the customer's face. As soon as my father had finished using the razor on the customer in his chair, I had to have the one in my chair ready for him to use the razor on there, and I would move quickly to his last customer, get a sponge out of a sterile box, and sponge the surplus lather off the face, then with both hands take hold of the towel to dry the face, especially around the ears, then ask the customer if he rquired his face powdered to dry up any dampness, or sprayed with antiseptic lotion. Finally pulling the towel from his neck and holding it out for him to take, saying "Thank you Sir". Then if it was winter time you helped him into his overcoat, took his money and gave him his change if necessary. Quickly got the next customer into the now vacant chair and proceeded as before. If the customer required a haircut you had to get him to sit up, put a gown around him, and tuck neck wool around the back of the neck to stop any cut loose hair going down his back. Nearly all customers' clothes were brushed after service, all for a few coppers, and looking back on it I don't

221

wonder that no hairdresser made other than a living.

The 1914/18 war was finished and the men came home, but conditions were very bad for quite a long time. Some haidressers re-opened, others took over new premises, and we were bound to lose some customers.

Everyone was gradually finding out that the country's promise of "a land fit for heros to live in" was a myth and it was of case of helping yourself.

My father died in 1920. I was then only sixteen and a half years old, and although I had been a great help to my father I could not be put in charge of the business so we advertised for an assistant.

In those days shaving was the main moneymaker and my father employed a lather boy as a well lathered face was a great help. He had several boys to start with him. Some got on fairly well, but the pay was so poor in the hairdressing trade, that the boys would come on trial but leave as soon as they got a better offer in some other job. A man would have his hair cut then only once a month. It was not the done thing to go and ask for just a haircut, even if a man did shave himself. Singeing of the hair was an extra which some would have done, the belief being that it was good for the hair and prevented catching cold.

I myself only took a few shillings more than we paid the staff and kept ploughing back profits into the business.

Les Bennett was a real good one and used to keep the others on the move. If one of us got too involved with talk with a customer, with just a glance, or a tap on the heel of his shoes, he would convey the message "You're taking too long, pull your weight", but the customer didn't know for no words were spoken. This art seems lost on today's assistants; they do not know how to deal with one customer and move on to the next when required.

When my father opened his shop in Gloucester Road he only had one source of supply for his tobacco, cigarettes and sundries and that was W. D. & H. O. Wills. They had premises in the centre of Bristol, and besides making their own brands, which at that time were only a few, they wholesaled other brands, plus extras. Then the Imperial Tobacco Co. Ltd. was formed, which embraced nearly all the Bristol manufactuers and they sold only their own brands which disposed of the general wholesale business. The Imperial Tobacco Co. was formed, because there was a threat that the British American Tobacco Co. were going to come over from America and develop their own trade. This all fell through when by mutual consent Bristol manufacturers agreed not to compete on the American market and vice versa. The outcome was that as trade developed we opened accounts with more firms to buy under better terms. Players, Ogdens, Carreras and Murray's goods were all selling well in our area.

In the last few years of our trading we added chocolates and sweets, and besides wholsale accounts we bought direct from Frys, Cadbury, Rowntrees, Callard & Bowsers, Bensons etc. On the toilet side many firms developed during our years: C A Strokes Eclipsol Works in Lower Castle Street, Bristol, Skinetolin Co., Louvain Co., Kolene, made by Pannett and Nedon, London, and County Perfumery Co. of Birmingham; ultimately these people then brought out Brylcreem which became a top seller.

In my father's day there was a Mr. Jennings, who lived in Dongola Road. He was an insurance agent and was in what was called our Toilet Club. On the first of every month he paid a pre-arranged amount and this entitled him to a daily shave, haircut as required, clean towel and brush and mug kept for his exclusive use. Many people think that styled Gents hair is something new, but even in the early days we had customers who kept their hair to a special style. This Mr. Jennings had little hair on top but wore the rest back and sides — in a bouffant style.

It was during the First World War that bobbed hair came in for women. It was a craze that took on but there were only about a dozen Ladies hairdressers in the whole of Bristol. We were admirably placed because we had made alterations in our premises. Besides having a fair sized front shop we had three basins and mirrors put up on the other side of the shop, and a nice wood and glass screen with a door at both ends, so, with curtains, we could screen off these chairs and the girls could go straight into a private cubicle and receive hairdressing service. I expect we bobbed/first cut as many girl's hair as any other shop in Bristol. We were charging the men one shilling for a haircut but we charged the girls five shillings and the word soon got passed on, for most Ladies hairdressers charged fifteen shillings.

In the course of continuous trading from 1896 to 1961 we must have served a tremendous number of customers. In lots of cases, although we were on very familiar terms, and saw them regularly, we never knew their names or where they worked or lived. Many others I remember clearly and got to know a great deal about them.

We certainly had lots of local trade, but some came from other parts of Bristol and district. Farmers from Stoke Gifford, Olveston and Thornbury bringing their women into Bristol were common. I remember Mr. Baker who used to breeze in about twice a week to have a barber shave; he didn't have a lot of hair. He was of working class and we never knew what he did or where he came from, but there was no doubt about it he enjoyed coming to us as much as we enjoyed serving him. This atmosphere prevailed all through my working life. Ours was a happy shop and in the main we had quite a nice lot of customers. Our time off was very limited; only one week's holiday a year plus the usual Bank Holidays. We made the most of weekends and made our own fun with little to spend.

Back in Edwardian days we had electric trams on the streets of Bristol. A Mr. Harry Lee lived in Manor Road — the road behind our shop — and every week-day morning he would come round to our shop at 7.45am to be shaved before catching a tram to the Tramway Centre. He was the commissionaire at the Waterworks Company offices, then in Marsh Street off Baldwin Street, and his first jobs were to open up, collect the mail, sort it and place it on the various desks before the clerks came to work at 8.30am. Therefore, you will see it was essential that we were ready, on time to shave him, so that he could catch the same tram at the same time every day.

Quite a large number of past-pupils of Bishop Road School were life long customers, and when I gave up the business I was working on quite a few of the fourth generation, which is in itself remarkable. Men like Sammy Ball and Phillip Hooper, who both worked on the railway engines, would call in regularly when cycling home after doing their shift. They would be wearing their greasy overalls and if they called in during the winter time they would strip them off before sitting down, even in the waiting seats; but in the summer and hot weather, because they had to work in the heat of the fire-box they had little or only underclothes on, and we used to put old newspaper on both waiting seats and our barber chairs for them. Some barbers had notices up stating that either they removed overalls or they could not be served. Our trade was very varied: from labourers to City councillors, County cricketers, Prison Officers, Police Officers, office workers, in fact from the highest to the lowest in their own world. I well remember on one occasion I had cut a gentleman's hair who had told me had become a regular customer by recommendation. He had already been to us several times but had never divulged his calling and we always tried not to appear inquisitive. As he walked from my chair to get his hat the next gentleman coming towards hims said "Good afternoon Bishop, how are you?" and proceeded to talk about church matters. That's how I found out he was a Bishop, for he wore no clerical collar when he came in for a haircut.

Oh, for the days when a tobacconist knew more about the commodities he was selling. A real tobacconist had knowledge of different types of leaf used in making tobacco mixtures, and he also

bottom waistcoat pocket, which he had specially chamois lined. Thus he dispensed with a snuff box and had his snuff always with him and could take a pinch by using his right hand, first finger and thumb.

". . .'Cabin Boy required – SS 'So and So'. ."

R. Buck

Pill, Bristol

THE DEEP BLAST OF SHIP'S SIRENS

My father came from an old Pill family of pilots and sailormen (although, alas, my father never went to sea). My mother came to live at Pill in 1917 and they were married at Christ Church, Pill in 1920, separated through his death in 1974, a long love match, devoted to each other. They set up house at Pond Head, old cottages in the centre of Pill by Victoria Park. I was born at Pill on the eighteenth of July in Nineteen Twenty One.

My earliest recollections of life is of a Gladiator contest with a mouse which I despatched with a boiler stick, thus saving my infant sister and rescuing my mother from her astral solitude on the nearest chair, aged about three and a half. The cottage where we lived nestled by a stream, at the back, and Mr. Raikes the farmer's property, on the opposite side of the road with a large old barn and orchard.

Pill — then an enchanting village. Narrow dark streets, cobbled in the lower half of the village, quaint old pubs, some like the "Waterloo" almost in the river. At that time there were still a few old Pill pilot cutters riding at their moorings, and clusters of pulling boats used by the hobblers plying their ancient maritime trade in the river and the nearby docks at Avonmouth.

On the spring tides our cottage, in company with a lot of others, was besieged by the tide pouring in from the creek helped by a westerly gale. I have seen it reach the bottom of Ham Green Hill at times. On those days I would accompany my grandad, an old square-rigged sailor and westerman, down to the Arch where he would dig up a bucket of mud, and this would be used to seam up the joints on the boards outside the front door. As far as I can remember this was not always effective.

230

a) Victoria Park, Pill, where Mr. Buck's parents set up home in 1920.

In these hard times my father, a literate sensitive man, had obtained a stokers job at Ham Green Hospital. He was worth better things but jobs in those days were at a premium and opportunities scarce. After 5 years at Pond Head, we were given the tenancy of No 4 Rock Cottages. A rank of eight very fine houses that had just been built about a quarter of a mile down past the Hospital itself. A beautiful spot, the front sloping down to the artificial reservoir, and in the rear a large field running alongside the river Avon.

In 1926 came the momentous moving day. For this the hospital sent Mr. George Wilson, a gardener at the hospital, and his horse "Captain" and a large wagon. Incidentally this horse had served in the R.H.A. with his master in France, 1914-18. Off we went to the new abode my father in the front, with my brother and me safely stowed in the tin bath, wedged alongside the other bits and pieces. My mother choosing to walk with my sister in the wicker pushchair. What a thrill, as peering over the top of the wagon we watched the horse galloping up over Ham Green Hill out of the village. So to our new home which was quite advanced for those days. It had three bedrooms with a coal-fired boiler in the kitchen and a bathroom, inside toilet and large gardens front and rear, (much to the dismay of my father). But no electricity of course. Double burner oil lamps for the front room, single ones for the kitchen.

The first four houses in our street were occupied by hospital staff and the last four by the farm workers, a wonderful healthy environment for children. The farm and hospital grounds were beautifully kept and tended, patchwork fields with neat hedges, a great variety of wildlife, the lake a haunt of wildfowl. What an untidy mess it all is today; so much for Bloody Progress and Town Overspill.

Ham Green Hospital in those days was practically a self-contained unit, the farm supplying beef, lamb, milk, pigs and poultry. So began a truly splendid childhood. In the summer evenings it was sheer magic for us children to help with the hay-making, all done by horses and by hand, and we would sneak alongside the hedgerows and take a surreptitious swig from the wicker encased stone cider jar the farm labourers kept under a moist heap of hay. Leading in the huge dray horses to the watering trough and kept busy on the pump whilst they drank, then into the stables where the sweat-stained harness was removed and the horses rubbed down and left contented for the night with their feed. If the hay-making was by the towpath where the river Avon sweeps around Horseshoe Bend we would enjoy seeing the steamers, large and small, navigating the river as an added bonus Campbell's paddle steamer going fullspeed with her happy throng of day trippers aboard.

After haymaking — threshing. The huge steam tractor towing the machine and behind the machine the men's little red caravan, their home on wheels. During this period I would be up at five o'clock and steal out of the silent house, down the road to the farm where the machine was stationed and receive a warm welcome from the men. A little bogie stove would be burning brightly in their little home and no tea and toast ever tasted as good. Then I would run to the village and get the men their tobacco and papers, no transistors blaring out in those days. During this period of the year these men would travel the counties.

A hundred yards up from the cottages was the slaughterhouse where the animals were dressed for the hospital and every Thursday a steer, four sheep, sometimes a calf, and four pigs were slaughtered. I must confess we were quite bloodthirsty and on the instructions of the butcher I used to put my foot on the animal's carcass after its throat was slit to pump the blood so that it was ejected quicker. Looking back on it I now realise this man was very cruel. By late afternoon, if he was getting late, he wouldn't bother to stun the pigs but would just up-end them and slit their throat. Years later he committed suicide. Life was indeed harsher in those days.

During the summer we boys used to camp out in a 'Pup' which was a tent behind the houses along with the girls, nurses and maids. They all resided in the hospital in those days. A lot of these girls were Welsh and there was marvellous singing, no discos, maybe a private gramophone or Mr Hunt with his guitar, beautiful melodious evenings and no funny business. (The girls had to be in at ten, a late night pass was an infrequent privilege).

Winter evenings would be spent around the fire and in the early 'twenties my father made radio sets from the plans in the *Evening Times & Echo*. There were three sets of earphones and my sister and I used to take it in turns to share before we went to bed, always early unless there was some social treat. What a difference today when children are allowed to sit up late, constantly assailed by inane trash too adult for their tender years. One of the treats of winter mornings was the early visit of the Hot Roll Man (6.30am) from the Bill Holbrooks bakery at Pill. The bin on the front of the carrier bike would contain steaming hot rolls covered by a clean white flour sack.

School was a long walk, especially in winter time. No coaches in those days. We stayed in for lunch and a hot meal would consist of toasting your sandwiches before a huge coke-burning stove. When they brought in cheap school milk in the 'thirties we thought it was fantastic. Although times were hard we had a wonderful childhood. A copper or two earned was indeed manna from heaven.

Momentous days were the annual trip to Western-super-Mare through the medium of the particular Sunday School you attended and the Rag on the 5th of November, when the village would be invaded by people from the surrounding villages and from the aliens across the water in Gloucestershire. There was Regatta day, a terrific occasion for us children — when everyone let their hair down and the pubs did a roaring trade. Then there was the Flower Show, complete with dodgems and musical roundabouts. The tractors hissing and spluttering steam and all the variety of miniature figures performing wonderful antics on the music *Wurlitzer*. How soon the precious few pence disappeared, little money we had but it was a temporary enchantment. Saturday afternoons we would cross the ferry wall, down the Green to Avonmouth (the nearest cinema or bug house — a magic expedition into another world.) I always remember before the performance started the proprietor's wife would come round with a huge Flit gun spraying copious amounts of antiseptic all over us. Then back up, across the Ferry and the well-endowed would have two pennyworth of chips in Gomer Sharp's. Sometimes the village would be visited by a travelling

b) Drying Sails – the harbour at Pill.

Repertory Company. The last one I remember was "East Lynne". A couple of us had a free ticket in exchange for going around collecting the handbills; and we had great fun helping unload the props from a rickety old lorry. The street barrel organ was pushed out from Bristol complete with monkey, and there was a blind lady of genteel type who used to sit on a canvas stool outside the pubs playing her guitar and singing in a beautiful contralto voice.

Life was hard by todays standards but there was total respect for elders and the Constabulary were held in awe. Once I was summonsed for trespassing on the railway line with an air gun and appeared in front of the Local J.P. at Flax Bourton. It cost my father £2, nearly a weeks wages in those days. At the same Court a boy from North Weston appearing for a second time was sentenced to two years at a Reformatory School and he was forcibly separated from his parents, his crying entreaties of "No, no" rang in my ears for days.

I was about thirteen when I obtained my first job delivering the evening paper for 2/6d per week, 6d extra if I was available to deliver telegrams. Saturday mornings I had to go down and bundle up the unsold papers. From this remunerative salary I bought my first cycle from Freeman's Club, a 26" Standard Upright with a carbide lamp. I left school in August 1935 and obtained my first job as errand boy at Sibley's the grocers next door to the Star Inn delivering the weekly groceries, chopping firewood etc. My pay was seven shillings and sixpence per week and threepence extra for each new customer introduced, of this I gave five shillings to Mother. Alas I wasn't cut out to be a Tesco Manager, so, a week's notice and another job with the gamekeepers on Sir Melville Wills estate at Abbots Leigh. Fifteen shillings per week, 8am-5pm, 12 o'clock on Saturdays. Wonderful job for a young country lad. The estate beautifully maintained, a good employer, four gamekeepers kept. When I hear these Left Wing Intellectuals running down these people it makes me mad. Sir Melville Wills, in keeping with the majority of his class was an enlightened and caring employer. What a difference today with these ignorant crude Pop Stars who buy country estates. "Obscene". They think Conservation's the name of a Group.

All this time I was yearning for the sailor's life and in the darkness of my bedroom would listen to the deep blast of ships' sirens at Avonmouth and the answering response of the tug, especially when the wind was N.W, or I would sit up in the window watching the river traffic on the stretch between Pill and Horseshoe Bend.

At this time my two cousins were both at sea and one evening down at the village they prevailed on me to come to Avonmouth. Next morning I met them outside the Federation at Avonmouth to learn of a Cabin Boy's job vacant in one of Roper's old tramps, the SS "Carperby" lying at West Wharf 3. So into the dock I went, yet another marvellous incursion into a new world. Tramps, Federal boats, four-masted ships, tugboats, engines hooting and fussing, ships winches rattling away. Cranes and derricks discharging cargo from across the world.

So aboard the SS "Carperby" I went. She looked mountains high to me, climbing up a rickety accommodation ladder into a dimly lit alley and a tiny cabin where I introduced myself to the Chief Steward. After pleasantries about my seafaring family and the rejoinder that I was very lean, he told me I could have the job; £2.15 per month, join her that night with a 'donkey's breakfast'*, and that the ship was going to Swansea where I would sign the Articles.

Then home to Pill, a letter of apology to Mr. Monk the Chief Gamekeeper, tears from Mother, farewell to my two sisters and small brother and by 4 o'clock back across the Ferry to Avonmouth with a small suit-case, into the Chandlers at Avonmouth to buy my 'donkey's breakfast', costing 1/6d. And, struggling with this monstrosity nearly twice as big as me, I presented myself aboard my new home. I was given a dingy little cabin starboard side on the engine housing abaft No 3 hold. The bottom bunk was occupied by the Cook's son, about 18, a large robust bloke. His resentment showed in no uncertain manner.

We left next morning at 5am and, whilst endeavouring to learn the duties of Cabin Boy, the Cook, in no uncertain terms, let the Chief Steward know that this position (mine) had been promised to his other son in their home port of Swansea. So, alas, when we arrived at this port late that night the Chief Steward, who did not want to lose a first class Cook acceded to his demands and gave me two days wages and a railway warrant home to Bristol. Thus ended my first sojourn afloat. My father said "You wait a while."

After two days I heard about a boy's job in the Commonwealth Steam Tug Company and presented myself at the counter of the dingy office in Avonmouth. Mr. Clone, the man who engaged me was clerk cum skipper, runner etc., "Start tomorrow at 0800 my son" he intoned, "Join the SS "Triton" in Avonmouth Dock".

Next morning it was blowing a gale from the S.W. The SS "Llannashee", a Cardiff tramp, had left the berth at Spiller's Mill and was just coming through the junction cut. The "Triton" was made fast off by two rope bridled right down. Old Tug Wilson, the Mate, was sat on or crouched on the after focsle entrance, the bridle rope in his hands, ready to slack off or haul down, whichever quarter the tug was needed, a short stemmed pipe in his mouth and heavy-weather gear on. As the tug's stern quarter came into the busy wharf I leapt smartly aboard. "New boy, eh? Make a pot of tea and then get ready to scrub the cabin out." Thus my introduction to tug-boating.

What a lovely craft the "Triton" was. 129ft long, built and engineered by Cox & Company of Falmouth. An after focsle with four bunks and two separate cabins, a forrard focsle with beautiful hanging chandelier-type oil lights, a mahogany Saloon table and two cabins for Master and Chief Engineer (never used). Alas no dynamo. Coal bogie aft and forrard, small Galley and toilet amidships, also Lamp and Store Room. She

* Bedding Roll.

carried Captain, Mate, Chief Engineer, two Firemen and a boy plus an extra deck hand if long towing.

Whilst I was in her we went down channel and picked up the SV "Viking" and took her up up to Sharpness, also towed the SV "Archibald Russel" and "Abraham Ryeberg", both square-rigged ships, away from Barry to west of Lundy. The "Triton" never had a capstan aft, thus when the 120ft manilla tow rope was let go it was heaved in by messenger through sleeve on focsle bulwark, through blocks, then heaved to aft and to windless, then heaved in along the deck. Then the chase after the sailing ship, come up astern of her, throw the heaving line aboard, three blasts farewell and off she went, crowding on sail in a favourable wind, a beautiful sight and us full speed back up channel for Avonmouth to resume mundane towing at Bristol Sharpness.

Commonwealth Towing Company had four other smaller tugs at this time, "Falcon", "Steelopois", "Wolfhound" and "Mercia". They kept two manned, "Triton" and "Steelopolis", and they would light up the fires of the two extra tugs and get hands off the dole for one day's pay. They were always short of any stores, just the bare minimum to keep the boats going.

My job was to keep the navigation lights trimmed, cabin lights, bogie stove lit, and scrub the cabin and wheelhouse and help the Mate to haul the ashes up from the stokehold.

We did all our ablutions in our own bucket, down on the stokehold plates in the warm, but after a long tide how snug and warm the wood-panelled focsle was. The bogie bright red, wind howling and rain lashing down, but God help you if you were not up before the hands next morning to stoke up and make the tea. The lifting of the port and starboard lights into their respective lamp boxes used to tax my slender little frame to the limit and when the Extra Mast Head light had to go in the cage and be hauled up to denote towing, it was only just humanly possible for me to do it.

If I had to be ready for tide any time before 6am in the morning I used to have to come down the night before, because, living across the water, the last ferry went at 10.30pm. Last thing at night I would come over and our tugs were always moored up at the north end on the jetty out of the way, because they were eye-sores I suppose. How my heart used to pound as I climbed over each tug in eerie pitch blackness; found the scuttle hatch key and descended the Stygian gloom. Then with shaking hands lit the single burner oil lamp and got the bogie going, then turning in, would sleep restlessly listening to the lapping of the water on hull plates and the creaking of her moorings as she gently ranged. But life was not too bad, hard work for boys, you did not last five minutes if you were a shirker, and thirty shillings a week, nearly half as much as my father was receiving to maintain a wife and three children.

After about nine months satisfactory work I obtained a job in Corys' Tugs as boy in the small tug "Islegarth" (used principally in the towage of their coal barges, "Kenn", "Teme", "Axe", "Avon", and "Usk" to transport finest Welsh steaming coal to rebunker the banana boats.

These tugs were very well kept plentifully supplied with paint, stores of every description, standard compass cover polished, Bell Telegraph, navigation lights copper polished. Cabins, wheelhouse, all gratings scrubbed white.

A typical Monday morning would be:- away with a barge from Old Dock, down around the lightship EW, first across the sands Newcombe Buoy, to Goalcliffe, and on to the Springs and Risers. I have known us many times to tow barges all week with perhaps one short night home. Come back, up channel on a Saturday morning, approach the Old Dock pier and locks and the runner would approach the pier. "Ahoy Fred, let her run (the barge)".

The Fireman and Chief would then be heard muttering the most obscene profanities because preparing to bank down after a hard two and a half hours, they now faced another two and a half hours run down to Barry Roads; so, swing the bow on to the Pier, get ashore to collect wage packets and away. Then back aboard, out to anchor off Sully Hospital, heads down, no watch kept, only on dockable times; perhaps we would be down there all weekend, no ships arriving; there was no up-to-date communication system then and the Skipper used to go to the pier at Barry and ring the Cardiff Office Coast Guard Station for information.

Summer evenings, tramps loaded with coal outward bound, one after another, flat irons, dandys, Niel & West's trawlers out of Cardiff, French schooners, Federal boats, N25's, banana boats, beautiful 4 sticker Shire boats from Rangoon for Avonmouth. If the Haines boat, or whatever we were down there for, did not dock it would be back to Old Dock, find our orders in the Dock Gateman's Office and it would invariably be away Monday with a barge.

These barges were very well found craft, a long hatch, deep coamings, a mast fore and aft of the hatch and two long five ton derricks. The masts carried rigging and ratlines just like a DW ship. Foscle forrad and winch fore and aft, steam supplied by a donkey boiler aft. They carried their own towing junk and 3ft wire.

So then about three and a half hours to flow tide, the fireman would be up, fires away call the boy if he warn't already up, make the tea, light the navigation lights ready. The Mate would be up, pay a little slack on the anchor and await the barge being ready, steam up, and away to starboard against the flood. It seemed you no sooner turned in than you were out, and you couldn't win.

I couldn't see today's generation of youth standing up to it. Standing on the belting of a tug winter time, coming into the docks, jumping into the recessed ladder to take the ropes on low ebb. Some experiences stand out during my time in the "Islegarth". The first was when we arrived back, were hailed by the runner and told to run down to Barry, despite the bottom falling out of the glass and the old man telling them we had no food — we didn't either. To no avail.

Off we set this Saturday afternoon on the ebb, the gale storm force, howling and shrieking in from the NW. Time we got down to the Welsh Hook buoy there was an angry sea running and things were bad. She was filling up. Captain had no choice but to turn back, a tricky manoeuvre. Time we got back to Black Hole it was too late to go on to the Old Pier, so we decided to drop the hook in Portishead Hole, pitching and tossing, with an occasional dollop of mud-spattered spray down the skuttle hatch, an uncomfortable place with the wind northerly. We had no grub but plenty of tea and sugar. Anyhow Jasper dug up a 1lb of flour, a bit of marge, a few old sultanas lying in the locker of the Chief, got a saucepan boiling on the bogie and kneaded this — my introduction to sea-going Spotted Dick — concoction up, wrapped it in a bit of muslin we used for cleaning, and into the pot. By God it tasted delicious, never had substance been so welcome. Midnight the gale died away and we got under way and ran down to Barry.

The second occasion was when we had to tow a derelict French fruit schooner from Barry to Newport, ordered out in a SW gale. It was all we could do to get past the West Cardiff buoy. We had our hook down and lashed alongside this schooner. The Mate went aboard with myself following down into the Captain's cabin aft. Exquisite scrollwork, beautiful panelling and during his rummaging he found a bottle of doubtful ancestry. Anyhow he and the Old Man polished it off and apart from excessive verbosity, seemed to fare none the worse for it.

The third time we were sent to Barry to spend one tide looking for a Yank schooner bound for Newport. It was November, fog coming down and clearing. No Radar in those days. Ships bells ringing whilst they prudently remained at anchor, blasts of whistles and sirens and an occasional honk from a dandy's hand-operated fog horn, the "bay" of the different light ships (all these years after I can still reproduce the two-toned boom of the English and Welsh), the more Drake-minded mariners under way. Fog in busy shipping lanes always seems to produce its own peculiar cacophonous sound. A mournful discord in keeping with the weather about. On coming near the light ship and interlaced with its time-patterned baying, we were amazed to hear the sound of a banjo playing Negro spiritual music, dead slow, and approaching the direction we hit a clear patch. There, about two cables from the light ship, anchored snugly, was our quarry — the five masted schooner "Edna Hoyt".

Built at Thomaston, Maine, gross tonn 1512 length 224, beam 91.9, depth 28.8, Master, Captain Elmer Beal, her stern revealing her port of register as Savannah, USA and just forrard of her jigger mast a venerable old gentleman was seated in a wicker chair (he turned out to be the Captain) playing the banjo surrounded by Negros in various attitudes repose, singing. What an absolutely amazing sight.

Not long after, I left the "Islegarth" and joined the "Reagarth". She was principally employed at Avonmouth with an occasional run to Newport or to do a Federal boat. It meant a lot more time home. The only time she deigned to tow a barge was if we had to go down channel for bunkers.

One forgotten practice then was taking a ship from Avonmouth, after part cargo discharge, to the buoys off Severn Beach to await the right tide for Sharpness. If we shifted ships between tides we used to get seven and sixpence, extra, five shillings for the boy. Busy, bustling port Avonmouth in those days. Meat boat on O shed or P shed, Shire on Q1, usually two or three well known tramp steamers with grain or iron ore. Ellermans, Brocklebanks, Dandys all up the old dock, barges and they used to move them about all over the place *by hand*. Sar tankers, BTG tankers and always a couple of banana boats under repair.

Thus up to December 1938 and moored on R shed I decided to go down to the locks to see the "Cavina" docking. My cousin was serving as lookout man in her. When she was tied up in the locks I went aboard and forrard where he informed me there was a deck boy's job vacant. So after the ship discharged her passengers I approached the Bosun who gave me the job.

Back to the rear office, explained the circumstances, and they generously agreed to 48 hours notice. It had been a happy but hard introduction into the nautical world. Barry, dismal grey place, Cardiff and the cosmopolitan atmosphere of Bute Street. . . .

On Friday, late December 1938, under the patronage of my cousin Swisher, a real sailor, hard drinking all his life, still is (jumped ship 1954 and is now in Australia somewhere). . . I went aboard the "Cavina" with my P65 and signed on as deck boy, wages £3.10.0d a month. A motley crowd, fireman, sailors stewards; firemen always seemed to be dressed in blue serge suits, the sailors dressed in scrubbed blue dungarees. And Levi dungarees, or jeans, as they are called today — they *did* denote a sailor, no one else wore them. After cashing up their advance notes they would end up in the Royal Hotel, no such niceties as Merchant Navy Club in those days.

Over the Ferry 7.30 Monday morning, suitcase, sea bag, pair of three quarter sea boots strapped on the outside (badge of office), I felt 10ft tall.... Aboard was a bustling scene, last minutes of activity, then 8am stations fore and aft (round hats on), down through the dock in the December gloom, my mate Ted Cox waving a white flour sack in adieu. Past the junction cut, down into the locks to take passengers from the Old Passenger Station. The Boat Train from London came right into the dock. Gangway down aft for the crowd of immaculately dressed passengers, forrard end of the Prom deck for VIP passengers — in those days Fyffes carried the cream of British Society.

What a beautiful picture Elder & Fyffes ships were in those days. Buff masts; funnel vents and upper main top mast black; stays white lead, and tallowed ratlined rigging black; white hull upperwards; coamings, bollard and scuppers battleship grey. All brasswork highly polished; boat covers scrubbed white; on the Boat Deck hatch covered duck canvas. Wedges, ballins all white, Jamaica flag flying from the fore topmast. Royal Mail pennant, Port Yard Blue Peter, Starboard Yard House Flag, Mainmast Truck Ensign; aft, bunches of flowers coming aboard for the passengers. Stay in the docks all day, then as evening tide came, back up the Bristol Channel.

Slowly out the docks, three blasts on ship's whistle and she's under way. The Master was Captain Forester, Chief Mate John Summerley, ex square-rigged man, very hard; Bosun Jack Nickels; Carpenter Bill Cramer, huge Cornwall man. Watches set, the ship settled down to another voyage to the West Indies.

There were six Quarter Masters, three lookout men, bosun's mate, carpenter's mate, two deck boys, two Senior Officers, two Junior Officers, two Able Seamen. One room for the six quarter masters another for three lookout men. Bosun's mate and carpenter's mate in together; likewise, bosun and carpenter (sumptuous compared with the hands); and the day workers together forrard; port side Pilot Officers toilet, and hands starboard side; tiny messrooms and steel locker, bare steel with cork on to prevent condensation (and hence rust). Minute heater on ship side (about the strength of an electric iron), steel bunks, deck table and forms (wooden) scrubbed white; linen sheet and pillowslip changed once a week. One paper-thin grey blanket, one towel, miserable surroundings.... Winter time as she plunged down

241

into it (it had to be very severe weather conditions for Fyffes to ease, they maintained a meticulous schedule). . . no radios or transistors in those days.

On my first sea voyage I was desperately sea sick (I always had been on the tugs). I vomited green bile continuously and could not have cared less if she had foundered. All these first few days, the ship laboured against Force 10 gales. Forrard continuously awash. There was no respite if you were ill, unless dying you were a malingerer. After four days I laid out on No 1 hatch soaked in icy spray, quite ill. Old shellback Charlie Jay said "throw the bastard over the side". I was beyond caring. Finally the Bosun told me to go along and see the doctor. The dour angular physician who could spot shirkers a mile off gave me a thorough examination. "You've a temperature laddie" he said, "take this chit up to the Mate". How cosy and warm this haven of rest — the surgery — looked compared with the bleak Dickensian conditions forrard. So up the bridge I went and Summerly CC, a very hard man made me go forrard and turn in. Which I did, intermittently crawling out and staggering to the heads violently vomiting. It lasted six days then I found my sea legs and the cold was better. I was never sea sick again, and, unfortunately, through my own experience, cast a jaundiced eye at other sufferers.

You learnt seamanship off the old hands, got conned into relieving the lookout man on the focsle head. I remember joyously when the 8-12 lookout man first let me ring 8 bells on the huge focsle bell, repeating it from the Bridge bell (and shrieking out "Lights are bright Sir"). . . .

Another time in the same ship, "Cavina" I was ordinary seaman and we were holy-stoning the deck by No 3. Summerley was on the after end of the Prom looking down. It was a freezing NE blusterly squall. I must have temporarily eased up in the mechanical rhythm of the stone. "Buck" he hailed, "How old are you?", prior to some sarcastic innuendo no doubt. An old AB next to me whispered sotto voice "say you don't know". "I don't know Sir" I said. "Well my son, go up on the main mast table and when you do know come down and see me." I clambered on to the bulwark and up the weather rigging on to the table, trying to crouch behind the tops of the No 3 derricks housed in the hutch clamps. Half an hour up there, a vast expanse of turbulent seascape, ship lifting and falling, was enough especially seeing the lads going forrard for smokes. Up to the Chief Officer, rather contrite for being stupid, and very subdued, gave him my age. "Listen Buck" he said, "never be led by other people, away you go". It was over as far as he was concerned.

I returned to working on the river, to the job I am doing at the present time, a hobbler. You are granted a licence by the Bristol Corporation, the job consisting of mooring ships at Avonmouth, Portishead and Bristol, also helmsman, steering the vessels up the treacherous Avon. The river work is the most interesting about, with wooden boats kept moored in the creek.

We worked on a rota system, you could have a tide off but you had to put 'NOT' on your number on our board in the Boatman's Shelter which nestled down by the side of the river. Here there was a phone and a coal tortoise stove, wooden panelled interior, a snug abode maintained during the day by a little, cherubic character called Frank Cox, a deft pianist — and often we would have a sing-song in the pubs nestling by the creeks, alas all gone. You could sit in the Bar Parlour of the Waterloo Inn and look down the river awaiting your ship to enter the straight stretch. Very often I have known the last train, 11.30pm from Clifton Bridge, wait five minutes for us whilst we hurried from the Cumberland Basin. I have known that Basin a mass of shipping. You could walk from one side to the other across ships during days of fog.

Summertime river work was enchanting, towing up the boat, the sun on your face, dabbling your hand in the cool river, hearing the nightingales in profusion singing when coming down past Nightingale Valley. Pill was then a close knit community, pretty cottages, Inns, Pilots, many still living in the village. Hobblers, many of them descended from Pilots, yachtsmen, westermen, who had crewed the famous Pill Pilot cutters. . . . Alas, the call of the sea was still strong in me and I shipped out in a banana boat twelve months later. . . .

People today have no conception of life in those pre-war days with a complete absence of radios. The only radio I knew was owned by the Captain of the "Plumgarth". (This was because she was often away long towing.) No VHF. Weather depended on the Captains's nautical lore and the barometer. Gales of wind, where and when imminent, would be signalled by the appropriate cones hoisted on the signal masts around the coast.

Another aspect of the boy's job, which readers by now probably realise was tough and could be dangerous, was the maintenance of the night-time illumination. In pre-war days the only tug with a dynamo was the "Eastleigh". All navigation lamps were copper and kept, like the bell and wheelhouse telegraph, highly polished. For instance, after a winter's night, the next day I would have to trim, refill and clean two masthead lights, a stern light, port and starboard lights, compass light, Captain's and Chief's cabin light, forrard after cabin light, and if we were down channel, the all round anchor light. The navigation lights demanded special attention because they had reflectors that were highly polished. Another must was the placing of the axe by the towing hook, especially important in winter time.

But it was, all in all, a marvellous life, challenging, especially pre-war, when a simple notice on the Shipping Federation door at Avonmouth —"Cabin or Messroom or Deck boy required SS "So and So" " — could transport a green boy to romantic places. Ah, but I think the magic allure has gone.